BABY NAMES

A NEW GENERATION

Barbara Kay Turner

BERKLEY BOOKS, NEW YORK

BABY NAMES

A Berkley Book / published by arrangement
with the author

PRINTING HISTORY
Berkley edition / February 1998

All rights reserved.
Copyright © 1998 by Barbara Kay Turner.
Book design by Casey Hampton.
This book, or parts thereof, may not be reproduced
in any form without permission.
For information address:
The Berkley Publishing Group,
a division of Penguin Putnam Inc.,
375 Hudson Street, New York, New York 10014.

The Penguin Putnam Inc. World Wide Web site address is
http://www.penguinputnam.com

ISBN: 0-425-16238-9

BERKLEY®
Berkley Books are published by The Berkley Publishing Group,
a division of Penguin Putnam Inc.,
375 Hudson Street, New York, New York 10014.
BERKLEY and the "B" design are trademarks belonging to
Penguin Putnam Inc.

PRINTED IN THE UNITED STATES OF AMERICA

18   17   16   15   14   13

NAMES FOR A NEW GENERATION...

More than ever before, your options for baby names are wide open. You can choose a traditional name, keeping the classic spelling . . . select a name that reflects your baby's ethnic heritage . . . update an old favorite . . . try something with a futuristic flavor . . . or create something completely unique!

This A-to-Z guide covers...

- The difference a middle name can make

- What to think about when naming your baby

- Popular names from regions throughout the country

- Names with lasting appeal: what makes them stay in style?

and much more

BABY NAMES
A NEW GENERATION

Berkley Books by Barbara Kay Turner

THE VERY BEST BOOK OF BABY NAMES
BABY NAMES FOR THE '90s AND BEYOND
NAME THAT BABY
BABY NAMES: A NEW GENERATION

To my niece Melissa Benbrook Williams for her invaluable assistance with this book, and to my brother Timothy Benbrook, who understands my database.

To Miranda Coffey, who knows why, and to my husband, Dick, for the rose he brings me every second Friday.

CONTENTS

BEAM ME UP, PR'ZYLLA!

What names do you think are likely to top the popular lists in the new century? Michael and Amanda or R2-D2 and Pr'zylla? With visions of Star Trek voyages dancing in your head, the important task of choosing a name for your baby becomes even more challenging.

You may be concerned that a new era in personal names is awaiting us as we start writing January 1, 2000, on our checks and letters. Naturally, you want to protect your child from the handicap of growing up with a name that too soon becomes hopelessly old-fashioned.

In 1900 Agnes, Bertha, Chester, and Dexter were fashionable names for newborns. Today those names rarely appear on birth registrations. They've yielded to Ashley, Brianna, Cody, and Dylan. If you choose a popular name like Ashley or Dylan, will it sound dated early in the new century? To avoid this problem, you need to know how radically name choices will change over the next few decades. Will they change faster than they did in the 20th century?

To answer these questions, let's take a quick look backward to the 1900s for clues about the patterns of name change. What we learn will help us predict changes in the future. Then, with perfect confidence, you can choose a name that will serve your child well for a lifetime.

THE 20TH CENTURY IN REVIEW

1900–1925: English Traditional Names

Popular name choices in America at the beginning of the century were almost entirely dominated by traditional English names. Some names, such as Arthur, Walter, Frances, and Lillian, are less used today but are still on the active lists. Others, like the names that follow, are still popular at the end of the century.

TOP NAMES IN 1905 AND STILL IN THE TOP 100

BOYS

Andrew	Edward	Joseph	Richard
Charles	Jacob	Kenneth	Robert
Daniel	James	Paul	Thomas
David	John	Peter	William

GIRLS

Anna	Emily	Katherine	Nancy
Catherine	Grace	Laura	Rebecca
Elizabeth	Julia	Mary	Sarah

1925–1950: Irish Names and Movie Stars

Due to the great immigration wave near the beginning of the century, favored Irish names such as Michael, Dennis, Patrick, Brenda, Eileen, and Kathleen appeared on the most frequently used name lists. Since 1940, Michael has been at or near the top of the list of most popular boys' names; it's been one of the enduring favorites of the century.

Movies and movie stars of the thirties and forties brought less commonly used names into the spotlight, and parents began choosing them more frequently as names for their babies, particularly for girls.

FAVORITE "STAR" NAMES AT MID-CENTURY

GIRLS			BOYS
Arlene	Gloria	Marlene	Alan
Deborah	Joan	Patricia	Bruce
Dolores	Joyce	Paulette	Douglas
Donna	Judith	Sandra	Gary
Gail	Karen	Sharon	Larry
Geraldine	Linda	Shirley	Ronald

1950–1975: Classic Revivals

Parents developed a taste for names that were a little more unusual than the traditional favorites, particularly for girls. Almost all of these newly popular names came from the existing name pool. Other older, traditional names for boys rose to the top of the lists.

NEWLY POPULAR NAMES IN THE SEVENTIES

GIRLS		BOYS	
Amy	Kimberly	Darryl	Marcus
Angela	Lisa	Derrick	Mark
Christina	Lori	Eric	Scott
Dawn	Michelle	Jason	Sean

Denise	Nicole	Jeffrey	Todd
Heather	Shannon	Jonathan	
Jennifer	Stacey	Justin	
Julie	Tammy	Keith	
Kelly	Tracy	Kevin	

1975–2000: Multiple Choices

In the last quarter of the 20th century, an explosion of popular name possibilities has offered a bewildering array of choices for parents in search of baby names. Where did they come from?

"New" classics

Unusual or rarely used traditional names, or variants built on classic names, were promoted to the list of most popular choices.

	GIRLS		BOYS
Alexis	Karina	Monica	Brandon
Alyssa	Kelly	Natalie	Brett
Ashley	Kylie	Sabrina	Cameron
Danielle	Lauren	Samantha	Christian
Erica	Mariah	Sara	Dustin
Erin	Marissa	Savannah	Jeremy
Jasmine	Megan	Stephanie	Jordan
Jenna	Melissa	Tiffany	Kyle
Jessica	Michaela	Vanessa	Ryan

Old-fashioned and biblical

The popularity of names such as Amy, Sarah, and Molly has led to the revival of more "old-fashioned" names for girls.

This trend paralleled the trend for reviving biblical names for boys.

GIRLS		BOYS	
Abigail	Katie	Aaron	Jesse
Amanda	Leah	Adam	Joshua
Emily	Miranda	Caleb	Matthew
Emma		Elijah	Nathan
Grace		Gabriel	Samuel
Hannah		Jacob	Zachary

Gaelic variants
Names with Gaelic roots have become very popular and quickly acquired multiple spellings and variants. Some of the samples listed here have more variants than the ones shown.

NAME	VARIANTS
Brianna	Breanna, Briana, Briannon, Brienna, Brienne, Brionna
Brittany	Britney, Brittani, Brittney
Caitlyn	Caitland, Caitlin, Kaitlin, Katelin, Katlyn
Dylan	Dillen, Dillon, Dyllan, Dyllon
Shawn	Sean, Shaun, Shaughn, Shonn

Westerns and television
Names with connotations of the American West have achieved new status, thanks in part to television's daytime (and night-

time) series, particularly the "soaps." Most of the names listed here made their debut on these shows or gained in popularity due to the continuing exposure.

GIRLS		BOYS	
Ariel	Kayla	Austin	Damian
Blair	Krystal	Cheyenne	Dylan
Brandy	Kylie	Cody	Kyle
Brooke	Macy	Colton	Quinn
Carly	Savannah	Connor	Ryan
Chelsea	Shana	Dakota	Skylar
Dru	Sierra	Dalton	Travis

The last shall be first

The entertainment industry has also influenced the use of more surnames as first names, notably for girls, but also for boys. The samples listed below are mostly cross-gender names, used for boys and girls. Dillon and Tanner so far are used for boys only. Girls' usage predominates for Ashley, Courtney, Haley, Payton, and Whitney.

SURNAMES/CROSS-GENDER NAMES

Ashley	Dillon	Logan	Shelby
Bailey	Haley	Mackenzie	Sheridan
Blake	Harley	Madison	Tanner
Chase	Hunter	Morgan	Taylor
Connor	Jordan	Payton	Tyler
Courtney	Kelsey	Riley	Whitney

Made in America

American parents have created many new names during the last decade of the 20th century. Three types of created names are most favored. *Prefix* names combine various name endings with a preferred prefix sound, such as *da-*, *la-* and *sha-*. *Rhym-*

ing names are new names that rhyme with an existing name. *Blends* or compound names combine two names to make one new name. The names shown here demonstrate some results of these kinds of name creation.

PREFIX	RHYMING	BLENDS	
Shadonna	Daralyn	Ava/Ana	= Aviana
Shakira	Jerilyn	Cara/Lisa	= Caralisa
Shalynn	Kerrilyn	Dana/Lee	= Danalee
Shamaine	Marilyn	Rex/Ann	= Rexanne
Shaquise	Sherilyn	Trevor/Devin	= Trevin
Shawanda	Terilyn	Trevor/Travis	= Trevis

Ethnic heritage

Ethnically distinctive names, particularly Hispanic names, have appeared in greater numbers on the top names lists. In California and Texas, Jose and Juan are among the top 25 boys' names, with Luis and Jesus not far behind.

Birth registrations show an increase in African-American choices of African and Islamic names. Asian names, sometimes combined with English-American first or middle names, have also increased in number.

Informal names and nicknames

Popular trends in naming have allowed for a less traditional sound and look. Names such as Casey, Corey, Jamie, and Katie have taken their places as independent names.

Nature names and place names

Distinctive names using places, nouns, and images have followed the trend set by names like Heather and Dawn. All except River are girls' names.

Amber	Brandy	Destiny	Misty
Autumn	Crystal	Diamond	River

WHAT'S AHEAD IN THE 21ST CENTURY?

Tradition Continues to Count

Of all the names in popular use at the end of the 20th century, a substantial number have been around for centuries, some for thousands of years. They are links with the past that we value greatly, however much the world changes around us. So you can feel confident that Michael and Amanda will be piloting spaceships along with R2-D2 and Pr'zylla.

Flexibility Keeps Names Alive

Modern tastes allow for changes in a traditional name without sacrificing the name itself—Schuyler to Skylar, for example. Names can adapt to future tastes as well. If Dorotea prefers to use the short form Tea, and Geneva prefers Neve for everyday use, few will object to such choices. Spelling changes, rhyming variants, and name blends may increase in number, but that's been going on for centuries. Connections with origins and definitions may be stretched thin, but the connections are there.

The 20-Year Factor Favors Name Survival

Due to more frequent exposure in media coverage of news, sports, and entertainment, fewer names will fall out of fashion with the coming of each generation. Babies given very popular names grow up and become stars in various fields. A new generation of parents across the country hear and see the names in the press and on TV, are reminded of the good qualities of the names, and use them for *their* babies. More names in the 21st century won't be left behind by association with a single time period.

New Favorites Don't Make Older Names Obsolete

The greatest change in modern naming trends is not that older names are in danger of fading out of use, but that parents are now choosing from a longer list of favorites. The decreased percentages of choices made from the top-25 name lists show the change.

PERCENTAGE OF NAMES CHOSEN FROM TOP-25 LISTS

YEAR	BOYS	GIRLS
1989	40%	30%
1996	33%	22%

The Good News about Names? Go for It!

More than ever before, your options are wide open. Choose a name with a grand old tradition, keeping the classic spelling. Select a name with a meaningful ethnic heritage. Redesign a traditional name or create a new form. It's up to you!

MORE HELP ON YOUR PERSONAL NAME TREK

Baby Names: A New Generation provides information that will help you reach your goal of finding the perfect name for your baby. Read on; here's what you'll find in the pages ahead.

- The 200 most popular names across the United States.
- Regional differences in name preference.

- Qualities that help a name to stay in favor; a brief overview.

- Futuristic names from today's science fiction—just in case.

- A closer look at the magic of middle names.

- Naming goals for parents and some useful tips.

- The most helpful index of boys' and girls' names you're likely to find anywhere.

Children entering kindergarten in the year 2000 will set the pace for names at the starting gate of the new century. The following lists show the 100 most popular girls' and boys' names that will appear on enrollments for that year. Ties are indicated when no number appears next to a name. For example, Amanda and Elizabeth tied for 11th place.

Top 100 Girls' Names in Kindergarten in the Year 2000

1. Ashley	17. Brianna	32. Haley
2. Emily	Nicole	Katherine
3. Jessica	19. Morgan	34. Abigail
4. Sarah	20. Alyssa	Allison
5. Taylor	Amber	36. Jasmine
6. Samantha	Rebecca	Kaitlyn
7. Hannah	Victoria	38. Chelsea
8. Megan	24. Danielle	Sara
9. Brittany	Jennifer	40. Jordan
10. Kayla	Kelsey	Mary
11. Amanda	27. Alexandra	Olivia
Elizabeth	Stephanie	Sydney
13. Rachel	29. Madison	44. Miranda
14. Courtney	30. Anna	45. Brooke
Lauren	Shelby	Heather
16. Alexis		

47. Erin	Lindsey	Jamie
48. Tiffany	66. Erica	Shannon
49. Katelyn	67. Amy	85. Angela
Marissa	68. Bailey	Jenna
Michelle	Destiny	87. Briana
Paige	Madeline	88. Kaitlin
53. Sierra	71. Alexandria	89. Molly
54. Christina	Caitlin	90. Hailey
Kimberly	Cassandra	91. Leah
56. Mariah	74. Breanna	92. Autumn
Melissa	75. Cheyenne	93. Michaela
58. Andrea	Mackenzie	94. Brittney
Laura	Maria	Crystal
60. Natalie	78. Kelly	Kaylee
61. Katie	Savannah	97. Catherine
62. Emma	80. Kathryn	Sabrina
63. Gabrielle	81. Julia	Whitney
64. Kristen	82. Alicia	100. Bethany

Top 100 Boys' Names in Kindergarten in the Year 2000

1. Michael	14. Daniel	26. Dylan
2. Jacob	James	27. Aaron
Matthew	John	28. Thomas
Tyler	17. David	29. Benjamin
5. Joshua	Justin	Samuel
6. Christopher	19. Alexander	31. Jonathan
7. Brandon	20. Cody	Nathan
8. Austin	21. William	33. Christian
9. Andrew	22. Kyle	34. Eric
Zachary	23. Jordan	35. Adam
11. Joseph	Robert	36. Steven
Nicholas	25. Anthony	37. Timothy
Ryan		

38. Brian	60. Tanner	82. Marcus
39. Jason	61. Ethan	83. Mason
40. Jesse	62. Evan	84. Lucas
41. Patrick	63. Ian	85. Brett
Richard	64. Jeffrey	86. Shane
43. Sean	65. Blake	87. Cole
44. Caleb	Garrett	Isaac
Cameron	Nathaniel	Spencer
46. Charles	68. Derek	90. Shawn
Connor	69. Paul	Tristan
48. Logan	70. Kenneth	92. Elijah
49. Trevor	Mitchell	93. Noah
50. Jeremy	72. Bradley	94. Peter
51. Devin	Seth	95. Dillon
Taylor	74. Chase	Grant
53. Dakota	Corey	Jake
54. Jared	Dalton	98. Edward
55. Stephen	77. Colton	99. Jack
56. Hunter	Luke	100. Alec
57. Mark	79. Gabriel	
58. Dustin	80. Bryan	
Travis	81. Scott	

Regional Differences in Name Preference

Do parents in California choose the same names as parents in Texas or New York? In the four main regions of America—West, Midwest, South, and Northeast—remarkably few major differences in naming practices can be identified. Some general trends can be observed, however. For example, names come into fashion somewhat earlier on the West Coast than in other parts of the country.

More surnames are used as middle names in the South. Also, diminutives of boys' names, such as Billy, Bobby, and Jimmy, are used as independent names more frequently in the South than in other regions.

Birth registration lists show fewer rare and unusual names in the South, as well as in New England and Alaska. Parents in Hawaii choose both standard English-style names and native Hawaiian names.

In California and Texas, which have large Hispanic-American populations, more parents choose saints' names for their babies as a regular practice. A great advantage of this custom is that names are preserved in active use that otherwise might be lost.

Although considerable variation in the popularity of specific names does occur nationwide, almost all the same names show up on every state's top lists. Nationally, parents seem to come under the same influences and to share in similar patterns of name preference. In the following list, names without a number are ties. For example, Austin and Matthew are tied for fifth position in the West.

1995 TOP FIVE NAMES BY REGION

WEST	MIDWEST	SOUTH	NORTHEAST

BOYS

WEST	MIDWEST	SOUTH	NORTHEAST
1. Michael	1. Jacob	1. Christopher	1. Michael
2. Jacob	2. Michael	Joshua	Nicholas
3. Joshua	Tyler	Michael	3. Christopher
4. Tyler	4. Austin	4. Austin	4. Ryan
5. Austin	5. Matthew	5. Jacob	Tyler
Matthew			

GIRLS

WEST	MIDWEST	SOUTH	NORTHEAST
1. Jessica	1. Emily	1. Ashley	1. Emily
2. Ashley	2. Ashley	2. Emily	2. Ashley
3. Emily	3. Jessica	Jessica	Samantha
4. Samantha	Taylor	4. Brittany	4. Sarah
Sarah	5. Sarah	5. Sarah	5. Jessica
		Taylor	

What Qualities Help a Name Stay in Favor?

When a street reporter in San Francisco asked people passing by what they liked about their names, Catherine C. replied, "My first and last names go together well. The first name is pretty, and I like the history of the last name."

Catherine C.'s response illustrates the three qualities people most look for in names:

- Harmonious sound

- Appealing look

- Personal meaning

Listen for the rhythm in a name
If you're considering names for your new baby, do you sound them out, matching them with your surname to see how they fit together? Do you listen for the rhythm of the names until the effect pleases you? You're on the right track. Names have countless variations of rhythmic effects and pleasing sounds.

The softer consonants and vowel sounds have a distinctive effect on a name. Melissa and Patricia demonstrate this softer effect, which is often found in girls' names. Boys' names like Alan, Paul, and Lowell also use the softer consonants and achieve pleasing effects.

Stronger consonants like *K, D,* and *T* make syllables more forceful when pronounced, as in names like Kate and Garrett. If you listen for these soft and hard sounds as you say a name, you'll detect the different effects and decide which would be appropriate for your baby's name.

For an example of a name sound that is universally favored by parents from many cultures, notice the *sha* and *shan* sounds in the following list.

American: Shavonne	Hindi: Shanti
Arabic: Aisha	Irish: Sean, Shawn
Chinese: Xia (sha)	Latin: Alicia, Felicia

| English: Sharlene | Russian: Natasha |
| Hebrew: Elisha | Swahili: Shan |

The number of syllables used and where the emphasis is placed influences how you feel about a name. For example, pronounce the name Marjorie Morningstar. Notice the effect of the repeated three syllables, and the emphasis on the first syllable of each name. A first name like Marguerite, for example, with its emphasis on the third syllable, isn't quite as harmonious combined with Morningstar. Also, the full name seems rather long.

Now try Margo, Katherine, and Kate with Morningstar. Each version achieves a different effect, doesn't it? The two-syllable Margo works well with its emphasized first syllable. Kate, a single-syllable name with strong consonants, has a strong, immediate impact. Katherine has a softer and more leisurely effect.

There's no rule for the best combination of syllables. Generally, a long last name works well with a short first name and vice versa. James Masterson and Jonathan Smith are good examples of this guideline. Keep in mind, however, that most first names get shortened in everyday life, and women will probably change their surnames at marriage.

Names with fewer syllables and simpler pronunciations will probably have an edge in the next century, unless a reverse fashion trend develops. Name evolution seems to favor names that are less complicated to spell and pronounce. For example, Killashandra is an Irish name from the past. Adalheid is German. You'll recognize them today in their shortened forms Shandra and Heidi. Adam, David, Sarah, and Hannah are prime examples of very old names that are still popular today. Melchizedek and Hepzibah, equally venerable biblical names, are virtually obsolete in America.

One reason new names come into fashion and stay in use for a long time is that they fit a familiar, well-liked pattern. The following lists demonstrate some names with very popular sounds and effects in common. Note the number of syllables, where the emphasis is placed, and certain repeated consonant sounds or vowel sounds. Start from the top of the lists and read downward. Can you see the patterns?

GIRLS

Bethany	Diana	Kelly	Amanda
Stephany	Briana	Kaylee	Samantha
Tiffany	Kiana	Kayla	Savannah
Brittany	Leeanna	Kellen	Miranda
Kimberly	Rhiannon	Kelsey	Jordana
Destiny	Tiana	Kylie	Madonna

BOYS

Nathan	Cody	Dalton	Jason
Ethan	Corey	Colton	Jesse
Ian	Caleb	Justin	Jeremy
Evan	Connor	Dustin	Jared

Final caution: try not to repeat the same sounds in first, middle, and last names. A name like Shannon Anne Anderson or Corey Cody Corcoran can be a tongue twister.

The impact of a name—negative or positive?
Part of the impact of a name is in the way it looks on paper, typed, or in a handwritten signature. Signatures can be casual, formal, friendly, impressive, and so on. Short forms of a given name can vary the effect, such as Kate for Katherine. Use of initials makes a name seem businesslike, more formal. Be sure to try out your name possibilities on paper and take into account how a name looks in all its combinations.

The personal impact of a name on other people can vary widely. Names impress others as dignified, frivolous, feminine, masculine, strong, gentle, exotic, plain, trustworthy—the list goes on. You and others will make judgments of a name according to personal feelings and experiences you've had with people bearing that name, or from impressions gathered from the media.

It's difficult to predict how those judgments will vary in the future. About all you can do is go with your feelings now and hope for the best. Unexpected events can influence how people perceive names. During World War II, many German-American citizens dropped or altered distinctively Germanic names like Adolf and Hildegard.

Logical spellings that look reasonably like the way the names are pronounced will have an advantage in the future—Margo instead of Margeaux, for example. As the global village continues to expand, more cultures will mix and communicate, and names that work best will be names quickly understood by others.

Meaningful names give lifelong satisfaction

"I like the history of my name," Catherine C. said to the street reporter. Michael G. made another point about name history and tradition in his response: "It was my father's name. . . . I have a lot of respect for him. I like sharing his name."

Family heritage—of a parent's or other relative's name, for example—is meaningful. The meaning will last into the next century, if only for that person and that family.

Your child may be proud of his or her name for other personal reasons, especially when you explain the reasons early in his or her childhood. The chosen name might have religious, ethnic, or patriotic associations. Perhaps the name was specially created for your child, or some incident of family history is involved, or the meaning is in the love and care with which the name was selected.

Names are also meaningful in themselves. The great traditional names used so widely in America have long, interesting, multinational histories, which is fitting for a nation of mixed cultures and backgrounds. In 1996 the *New York Times* published an analysis of data supplied by the city's health department about ethnic name choice in New York City. All top ten Hispanic-American and Asian-American choices included traditional names like Ashley, Stephanie, Jennifer, and Jessica for girls, and Kevin, David, Jason, and Daniel for boys, with the addition of Jose and Luis in the Hispanic top ten.

This book contains some 10,000 names, many of which are too new or too unfamiliar to most people to classify as traditional names. They're all in use today in America, and they have personal significance to the individuals who bear the names. We don't know which of these names will in time join the list of beloved classics. That remains to be seen by our great-great-grandchildren. The fact that they have significance to their name bearers *now* is what counts.

FICTIONAL NAMES—PREVIEW OF THE FUTURE?

Names from Science Fiction

Authors of science fiction novels and script writers of sci-fi films and TV series use their imaginations to name characters living far in the future. Since fiction often prefigures fact, it's worth taking a look at some of these names. Writers draw on their knowledge of existing names to invent names for their characters, in much the same way that parents might look for unusual names for their children. They also mix traditional Earth names with futuristic and "extraterrestrial" names.

See for yourself what you like and don't like about some of the following examples—just in case you might choose a similar name for your 21st-century baby. The *Star Trek* series list includes nonhuman names, which are interesting because they're meant to differ from Earth names and still be recognizable as names. Notice how the writers expect classic Earth names will still be circulating centuries from now.

CHARACTER NAMES FROM VARIOUS *STAR TREK* SERIES

WOMEN

Alexana	Guinan	Liva	Silva
Ardra	Jadzia	Lwaxana	Sonji
Ardrian	Jil	Nella	Soren
B'Elanna	Kareen	Nellen	Tasha
Beverly	Kathryn	Ohana	Tava
Dara	Kayron	Perrin	Tryla
Deanna	Keiko	Rachella	Uhura
Duana	Kes	Rishan	Valeda
Eline	Kira	Ro	Vash
Etana	Lanel	Salia	Yareena

MEN

Alrik	Geordi	Miles	Sarek
Benjamin	Hagan	Montgomery	Spock
Chacotay	James	Neelix	Sulu
Daimon	Jarok	Nel	Tom
Dalen	Jarth	Nog	Tuvok
Data	Jean-Luc	Odo	Wesley
Duras	Julian	Pavel	William
Elim	Kyril	Quark	Worf
Endar	Kyrus	Ramos	Zayner
Galek	Leonard	Rom	Zorn

Science fiction writer Anne McCaffrey created an entire world of distant-future Earth colonists in her *Dragonriders of Pern* and the *Rowan-Damia* novels. The names she created for her characters are acceptable to our 20th-century ears because they follow patterns we might logically expect to evolve from names in use today. Here are just a few examples from her novels.

WOMEN		MEN	
Adrea	Lessa	Afra	Mick
Almi	Mauli	Alemi	Perry
Aramina	Mavi	Curran	Reidis
Aranya	Menolly	David	Rojer
Damia	Mirrim	Ewain	Samvel
Durras	Morag	Fabry	Talmor
Hally	Morgelle	Hamian	Thian
Isthia	Petra	Jaxom	Tomal
Kaltia	Ramala	Jayge	Toric
Kami	Temma	Jeff	Torshan
Kitrin	Xahra	Kern	Worlain
Laria	Zara	Larad	Yanus

Elizabeth Moon, in her science fiction novel *The Hunting Party*, created names for her characters that are close to names we use today, yet are different in subtle ways. Moon also carries traditional names into the future, which is likely to happen in real life.

WOMEN		MEN	
Alicia	Heris	Allie	Kev
Amalie	Jalora	Arash	Miko
Andalanee	Kirsya	Brun	Nadrel
Aublice	Lorenza	Corey	Oblo
Berenice	Maris	Gari	Nils
Brigdis	Monica	Gavin	Padoc
Carly	Myrtis	George	Petris
Cecilia	Raffaele	Gerel	Piercy
Clarisse	Sorah	Herek	Ronnie
Devra	Vivi	Kentre	Tighe

THE MAGIC OF MIDDLE NAMES

A flamboyant middle name is like a hidden horn in your automobile that can play fanfares. You can be circumspect and never honk it, or just beep its initial, or you can turn heads when you use it. Every child should have one.
—Writer Robert Eugene Campbell attributed this quotation to G. Tallyrand Dubois, a fictional congressman from Louisiana. The points made in the quote are exceptionally apt to a discussion about middle names.

Whether flamboyant or more traditional, the middle name deserves credit for its all-around usefulness. Here are some of the gifts your child receives from a middle name.

Preservation of heritage
A family surname, the name of a beloved relative, or an ethnically significant name can be passed along in a middle name. If Melissa Maud appreciates the heritage sentiment but doesn't like the name Maud, she can simply use the initial instead of the full name.

Identification
When events in life require proof of identity, John Harrison Brown is more immediately identified than plain John Brown. In the 21st century, it's likely that more people will use two or even three middle names, for better identification in an ever-growing population.

Variety
Jared Jackson Garcia has quite a variety of name choices available as he goes through life. Jared, Jerry, Jay, J. J., Jack, Jackson, Jared J. Garcia, J. Jackson Garcia and Jared Jackson Garcia. For his e-mail address, the possible choices multiply.

Balance in the look and sound of the full name
The syllables in first, middle, and last names can add up to a balanced, pleasing effect, as in a name like Timothy Scott Daniels. Timothy Daniels, Tim Daniels, and Scott Daniels also appeal.

Compatibility
Middle names can provide a bridge between two less compatible names. For example, try saying Sheila Larue out loud. Then try Sheila Mae Larue. Which works better?

Peace
How better can you solve the problem of choosing between two grandparents' names for a new baby, or settle a dispute between two parents who can't agree on the names each prefers? There's room for two choices with a first and middle name. With good fortune, the names will work reasonably well together. If a special first name creates too many problems for your child in school, he or she could switch to the middle name, at least through the teasing years of childhood. As a teen or an adult, he or she probably will take pride in the distinction conferred by the more unusual name.

One last observation about middle names. Some parents like to make sure that their child uses both first and middle names in everyday life. Joining the two names with a hyphen encourages this kind of use. Friends and teachers quickly get used to saying "John-Paul" or "Carol-Ray." Birth registrations show that a trend is developing; more parents are hyphenating their babies' first and middle names. The John variants are especially favored for this treatment, as you can see by looking up those names in the index.

NAMING GOALS FOR PARENTS

Some Hints to Help Stay on Target

To keep this process simple, it's good to remember that whatever name you choose for your baby, ultimately he or she will imprint the name with his or her own personality and character. But you can start out with some basic goals that will increase your chances of picking out the best name. Maybe you can make things a little easier for your children as they find their places in life. Here are some suggested goals, with tips to ease the way.

Choose names for your child's benefit, not yours
This means no joke names, puns, or clever plays on words that might be funny for a little while, but would be a burden to your child for much longer. Don't overdo special pronunciation and spelling that require repeated explanations throughout life.

Look to your child's future, not just babyhood
Billy and Willie might be perfectly happy with those names all their lives, but it won't hurt if William is on their birth certificates if they're sitting on a judge's bench or in a corporate boardroom. Keep an open mind about your daughter's name; there are plenty of feminine names available that don't evoke stereotypes that might handicap a woman pursuing a career.

Build self-esteem
Your pride and approval when your child first learns to say and write his or her name will go a long way toward instilling self-esteem. During school years, offer help in dealing with any hurtful nicknames. Tell the stories of how carefully you chose the name, and why it's special to you. Sometimes a

teenager will go through a period of disliking a name, but be patient; that phase is almost always outgrown.

TIPS FOR SELECTING A NAME

1. Decide on the type of name you want
Do you want a classic traditional name, a more unusual name, or a combination of the two? Do you want a biblical name, an ethnic name, a very feminine name? As a starting point, look for a name that suits the type you want.

2. Heritage considerations
Have you already decided that the name you want must be specifically oriented to your family? Relatives' names, surnames, ethnic history, and personal favorite choices will guide you to names that fit your special family situation.

3. Consider cross-gender questions
Are you interested in some of the popular surname choices for girls? Does a name you're considering for a boy lean further toward usage for girls than for boys? Sometimes it's more difficult for boys to deal with teasing about having a name also used by girls.

4. Make lists
Start a list of possiblities for first and middle names. Don't argue too much with friends and relatives about choices; just add their suggestions to the list. Keep a special list of the names you and your parenting partner like.

5. Check the spelling of names on your lists
Don't take it for granted that you know the accepted spelling of a name. Familiar names like Brittany, Danielle, Dominic, and Zachary are misspelled on more birth certificates than you

might believe. Look up names in the index and check for the version you prefer.

6. *Examine names for potential disadvantages*

Is a name too common, not common enough, difficult to spell? Does it invite a disagreeable nickname? Does the name have negative associations that might make it difficult for the child to defend? Try to resolve the problems or just take the name off your list.

7. *Narrow your list to final choices*

This is when your name selection process can get tricky. It's important to come to mutual agreement with your partner on final name choice. If necessary, compromise on the final name choice. The father might choose the first name while the mother chooses the middle name, or the other way around. A good compromise, if neither parent likes the other's first choice, is to go with the next choice on their list that both can agree on. Or other solutions can be found. Your mutual agreement on the final choice, however achieved, is far better than having a child grow up hearing how much one parent dislikes the name.

Keep in mind that emotions at the time of birth frequently affect final name choices. One way of handling this might be agreeing in advance that you'll wait until the baby is born to decide. Or else you can make firm choices now and agree not to change later, no matter what. Remember also that unless you have reason to be certain of your baby's gender, be prepared with name choices for both.

If you have reason to believe you're expecting a multiple birth (twins, for example) your final choice will undoubtedly expand to include compatible pairs of names. Names that rhyme or begin with the same letter of the alphabet are popular with parents of twins and triplets. Some choose names whose only similarity is in the number of syllables and placement of emphasis; other avoid similarities in favor of individual distinction.

8. Verify the correct name after the baby is born
Check the birth certificate for correct spelling and birth details
as soon as you receive it. Register any needed corrections as
soon as possible.

THE NAME INDEX—HOW IT WORKS FOR YOU

The index in *Baby Names—A New Generation* is designed to
give you all the help you'll need. Look for these features:

Quick Reference to Traditional and Popular Names

Flip the pages of the index and look at the corner boxes on
the pages in each alphabetical group. The boxes titled "Quick
Reference: Names in the Top 300" feature names chosen by
some 80 percent of American parents in most states. If a Quick
Reference name interests you, look for the nearby main index
entry for more details.

Additional boxes within each alphabetical group in the index contain names under the title "Less Common Classics;
New, Unusual Names." These names are more rarely used,
generally ranking in the 300–500 most frequently used names,
or they're in the top 300 ranks in fewer states.

The Quick Reference boxes make it easier to sort through
the vast reservoir of available names. You may already have
an idea of the kind of name you want, and most likely it will
be among this group of names.

Whether you're satisfied with your first choices or not,
you'll also want to browse and read further in the index. The
name pool is wonderful in its variety and historical interest.
The index will give you a clearer picture of names in use
across the United States. You'll see how your choice compares

or fits into the world of American names. You might find a special name you like better than your first choice.

Pronunciation Key

Following each main name entry, a simplified pronunciation key in italics indicates how that name is most often pronounced in America. An all-capital syllable means that that part of the name should be emphasized. If no syllable is capitalized, all parts of the name should be stressed equally. Sometimes more than one pronunciation is shown. Opinions can vary on exact pronunciation, but the key does give guidelines. Rather than create a new spelling for a name when you're looking for a specific sound, check to see if what you want is already listed.

Origins

A single national origin follows the pronunciation key. Many names have gone from one people to another, changing as they go, and it's difficult to determine which origin has the priority. For example, names we call English came from a variety of sources. Pre-medieval Anglo-Saxon names had Germanic, Scandinavian, and Celtic roots. Danish and old Norse names were absorbed into English forms after Scandinavian raiders settled in England a thousand years ago. William the Conqueror brought Frankish names to his new country, and they became "English," although Frankish names actually were a mixture of Scandinavian, German, and French origins.

Meanings of Names

It's remarkable how many meanings of names have been preserved down through the ages. Other names have been altered or combined in various ways, or duplicated by other language groups, and their meanings become "possible," or are simply a matter of choice. The value of deciding on a particular meaning lies in keeping alive connections to the past, however tenuous and fragmentary a meaning might be.

Wherever possible, the definitions (set in quotation marks) that follow the origins in this index are meant to convey the sense of whatever meanings have come down to us, in language understood in our time.

Comments, Historical Notes, Information

Comments and information that follow the definitions provide some reasons why a particular name has stayed in use over the centuries. Most of Western civilization's names are related to biblical names and saints' names, for example. Writers such as William Shakespeare created memorable characters who greatly influenced name use. The index provides tidbits of information about these people of the past, the notable characters in literature and real individuals who made a name famous or added to its luster.

Names in the news today affect parents' awareness of names, so notes about many of these are included.

Variants and Associated Names

Variant forms of the main name are listed as subentries just below the main entry. If the first variant listed is in bold type, it's a version of the name that's used more frequently than the other variants. Variants may be contemporary created forms of the main name, blends with other name endings, or another language form of the name.

Some variants have an equal standing with the name they came from; you'll find many such names cross-referenced in their own separate main entries. For an example, see Mary, Marie, and Maria.

International Names

International names and their variants used today in America are identified in the comments or listed separately as main entries. Japanese, Hawaiian, and African/Islamic names in particular are included in the index, due to the increased interest of American descendants in examining names from their cultural heritage in an American context. Some of these names have similarities of favored sound and look patterns that work well in a multicultural nation. For example, the Japanese names Miki and Sachi are very similar to Mickey (Irish) and Sascha (Russian).

For those seeking further information about names from specific national groups, an excellent reference is *A World of Baby Names*, by Teresa Norman, a Perigee Book published in 1996 by the Berkley Publishing Group.

Sample Index Entry

Name   Pronunciation Key   Origin   Meaning

Aaron: (*AIR-an*) (Hebrew) "Lofty, inspired." Biblical: Moses' brother Aaron was the first high priest of Israel. See also Aron. [AAREN, AARYN, ARRON]

Cross Reference

Variants

Information

GIRLS' NAMES

A

Abigail: *(AB-ih-gayl)* (Hebrew) "My father rejoices." Biblical: the name of King David's third wife, described as "good in discretion and beautiful in form." See also Gail. [ABBY, ABAGAIL, ABBEY, ABBIE, ABIGALE, ABIGAYLE, AVAGAIL]

Abriana: *(ah-bree-AHN-ah)* (Italian) Feminine form of Abraham. Abra was the name of a fourth-century French saint. [ABRA, ABREE, ABRI, ABRIANNA, ABRIELLE, ABRIENNE]

Acacia: *(a-KAY-shah)* (Greek) "Honorable." Biblical: acacia wood was used to build the wilderness Tabernacle.

Ada: *(AY-dah)* (Hebrew) "Ornament." (Nigerian) "First daughter." Ayda: (Arabic) "Benefit." [ADAH, AYDA]

Adair: *(a-DARE)* (Scottish) "From the oak tree ford."

Adanna: *(a-DAN-ah)* (Nigerian) "Her father's daughter." Adana is a Spanish feminine form of Adam. [ADANA]

Adara: *(AH-dra)* (Arab) "Virgin." [ADRA, ADRAH]

Adela: *(a-DELL-ah)* (German) "Of nobility, noble." See also Adeline and Adelaide. [ADALIA, ADALIE, ADELE, ADELIA, ADELITA, ADELLA, ADELLE]

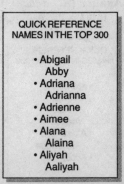

QUICK REFERENCE
NAMES IN THE TOP 300

- Abigail
  Abby
- Adriana
  Adrianna
- Adrienne
- Aimee
- Alana
  Alaina
- Aliyah
  Aaliyah

Adelaide: *(AD-a-layd)* (German) "Of nobility, noble." See also Adela and Adeline. [ADELAIDA]

Adeline: *(ADD-a-line, add-a-LEEN)* (French) Variant form of Adela. See also Alena. [ADALENE, ADALYN, ADDIE, ADELINA, ADELYNN, ADILENE]

Adelisa: *(ah-da-LEES-ah)* (French) A blend of Adela and Lisa. [ADALICIA, ADALIZ, ADELISA, ADELIZA]

Adinah: *(AH-dee-nah)* (Hebrew) "Noble." [ADENA, ADINA]

Adira: *(ah-DEER-ah)* (Arabic) "Strong."

Adonia: *(ah-DOHN-yah)* (Greek) "Beautiful lady." Feminine form of Adonis. [ADANYA]

Adriana: *(ay-dree-AHN-ah)* (Latin) "From Adria," the Adriatic Sea region. Also means "dark." **[ADRIANNA, ADRA, ADREA, ADREANNA, ADRIA, ADRIAN, ADRIANNE, ADRIELLE, ADRINA]**

Adrienne: *(AY-dree-en)* (French) Variant form of Adrian. [ADRIANE, ADRIENE, ADRIENNA]

Agatha: *(AG-a-thah)* (Greek) "Good." St. Agatha (third century) is the patron saint of bell-founders.

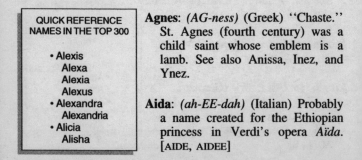

QUICK REFERENCE NAMES IN THE TOP 300

- Alexis
  Alexa
  Alexia
  Alexus
- Alexandra
  Alexandria
- Alicia
  Alisha

Agnes: *(AG-ness)* (Greek) "Chaste." St. Agnes (fourth century) was a child saint whose emblem is a lamb. See also Anissa, Inez, and Ynez.

Aida: *(ah-EE-dah)* (Italian) Probably a name created for the Ethiopian princess in Verdi's opera *Aïda*. [AIDE, AIDEE]

Ailani: *(ah-ee-LAH-nee)* (Hawaiian paraphrase) "High chief."

Aileen: *(eye-LEEN)* (Scottish, Irish) Variant form of Evelyn. See also Eileen. [AILEENE, AILENE, AILYN]

Aimee: *(ay-MEE)* (French) "Loved." Variant form of Amy. St. Ame of France (seventh century), also called Amatus, "beloved." [AIME]

Aisha: *(ah-EE-shah, AY-shah)* (Arabic) "Woman; life." Aisha was the name of the favorite wife of the prophet Mohammed. See also Asha, Asia, and Isha. [AISHAH, AYEISHA, AYESHA, AYISHA, AYSHA]

Akiko: *(AH-kee-koh)* (Japanese) "Light; bright."

Akilah: *(AH-kee-lah)* (Arabic) "Bright, smart." [AKEELAH, AKIELA, AKILI]

Alair: *(al-LEYR)* (French) "Cheerful, glad." Variant form of Hilary. [ALLAIRE]

Alana: *(ah-LAH-nah)* (Irish) "Dear child." (Hawaiian) "Awakening." Also used as a feminine form of Alan. Noted name bearer: Alanis Morissette, award-winning pop vocalist. [ALANAH, ALANI, ALANIS, ALANNA, ALANNAH, ALLANA, ALONA, ALONNA]

Alaina: *(ah-LAY-nah)* (French) "Fair one." [ALAINE, ALAYNA, ALAYNE, ALLAINE]

Alanza: *(ah-LAHN-zah)* (Spanish) "Ready for battle." Feminine form of Alonzo.

Alarice: *(AL-a-riss)* (German) "Rules all." Feminine form of Alaric. [ALLARYCE]

Alba: *(AL-bah)* (Latin) "Highlands." [ALBIA, ALBINA, ALBY]

Alberta: *(al-BER-tah)* (German) "Noble; bright." Feminine form of Albert. [ALBERTINA, ALBERTINE]

Alcine: *(al-SEEN)* (Italian) Literary: in the Orlando poems, Alcina is a mistress of alluring enchantments and sensual pleasures. [ALCEE, ALCINA, ALCINIA]

Alda: *(AHL-dah)* (Latin) "Wise; elder." Variant form of Aldo. [ALDANA, ALDARA, ALDENE, ALDONA]

Alena: *(a-LEE-nah, a-LAY-nah)* (Russian) A form of Helen. [ALEEN, ALEENA, ALENE, ALINA, ALINE, ALLENA, ALLENE, ALLINA, ALYNA]

Aletha: *(ah-LEE-thah)* (Greek) "Truthful." Mythology: goddess of truth. [ALATHEA, ALETA, ALETHEA, ALETHIA, ALITHEA]

Alessandra: *(al-ess-SAHN-drah)* (Italian) Variant form of Alexandra. [ALESSA, ALYSSANDRA]

Alexandra: *(al-eks-AHN-dra)* (Greek) "Defender of mankind." Feminine form of Alexander. See also Alondra, Alessandra, Alixandra, Alexis, Drina, Lexie, Lisandra, Olexa, Sandra, Sasha, Xandra, and Zandra. [ALEXANDRIA, ALEJANDRA, ALEKSANDRA, ALEXANDREA, ALEXANDRINA, ALEXSANDRA]

Alexis: *(a-LEX-iss)* (Greek) "Helper; defender." Short form of Alexandra. [ALEXA, ALEX, ALEXANNA, ALEXANNE, ALEXI, ALEXIA, ALEXINA, ALEXINE, ALEXIUS, ALEXUS, ALIX, ALYX]

Alfreda: *(al-FREE-dah, al-FRAY-dah)* (German) Feminine form of Alfred.

Ali: *(AL-ee)* (Arabic) "Greatest." A variant form of Allah, title of the Supreme Being in the Muslim faith. Allie is a short form of names beginning with *Al-*. Famous name

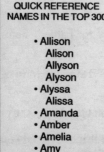

QUICK REFERENCE
NAMES IN THE TOP 300

- Allison
  Alison
  Allyson
  Alyson
- Alyssa
  Alissa
- Amanda
- Amber
- Amelia
- Amy

bearers: actresses Ali McGraw and Ally Walker. [ALEE, AL-IANA, ALLI, ALLIE, ALLY, ALYA]

Alixandra: *(al-eks-AHN-drah)* (French) Variant form of Alexandra. [ALIXANDRIA]

Aliyah: *(AH-lee-ah, ah-LEE-ah)* (Hebrew) "To ascend." Noted name bearer: singer Aaliyah. [AALIYAH, ALEA, ALEAH, ALEANA, ALEEA, ALEEYAH, ALIA]

Alice: *(AL-iss)* (English) "Of the nobility." Variant form of the old French name Adeliz, from Adelaide. See also Adelisa, Alicia, Alisa, Allison, Alyssa, and Elke. [ALEECE, AL-LISS, ALLYCE, ALLYSE, ALYCE, ALYS, ALYSA, ALYSE, ALYSS]

Alicia: *(ah-LEE-shah, ah-LEE-see-ah)* (Latin) Variant form of Alice. Phonetic forms to ensure a particular pronunciation are popular. Noted name bearer: actress Alicia Silverstone. See also Alyssa and Licia. [ALISHA, ALECIA, ALEECIA, ALEESA, ALEESHA, ALEEZA, ALESHA, ALESHIA, ALISHIA, ALISIA, ALLYSA, ALYCIA, ALYSA, ALYSHA, ALYSIA]

Alida: *(ah-LEE-da)* (Latin) "With wings."

Alika: *(ah-LEE-kah)* (Nigerian) "Most beautiful."

Alima: *(ah-LEE-mah)* (Hebrew) "Strong."

Alisa: *(ah-LEE-sah)* (Spanish) Variant form of Alice. [ALISE]

Alita: *(ah-LEE-tah)* (Spanish) Short form of Adelita.

Alizah: *(ah-LEE-zah)* (Hebrew) "Joy, joyful." [ALEEZA, ALEEZAH, ALIZA, ALIZE, ALYZA]

Allegra: *(ah-LAY-grah)* (Italian) "Lively; happy."

Allison: *(AL-ih-son)* (English) Diminutive form of Alice. [AL-ISON, ALLYSON, ALISANNE, ALYSON]

Alma: *(AL-mah)* (Latin) "The soul."

Almira: *(al-MEER-ah)* (Arabic) "Princess."

Aloise: *(AL-oh-eez)* (Latin) "Famous in battle." Feminine form of Aloysius, the name of a 16th-century Spanish saint.

Aloma: *(ah-LOH-mah)* (Latin) "Dove." Short form of Paloma.

Alondra: *(ah-LAWN-drah)* (American) Contemporary creation. Alondra and its variants may be based on the favored name sounds of Alana, Alexandra, and Sandra. [ALANDA, ALANDRA, ALLONDRA]

Alpha: *(AL-fah)* (Greek) The first letter of the Greek alphabet. May be used for a firstborn daughter.

Alta: *(ALL-tah)* (Spanish) "High." Short form of Altagracia, a reference to the "high grace" of Mary, the mother of Jesus. [ALTAGRACIA]

Altaira: *(al-TARE-ah)* (Arabic) "High-flying." In astronomy, Altair is a star of the first magnitude.

Althea: *(al-THEE-ah)* (Greek) "Wholesome." See also Thea. [ALTHIA]

Alva: *(AL-vah)* (Hebrew) "Sublime." Alvarita and Alvera are Spanish feminine forms of Alvaro, meaning "speaker of truth." Alvina is the feminine form of Alvin, meaning "wise friend." [ALVARITA, ALVEENA, ALVERA, ALVERNA, ALVINA, ALVITA]

Alyssa: *(ah-LISS-ah)* (English) Variant form of Alice. Noted name

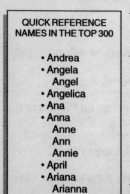

QUICK REFERENCE
NAMES IN THE TOP 300

• Andrea
• Angela
  Angel
• Angelica
• Ana
• Anna
  Anne
  Ann
  Annie
• April
• Ariana
  Arianna

bearer: actress Alyssa Milano. [ALISSA, ALISSE, ALLYSE, ALLYSSA, ALYSE, ALYSSE, ALYSSIA]

Ama: *(AH-ma)* (Ghanaian) "Saturday's child." [AMI]

Amabel: *(AM-a-bell)* (Latin) "Lovable." See also Anabel. [AMABELA]

Amada: *(ah-MAH-dah)* (Spanish) "Beloved." [AMADEA, AMADIA, AMADITA]

Amala: *(ah-MAL-ah)* (Arabic) "Hope." Amaliah *(ah-ma-LEE-ah)* is probably a variant form of Amelia. [AMALIAH]

Amanda: *(ah-MAN-dah)* (Latin) "Worthy of being loved." Literary: poets and playwrights brought this name into popular usage in the 17th century. May also be used as a feminine form of Amand, the name of a sixth-century French saint, also called Amandus.

Amantha: *(ah-MAN-thah)* (Greek) Variant form of Aramantha, a flower name, or a short form of Samantha.

Amapola: *(ah-mah-POH-lah)* (Arabic) "Poppy."

Amara: *(ah-MAHR-ah)* (Spanish) "Imperishable." Amaris, meaning "child of the moon," is the astrological name for Cancer. [AMARIS, AMARISSA]

Amaryllis: *(am-ah-RILL-iss)* (Greek) Flower name: poetically, a simple shepherdess or country girl.

Amber: *(AM-ber)* (Arabic) A jewel-quality fossilized resin; as a color, the name refers to a warm honey shade. Contemporary variants may be rhyming variants based on Kimberly. [AMBERLEE, AMBERLI, AMBERLY, AMBERLYN, AMBERLYNN]

Amelia: *(a-MEEL-yah)* (Latin) "Industrious, striving." See also Emily. [AMALIA, AMALIE, AMELIE]

Amethyst: *(AM-uh-thist)* (Greek) "Against intoxication." A purple- or violet-colored gemstone. According to ancient Greek superstition, an amethyst protected its owner against the effects of strong drink.

Amina: *(ah-MEEN-ah)* (Arabic) "Trustworthy." [AMEENA, AMEENAH, AMENA, AMINAH, AMINEH]

Amira: *(ah-MEER-ah)* (Hebrew) "Princess; one who speaks." [AMEERA, AMIRAH]

Amita: *(ah-MEE-tah)* (Hebrew) "Truth."

Amity: *(AM-ih-tee)* (Latin) "Friendship."

Amy: *(AY-mee)* (English) "Beloved." See also Aimee. [AMEE, AMI, AMIA, AMIE, AYMEE]

Ana: *(AHN-ah)* (Spanish) "Grace; favor." Variant form of Anna. Ana is often used in blended names like Analee and Anarosa. See also Anna and Anne. [ANALEE, ANALEIGH, ANALENA, ANAMARIA, ANAMARIE, ANAROSA]

Anabel: (Latin) "Beautiful; graceful." [ANABELLE, ANNABEL, ANNABELLA, ANNABELLE]

Anaïs: *(ah-NAY-us, ah-NYE-ess)* (Latin) Variant form of Ana. [ANAYAS]

Anastasia: *(ahn-a-STAH-shah, ahn-a-STAY-zhah)* (Greek) "Resurrection." The name of one of the daughters of Nicholas II, the last Russian czar. For decades some claimed that she alone survived the massacre of the royal family, but no claim has been proven. Also a saint's name. [ANASTACIA, ANA-

QUICK REFERENCE
NAMES IN THE TOP 300

- Ariel
- Ashley
  Ashlee
  Ashleigh
- Ashlyn
- Ashton
- Asia
- Aubrey
- Audrey
- Autumn

STASHA, ANASTASHIA, ANASTASSIA, ANASTAZIA, ANNAS-
TASIA] ·

Ancina: *(an-SEE-nah)* (Latin) A diminutive form of Ann. St.
Ancina (16th century) was a doctor of medicine and phi-
losophy.

Andee: *(an-DEE)* (Contemporary) Feminine short form of Andrea. Noted name bearer: actress/model Andie MacDowell.
[ANDENA, ANDI, ANDIE]

Andrea: *(AHN-dree-ah, AN-dree-ah)* (Greek) Feminine form
of Andrew, much favored for blended variants. See also
Ondrea. [ANDRA, ANDRANETTA, ANDREANA, ANDREANNA,
ANDREE, ANDREINA, ANDRENA, ANDREYA, ANDRIA, ANDRI-
ANA, ANDRIANNA, ANDRIANNE, ANDRIELLE, ANDRIENNE,
ANDRINA, AUNDREA]

Andromeda: *(an-DRAH-ma-dah)* (Greek) Mythology: an
Ethiopian princess, the wife of Perseus. Also a northern
constellation.

Angela: *(AN-je-lah)* (Greek) "Messenger." [ANGEL, ANGE-
LINA, ANGELE, ANGELEE, ANGELENA, ANGELENE, ANGELI,
ANGELIA, ANGELINE, ANGELISA, ANGELISE, ANGELITA, AN-
GELL, ANGELLE, ANGELYN, ANGELYNN, ANGIE]

Angelica: *(an-JEL-ih-kah)* (Latin) "Like an angel." Angelique is a French form; Anjelika is Russian. Noted name
bearer: actress Anjelica Huston. [ANGELICIA, ANGELIKA,
ANGELIQUE, ANJELICA, ANJELIKA, ANJELIQUE]

Anissa: *(a-NISS-ah)* (English) Variant form of Anne or Agnes.
Anysia is the name of a fourth-century Thessalonian saint.
[ANESSA, ANNICE, ANNIS, ANNISSA, ANYSIA, ANYSSA]

Anisa: *(ah-NEE-sah)* (Arabic) "Friendly." Anisha (Hindi)
means "end of night." [ANEECIA, ANEESA, ANEESAH,
ANEISHA, ANICIA, ANISHA]

Anita: *(a-NEE-tah)* (Spanish) Diminutive form of Anne. [ANEETA, ANITIA]

Anitra: *(a-NEE-trah)* (Scandinavian) A name created for the Princess in Ibsen's *Peer Gynt*.

Anjanette: *(an-ja-NET)* (American) "Gift of God's favor." Blend of Ann and Janet. [ANJANIQUE, ANJEANETTE, ANN-JEANETTE]

Anna: *(AN-ah)* (Latin) Variant of Hannah. Biblical: a devout woman who saw the infant Jesus presented at the temple in Jerusalem. Anna is often used in combination with other names. See also Ana and Anne. [ANNABETH, ANNALEE, AN-NAMARIE, ANNEMARIE, ANNMARIE]

Annalisa: *(an-a-LEE-sah)* (Latin) "Graced with God's bounty." [ANALICIA, ANALIESE, ANALISA, ANALISE, ANAL-ISIA, ANALISSA, ANALYSSA, ANNALISE, ANNALISSA, ANNE-LIESE, ANNELISA, ANNELISE]

Anne: *(an)* (English) "Favor, grace." Variant form of Hannah. A name favored by royalty and commoners for centuries. Among the royal name bearers: two queens of England, a queen of France, an empress of Russia and, today, Princess Anne of England. See also Ana, Anabel, Anissa, Anita, Anjanette, Anna, Annalisa, Anneke, Annette, Nana, Nancy, Nanette, and Ninon. [ANN, **ANNIE**, ANELIE, ANNI, ANYA]

LESS COMMON CLASSICS; NEW, UNUSUAL NAMES

- Alice
- Allie
- Alondra
- Anastasia
- Angelina
- Angelique
- Anita
- Annette

Anneka: *(AH-ne-kah)* (Scandinavian, Dutch) A diminutive form of Ann. [ANNEKE, ANNIKA]

Annette: *(an-NET)* (French) Diminutive form of Anne. [ANNETTA]

Annora: *(an-NOR-ah)* (Latin) English variant form of Honora.

Anthea: *(ahn-THEE-ah)* (Greek) "Lady of flowers." [AN-THIA]

Antoinette: *(ann-twa-NET)* (French) Feminine form of Anthony.

Antonia: *(ann-TONE-yah)* (Latin) "Highly praiseworthy." Feminine form of Anthony, with contemporary variants. See also Antoinette and Toni. [ANTONELLA, ANTONETTA, ANTONETTE, ANTONINA, ANTONIQUE, ANTONISHA]

Aphra: *(AFF-rah)* (Hebrew) "Dust." Biblical place name. Afra is the name of a fourth-century German saint. [AFRA]

Apollonia: *(ah-poh-LONE-yah)* (Latin) "Belonging to Apollo." Mythology: Apollo was the Greek god of sunlight, music, and poetry. A saint's name.

April: *(AY-prill)* (Latin) The month as a given name; often used to symbolize spring. See also Averil. Abril *(ah-BREEL)* is the Spanish form. [ABRIL, APRILLE, APRYL, APRYLL]

Arabelle: *(AIR-a-bell)* (Latin) "Calling to prayer." [ARA-BELLA]

Araceli: *(ar-ah-SAY-lee)* (Spanish) "Altar of heaven." [ARACELIA, ARACELY, ARCELIA, ARCILLA, ARICELA]

Arcadia: *(ar-KAY-dee-ah)* (Greek) "Pastoral simplicity and happiness." A feminine form of Arcadius, the name of two saints (fourth and fifth century).

Ardel: *(ar-DELL)* (Latin) "Eager; industrious." A feminine form of Ardo, the name of a ninth-century French saint. [ARDELLA, ARDELLE]

Arden: *(AR-den)* (English) "Lofty; eager." [ARDENA, AR-DENE]

Ardis: *(AR-diss)* (Scottish, Irish) Variant of Allardyce. [AR-DISS, ARDYCE, ARDYS, ARDYSS]

Aretha: *(a-REE-thah)* (Greek) "Virtuous; excellent." Noted name bearer: singer Aretha Franklin. [ARETA]

Argene: *(ar-JEEN)* (French) "Silvery." [ARJANE, ARJEAN]

Ariadne: *(ar-ee-AHD-nee)* (Greek) "Chaste; holy." Mythology: Ariadne helped Theseus escape from the Cretan labyrinth. St. Ariadne of Phrygia (second century) was a slave who became a saint. [ARIA, ARIADNA, ARIETTE]

Ariana: *(ar-ee-AH-nah)* (Greek) Variant form of Ariadne. [ARIANNA, ARIANE, ARIANNE, ARIONNA, ARRIANA]

Ariel: *(AYR-ee-ul)* (Hebrew) "Lion of God." Biblical; a name for Jerusalem. Shakespeare gave the name to a prankish spirit in *The Tempest*. Ariel was also popularized in the 1990s as the name of the mermaid in Walt Disney's cartoon feature film *The Little Mermaid*. [ARIELLE, ARIELA, ARIELE, ARIELLA]

Arleigh: *(AR-lee)* (English) "Meadow of the hare."

Arlene: *(ar-LEEN)* (English) Origin uncertain. Most likely based on Carlene and Charlene. [ARLA, ARLAN, ARLEANA, ARLEEN, ARLEENA, ARLEENE, ARLENA, ARLINA, ARLINE, ARLYNE]

LESS COMMON CLASSICS;
NEW, UNUSUAL NAMES

- Antoinette
- Arielle
- Arlene
- Audra
- Aurora
- Avery
- Ayana
  Ayanna

Arlette: *(ar-LET)* (French) A medieval given name of uncertain origin. [ARLETA, ARLETTA]

Arlinda: *(ar-LIN-dah)* (American) Blend of Arlene and Linda. [ARLENNA, ARLENNE, ARLYN]

Arliss: *(AR-liss)* (Irish) "High fort." A place name. [ARLISSA]

Armanda: *(ar-MAHN-dah)* (Spanish) Feminine form of Armando.

Arnelle: *(ar-NELL)* (American) "The eagle rules." Feminine form of Arnold. [ARNESSA, ARNETTA, ARNETTE, ARNIESHA, ARNISHA]

Arsenia: *(ar-SEE-nee-ah)* (Latin) Feminine form of Arsenio. St. Arsenius (fourth century) is famous for the saying, "I have often been sorry for having spoken, but never for having held my tongue."

Artemis: *(AR-te-miss)* (Greek) "Virgin goddess of the moon; huntress." Mythology: the equivalent of the Romans' Diana.

Asenath: *(a-SEE-nath)* (Egyptian) "Daughter." Biblical: Joseph's Egyptian wife. [ACENATH]

Asha: *(AH-shah)* (Sanskrit) "Hope." Mythology: the wife of a Hindu demigod. Ashia *(ah-SHEE-ah)* is a Somali name. See also Aisha. [ASHIA]

Ashley: *(ASH-lee)* (English) "Meadow of ash trees." An English surname. Also the name of an English saint (17th century). [ASHLEE, ASHLEIGH, **ASHLIE**, ASHLA, ASHLEAH, ASHLEI, ASHLI, ASHLY]

Ashlyn: *(ASH-lin)* (Irish) "Dream." [ASHLEEN, ASHLEENA, ASHLEN, ASHLIN, ASHLINN, ASHLYNN, ASHLYNNE, AYSLIN, AYSLYN]

Ashton: *(ASH-ten)* (English) "Town of ash trees." [ASHTEN, ASHTYN]

Asia: *(AY-zhah)* "The rising sun." The name of the continent used as a given name. According to the Koran, Asia was the name of the Pharaoh's wife who raised the infant Moses. Asia is also a variant form of Aisha ("life"), the name of Mohammed's favorite wife, one of the four "perfect women." See also Aisha, Fatima, Khadijah, and Mary. [ASIAH, ASIANNE, ASYA, ASYAH, AZIA]

Astra: *(AS-tra)* (Latin) "Star."

Astrid: *(AS-trid)* (Scandinavian) "Godly strength."

Athena: *(a-THEE-nah)* (Latin) Variant form of Athene, the mythological goddess of wisdom and war. [ATHEENA, ATHENE]

Auberta: *(oh-BEHR-tah, oh-BERT-ah)* (French) Feminine French variant of Albert. St. Aubert (eighth century) built the famous monastery Mont St. Michel.

Aubrey: *(AW-bree)* (French) "Rules with elf-wisdom." [AUBREE, AUBRI, AUBRIANA, AUBRIANNE, AUBRIE, AUBRY]

Audrey: *(AW-dree)* (English) "Nobility; strength." St. Audrey (seventh century) was a revered Anglo-Saxon abbess-saint who was also daughter of a king. [AUDELIA, AUDENE, AUDESSA, AUDRA, AUDREA, AUDREE, AUDRI, AUDRIA, AUDRIE, AUDRIELLE, AUDRINA, AUDRIS]

Audriana: *(aw-dree-AHN-ah)* (Latin) A blend of Audrey and Anna. [AUDREANA, AUDREANNA, AUDRIANNA]

Augusta: *(aw-GUS-tah)* (Latin) "Majestic, grand." Feminine form of August. [AGUSTINA, AUGUSTINA]

Aurelia: *(aw-REEL-yah)* (Latin) "Golden." [ARELA, ARELI, ARELIE, ARELLA, ARELY, AURELIE, AURENE, AURIEL, AURIELLE]

Aura: *(AWR-ah)* (Greek) "Breeze." Mythology: Aura was the goddess of breezes. [AURIA, AURIANA, AURIEL]

Aurora: *(aw-ROHR-ah)* (Latin) "Dawn." Mythology: Aurora was the Roman goddess of dawn. [AURORE]

Austine: *(aws-TEEN)* (French) Variant form of Augustine. [AUSTINA]

Autumn: *(AW-tum)* (English) The fall season.

Ava: *(AY-vah)* (English) Meaning uncertain; possibly a variant of Avis or Aveline, medieval given names. In contemporary usage, some forms may be intended as phonetic variants of Eva and Evelyn. See also Avis. [AVAH, AVALEE, AVELINA, AVELINE, AVELYN, AVLYNN]

Averil: *(AY-vril)* (English) "Opening buds of spring; born in April." See also April. [AVERILL, AVERYL, AVRIEL, AVRIL, AVRILL]

Avery: *(AY-vree)* (English) "Wise ruler." [AVRIE]

Aviana: *(ay-vee-AHN-ah, ah-vee-AHN-ah)* (Latin) Blend of Ava and Ana. [AVIA, AVIANNA]

Avis: *(AY-viss)* (English) A medieval name of uncertain meaning. [AVICE]

Aviva: *(a-VEE-vah)* (Hebrew) "Springtime." [AVIVAH, AVIVI]

Ayala: *(ay-AL-ah)* (Hebrew) "Doe." The name of a 17th-century Spanish saint.

Ayana: *(ay-AHN-ah)* (American) Meaning uncertain, probably a contemporary creation. [AYANNA, AYONNA]

Ayla: *(AY-lah)* (Hebrew) "Oak tree." Literary: Ayla is the heroine of Jean Auel's *Clan of the Cave Bear* series.

Azalea: *(a-ZAYL-yah)* (Greek) "Dry." A flower name. [AZALIA]

Aziza: *(ah-ZEE-zah)* (Arabic) "Beloved." (Swahili) "Precious." [AZIZI]

Azure: *(Ah-zhure)* (French) "Sky blue." The color used as a given name. [AZURA, AZUREE, AZURINE]

Azusena: *(ah-zoo-SAY-nah)* (Arabic) "Lily." [ASUCENA, AZUCENA, AZUSA]

B

Bailey: *(BAY-lee)* (French) Courtyard within castle walls; a steward or public official. Surname. Initial popularity of Bailey was due to a character in the 1980s television series *WKRP in Cincinnati*. [BAILEE, BAYLEE, BAYLEY, BAYLIE]

Bambi: *(BAM-bee)* (Italian) "Little child, *bambino*." Pet name.

Barbara: *(BAR-bra)* (Latin) "Traveler from a foreign land." Used since medieval times. In Roman Catholic custom, St. Barbara is invoked as a protector against fire and lightning. Barbra is a spelling variant made familiar by singer/actress/ film director Barbra Streisand. See also Bobbie. [BABETTE, BARBARELLA, BARBARITA, BARBI, BARBIE, BARBRA]

Beata: *(bee-AH-tah)* (Latin) "Happy; blessed."

Beatrice: *(BEE-a-triss)* (Latin) "Brings joy." Beatriz is a Spanish form; Beatrix is French. [BEATRIZ, BEA, BEATRISS, BEATRIX, BEE]

Becky: *(BEK-ee)* (English) Short form of Rebecca. [BECCA, BECKI]

Belen: *(bay-LEN)* (Spanish) "Bethlehem."

Belinda: *(ba-LIN-dah)* (English) "Very beautiful." Probably a poetic creation.

Bella: *(BELL-ah)* (Latin) "Fair, lovely one." Also a short form of Isabel. Noted name bearers: author/politician Bella Abzug and author Belva Plain. [BEL, BELLE, BELLISSA, BELVA]

Benecia: *(ba-NEE-sha)* (Latin) "Blessed one." [BENICIA]

Benita: *(be-NEE-ta)* (Latin) "Blessed." Feminine variant of Benedict.

Berenice: *(behr-a-NEE-see, behr-a-NEECE)* (Greek) "One who brings victory." See also Bernice. [BERENISA, BERENISE, BERRI, BERRY]

Bernadette: *(ber-na-DET)* (French) "Little strong bear." Feminine form of Bernard. Most famous name bearer was St. Bernadette of Lourdes (19th century). [BERNA, BERNADEA, BERNARDA, BERNELLE, BERNETTA, BERNETTE, BERNITA]

Bernadine: *(ber-na-DEEN, BER-na-deen)* (German) Feminine form of Bernard. [BERDINE, BERNARDINA, BERNEEN]

Bernice: *(ber-NEECE)* (Greek) "One who brings victory." Variant form of Berenice. [BERNICIA, BERNISHA, BERNISS, BERNYCE]

Bertha: *(BER-thah)* (German) "Bright." The name of two French saints (eighth and ninth century). Berta is a Spanish form. [BERTA, BERTHE]

Bertina: *(ber-TEEN-ah)* (English) "Bright." Feminine short form of

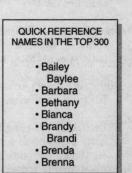

QUICK REFERENCE
NAMES IN THE TOP 300

- Bailey
  Baylee
- Barbara
- Bethany
- Bianca
- Brandy
  Brandi
- Brenda
- Brenna

names like Albert. May also be intended as a diminutive form of Bertha. [BERTINE]

Beryl: *(BEHR-el)* (Greek) A gemstone of varying colors, most often yellow-green. Biblical: the eighth foundation stone of the wall of New Jerusalem was made of beryl.

Beth: *(beth)* (Hebrew) Short form of Elizabeth. Literary: Louisa M. Alcott gave the name to the most beloved of the four daughters in *Little Women*.

Bethany: *(BETH-a-nee)* (Hebrew) The name of a village near Jerusalem where Jesus visited Mary, Martha, and Lazarus. [BETHANEE, BETHANI, BETHANIE, BETHANN]

Bethea: *(BETH-ee-ah, be-THE-ah)* (Hebrew) ''Maidservant of Jehovah.'' [BETHIA]

Bethel: *(BETH-el)* (Hebrew) ''House of God.''

Betty: *(BET-ee)* (English) Short form of Elizabeth. [BESS, BESSIE, BESSY, BETSEY, BETSY, BETTE, BETTINA, BETTINE]

Beulah: *(BEW-lah)* (Hebrew) ''Claimed as a wife.'' Biblical: a name symbolic of the heavenly Zion.

Beverly: *(BEV-er-lee)* (English) ''Beaver stream.'' [BEVERLEE, BEVERLEY]

Bianca: *(bee-AHNK-ah)* (Italian) ''White; shining.'' Variant form of Blanche (French). Blanca is the Spanish form. [BLANCA, BIANKA, BLANCHE, BYANCA]

Bibi: *(BEE-bee)* (Arabic, Persian) ''Lady.'' Bibiana is a Spanish form of Vivian. [BIBIANA, BEBE]

Billie: *(BILL-ee)* (English) ''Determination; strength.'' Originally a nickname for William. Now a feminine name, often combined with other names. Billy is used for boys. [BILLIE-JEAN, BILLIE JO]

Birdena: *(ber-DEEN-ah)* (American) "Little bird." May also be a variant form of Bernadine. See also Bernadette. [BIRDIE, BIRDINE, BYRDENE]

Birgitta: *(ber-GEE-tah)* (Scandinavian) "Strong." Variant form of Bridget. See also Bridget and Britt. [BIRGIT, BIRGITTE, BRITA]

Blaine: *(blayne)* (Scottish) Surname, meaning uncertain. Possibly a form of Blane. St. Blane (seventh century) was a Scottish saint.

Blair: (Scottish) "Field of battle." [BLAIRE]

Blake: *(blayk)* (English) "Black."

Bliss: (English) "Joy, cheer." Bliss and its variants date from medieval times. [BLISSE, BLYSS, BLYSSE]

Blondell: *(blon-DELL)* (French) "Fair-haired, blonde." Blandina is a Spanish name meaning "coaxing; flattering." St. Blandina (second century). [BLANDINA, BLONDELLE, BLONDENE]

Blythe: (English) "Blithe, lighthearted."

Bo: *(boh)* (Scandinavian) Nickname or short form. Made prominent by actress Bo Derek. Also a Chinese name meaning "precious."

Bobbie: *(BAH-bee)* (Contemporary) Nickname of Roberta and Barbara. Bobbie is sometimes combined with other names, with or without a hyphen. [BOBBI, BOBBIE-JEAN, BOBBIE JO]

Bonita: *(boh-NEE-tah)* (Spanish) "Little good one." In everyday

QUICK REFERENCE NAMES IN THE TOP 300
• Breanna
• Brianna
Briana
Brianne
• Bridget
• Brittany
• Brittney
• Brooke
Brooklyn

Spanish, *bonita* means "pretty." St. Bonitus was a seventh-century French saint.

Bonnie: *(BAHN-ee)* (Scottish) Diminutive of the French word *bon*, "good." In Scottish usage, *bonnie* means "pretty; charming." [BONNI, BONNIBELLE, BONNIE-JO, BONNY, BONNY-JEAN, BONNY-LEE]

Brandy: *(BRAN-dee)* (English) The name of the beverage used as a given name, with contemporary variants. Brandi is also an Italian surname form of Brand, "sword." [**BRANDI**, BRANDA, BRANDEE, BRANDELYN, BRANDICE, BRANDIE, BRANDILYN, BRANDYCE, BRANDYN]

Breanna: *(bree-ANN-ah)* (American) An alternate form of Brianna. See also Bree, Brianna, and Brionna. [**BREANNE**, BREANA, BREANN, BREEANA, BREEANN, BREEANNA, BREEANNE, BREONA, BREONDA, BREONNA]

Breck: *(brek)* (Irish) "Freckled."

Bree: *(bree)* (Irish) "Hill." May also be used as a short form of names like Brina and Breanna. See also Brianna. [BREA, BRIA, BRIELLE]

LESS COMMON CLASSICS;
NEW, UNUSUAL NAMES

- Bailee
- Berenice
- Beverly
- Blair
- Bobbie
- Bonnie
- Breana
- Breanne
- Bria
- Brook
- Bryanna
- Bryn
  Brynn

Breena: *(BREE-nah)* (Irish) "Fairy palace." May also be used as a short form of Brianna and Sabrina. [BREEN, BRENEE, BRINA, BRYNA]

Brenda: *(BREN-dah)* (Irish) "Princess." Feminine form of Brendan. [BRENDALYNN, BRENDOLYN, BRYNDA]

Brenna: *(BREN-ah)* (Irish) Variant form of Brenda. [BRYNNA]

Brett: *(bret)* (English) "Brit." A native of Britain (England) or Brittany (France). Lady Brett Ashley was Hemingway's heroine in the novel *The Sun Also Rises.* [BRET, BRETTA, BRETTANY, BRETTE]

Brianna: *(bree-ANN-ah)* (Irish) "She ascends." A contemporary feminine form of Brian. See also Breanna, Bree, Breena, and Brionna. [BRIANA, BRIANNE, BRIANN, BRIANNA, BRIANNAH, BRIANNON, BRIENNA, BRIENNE, BRYANA, BRYANN, BRYANNA, BRYANNE]

Brianda: *(bree-AHN-dah)* (American) Contemporary combination of Briana and Brenda.

Bridget: *(BRIH-jet)* (Irish) "Strong." Mythology: an Irish goddess. St. Bridgida, patroness of Ireland (fifth century) and St. Bridget of Sweden (14th century) are famous name bearers.

Brina: *(BREE-nah)* Short form of Sabrina. See also Breena.

Brionna: *(bree-AHN-ah)* Variant form of Brianna. [BRIONA, BRIONE, BRIONNE, BRYONNA]

Briony: *(BRY-o-nee)* (Greek) The name of a flowering vine used in folk medicine. [BRIONI, BRYANI, BRYONY]

Brisa: *(BREE-sah)* (Latin) Short form of the Spanish name Briseida, from Briseis, the Greek name of the woman loved by Achilles in Homer's *Iliad.* [BREEZY, BRISEIDA, BRISHA, BRISIA, BRISSA, BRIZA, BRYSSA]

Britt: *(brit)* (Scandinavian) "Strength." Short form of Brigit, from the Irish name Bridget. [BRIT, BRITA, BRITTA]

Brittania: *(brih-TAHN-yah)* (Latin) A poetic name for Great Britain. See also Brittany and Brittney. [BRITANIA, BRITTANYA]

Brittany: *(BRIT-'n-ee)* (English) From the name of an ancient duchy (Bretagne) in France. Celtic Bretons emigrated from

France and became the Bretons of England; later the name *Britain* came to signify the entire country. See also Brittney. [**BRITTANI**, BRITANI, BRITTANEY, BRITTANIE]

Brittney: *(BRIT-nee)* Very popular modern variant of Brittany; the phonetic spelling ensures a two-syllable pronunciation. [**BRITNEY**, BRITTNEE, BRITTNI]

Bronwyn: *(BRON-win)* (Welsh) "White-breasted." [BRANWYN, BRONWEN]

Brooke: *(bruk)* (English) "Water, stream." Actress Brooke Shields has made the English surname familiar as a girl's given name today. [BROOK, BROOKLYN, BROOKLYNN, BROOKLYNNE]

Bryce: (Scottish) Variant form of Bricius, a saint's name.

Bryn: *(bren)* (Welsh) "Hill." [BREN, BRENNE, BRYNN, BRYNNA, BRYNNAN, BRYNNE, BRYNELLE]

Cadence: *(KAYD-ens)* (Latin) "Rhythm."

Cady: *(KAY-dee)* (American) Possibly a combination of Katy and Cody. See also Kady. [CADEE, CADI, CADIE]

Cailin: *(KAY-lin)* (Gaelic) "Girl, lass." Possibly a contemporary variant of Cailean (Scottish). See also Kaylin. [CAELAN, CAELYN, CAILEEN, CAILYN, CAYLIN]

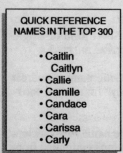

QUICK REFERENCE
NAMES IN THE TOP 300

- Caitlin
  Caitlyn
- Callie
- Camille
- Candace
- Cara
- Carissa
- Carly

Caitlin: *(KATE-lin)* (Irish) Variant form of Katherine. See also Catherine, Kaitlyn, Katelyn, and Katherine. [CAITLYN, CAIT, CAITLAN, CAITLAND, CAITLINN, CAITLYNN, CAITRIN, CATELINE, CATELYN, CATLIN, CATLINE, CATLYN, CATRIONA]

Calandra: *(ka-LAHN-drah)* (Greek) "Lark." Calinda and Calynda are contemporary variants or blends with Linda. [CALENDRE, CALINDA, CALYNDA]

Calista: *(ka-LEES-tah, ka-LISS-tah)* (Greek) "Most beautiful." Callistus was a third-century Roman saint. Mythology: an Arcadian nymph who metamorphosed into a she-bear, then into the Great Bear constellation. See also Kallista. [CALI, CALISSA, CALISTO, CALLISTA, CALYSSA, CALYSTA]

Callan: *(KAL-an)* (Gaelic) "Powerful in battle." See also Kallan. [CALLEN, CALYNN]

Callie: *(KAL-ee)* (Irish) Variant form of Cayley; also a short form of names beginning with *Cal-*. See also Kallie. [CALI, CALINA, CALLEE, CALLEY, CALLI]

Calliope: *(ka-LYE-ah-pee)* (Greek) "Beautiful voice." Mythology: the muse of epic poetry.

Calvinna: *(kal-VIN-ah)* (Latin) Feminine form of Calvin. [CALVINNE]

Calypso: *(ka-LIP-so)* (Greek) Mythology: a nymph who beguiled Odysseus for seven years. Music: a West Indian style of extemporaneous singing.

Cambria: *(KAM-bree-ah)* (Latin) The latinized name for Wales. See also Kambria. [CAMBREE]

Camelia: *(ka-MEEL-yah)* (Latin) A flower name often associated with the name Camille. See also Camille and Kamelia. [CAMELLA, CAMELLIA]

Cameo: *(KAM-ee-o)* (English) A gem portrait carved in relief.

Cameron: *(KAM-ren)* (Scottish) "Bent nose." Clan surname based on the nickname given a valorous ancestor. See also Kameron. [CAMERYN, CAMRYN]

Camille: *(ka-MEEL)* (French) "Free-born; noble." Literary: in Virgil's *Aeneid*, Camilla was a swift-running warrior maiden. See also Kamilia. [CAMILA, CAMILE, CAMILLA, CAMILLIA, CAMMI]

Candace: *(KAN-diss)* (Ethiopian) An ancient hereditary title used by the Ethiopian queens, as Caesar was used by Roman emperors. Noted name bearers: actresses Candice Bergen and Candace Cameron. See also Kandace. [**CANDICE**, CANDISS, CANDYCE]

Candida: *(kan-DEE-dah)* (Latin) "Bright, glowing white." [CANDIDE]

Candy: *(KAN-dee)* (English) Short form of Candace; also used as an independent name meaning "sweet." [CANDI, CANDIE]

Caprice: *(ka-PREESE)* (French) "Whimsical, unpredictable." Capri, as in the Isle of Capri, is occasionally used as a given name. [CAPRI, CAPRIANA, CAPRICIA]

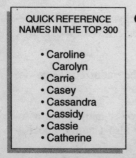

QUICK REFERENCE
NAMES IN THE TOP 300

- Caroline
  Carolyn
- Carrie
- Casey
- Cassandra
- Cassidy
- Cassie
- Catherine

Cara: *(KAR-ah)* (Latin) "Beloved." Cari is a Spanish short form of *caridad*, "dear, darling," and is also the name of a star in the Orion constellation. Variants are blends of Cara and various name endings. See also Caroline and Kara. [CARALEA, CARALEE, CARALINA, CARALINE, CARALISA, CARELLA, CARI, CARILLE, CARITA]

Caresse: *(ka-RESS)* (French) "Tender touch." See also Charis. [CARESS, CARESSA, CARRESSA]

Carina: *(ka-REEN-ah)* (Latin) "Little darling." See also Karina. [CARENA, CARIANA, CARIN, CARINE, CARINNA, CARRINA]

Carissa: *(ka-RISS-ah)* (Greek) "Very dear." See also Karissa. [CARISA, CARRISA, CARRISSA]

Carla: *(KAR-lah)* (Latin) Feminine form of Charles. Much favored in name blends with various endings. See also Carol, Charla, and Karla. [CARLY, CARLEE, CARLEEN, CARLEIGH, CARLENA, CARLENE, CARLETTA, CARLEY, CARLI, CARLIE, CARLINA, CARLISA, CARLITA, CARLYN]

Carlotta: *(kar-LAH-tah)* (Italian) Variant form of Charlotte. [CARLOTA]

Carmela: *(kar-MAY-lah)* (Latin) "Fruitful orchard," a reference to Mount Carmel in Palestine. See also Karmel. [CARMEL, CARMELITA, CARMELLA, CARMELLE, CARMILA, CARMILLA]

Carmen: *(KAR-men)* (Spanish) Variant form of Carmel. See also Karmen. [CARMENCITA, CARMINA]

Carol: *(KARE-ul)* (English) Feminine form of Carl. See also Caroline and Karol. [CAROLA, CAROLE, CARROLA, CARROLL, CARYL]

Caroline: *(KARE-a-line, KARE-a-lin)* (English, French) Feminine variant form of Charles. Carolan is an Irish surname. See also Cara, Carla, Carlotta, Carol, Carrie, Charla, Charlene, Charlotte, Karla, Karol, and Sharlene. [CAROLINA, CAROLYN, CARALYN, CARILYN, CARILYNNE,

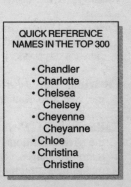

QUICK REFERENCE
NAMES IN THE TOP 300

- Chandler
- Charlotte
- Chelsea
  Chelsey
- Cheyenne
  Cheyanne
- Chloe
- Christina
  Christine

CARO, CAROLAN, CAROLANN, CAROLANNE, CAROLIANA, CAROLIN, CAROLYNE, CAROLYNN]

Carrie: *(KARE-ee)* (English) Short form of Carol and Caroline often used as a given name. The Irish surname Carey is used more for boys than for girls. [CAREE, CAREY, CARREE]

Carson: *(KAR-sun)* (Scottish) Surname.

Caryn: *(KARE-en)* (Scandinavian) Variant form of Karen. [CARYNN]

Casey: *(KAY-see)* (Irish) "Vigilant." Caycee and Cacia are short forms of Acacia. See also Kasey. [CACIA, CASEE, CASEY, CAYCEE]

Cassandra: *(ka-SAN-dra, ka-SAHN-dra)* (Greek) "Unheeded prophetess." Literary: in Homer's *Iliad*, Cassandra foretold the fall of Troy but was unheeded. See also Cassie and Kassandra. [CASANDRA, CASSANDREA, CASSAUNDRA, CASSONDRA]

Cassia: *(KASH-ah)* (Greek) "Spicy cinnamon." May also be used in reference to St. Cassian, a fourth-century French saint. See also Kassia.

Cassidy: *(KASS-ih-dee)* (Irish) "Curly-headed."

Cassie: *(KASS-ee)* (English) Short form primarily of Cassandra frequently used as an independent name. See also Kassie. [CASSI, CASSY]

Catarina: *(kah-ta-REEN-ah)* (Latin) Variant form of Catharine. See also Katherine. [CATALINA, CATERINA]

Catherine: *(KATH-rin, KATH-er-in)* (Greek) "Pure." One of the great traditional names for women, with variations in many languages. The name of several saints and queens, including Catherine the Great, empress of Russia. See also

Caitlin, Catarina, Cathleen, Cathy, Catriona, and Katherine. [CATHARINE, CATHRINE, CATHRYN]

Cathleen: *(kath-LEEN)* (Irish) Variant form of Catherine. See also Kathleen.

Cathy: *(KATH-ee)* (English) Short form of Catherine. See also Kathy. [CATHI, CATHIA, CATHIE]

Catrice: *(ka-TREECE)* (American) Blend of Catrina and Patrice.

Catriona: *(kat-tree-OH-nah)* (Scottish) Variant form of Catherine. See also Katrina. [CAITRIONA, CATRIN, CATRINA]

Cayla: *(KAY-lah)* (American) Variant form of Kayla. Cayley and other variants follow the rhyming patterns of Bailey and Kaylee. Gaelic association may be due to an old Gaelic name meaning "slender." See also Callie, Kayla, and Kaylee. [CAELA, CAILA, CAILEIGH, CAILEY, CALEIGH, CALEY, CAYLEE, CAYLEEN, CAYLEY, CAYLIA]

Cecilia: *(sess-SEEL-yah)* (Latin) "Blind." The blind St. Cecilia (c. second to fourth century) is known as the patron saint of music. The English variant Cicely *(SISS-a-lee)* is familiar due to actress Cicely Tyson. See also Celia and Celina. [CECELIA, CECILE, CECILEE, CECILIE, CECILLE, CECILY, CICELY, CICILIA, CICILY, C'CEAL]

Cedrica: *(sed-REE-kah)* (American) Feminine form of Cedric. [CEDRA, CEDRIANA, CEDRIKA, CEDRINA]

Celeste: *(seh-LEST)* (Latin) "Heavenly." [CELESSE, CELESTA, CELESTIA, CELESTIEL, CELESTINA, CELESTYNA, CELISSE]

QUICK REFERENCE
NAMES IN THE TOP 300

- Ciara
  Cierra
- Claire
- Claudia
- Colleen
- Courtney
- Crystal
- Cynthia

Celia: *(SEEL-yah)* (Latin) Short form of Cecilia. [CEIL, CELE, CELIE]

Celina: *(seh-LEEN-ah)* (Latin) Variant form of Celia or Selena. Mythology: one of the seven daughters of Atlas who were transformed by Zeus into stars of the Pleiades constellation. Noted name bearer: Celine Dion, singer. See also Selena. [CELENA, CELENE, CELENIA, CELENNE, CELICIA, CELINE, CELINDA, CELINNA]

Ceres: *(SAIR-ees)* (Latin) "Of the spring." Mythology: the Roman goddess of agriculture and fertility.

Cerise: *(seh-REESE)* (French) "Cherry; cherry red." [CERISA]

Cha-: (American) Blends of *Cha-* and *Che-* plus various name endings, with pronunciation emphasis on the second syllable. See also Charis, Cherie, and *Sha-*. [CHALIA, CHALISE, CHALON, CHALONN, CHALONNE, CHALYSE, CHANAE, CHANEE, CHANICE, CHANISE, CHAQUITA, CHARELLE, CHARICE, CHAVONNE, CHENAY, CHEVELLE, CHEVON, CHEVONNE]

Chalina: *(sha-LEEN-ah)* (Spanish) Diminutive form of Rosalina.

Chana: *(KAH-nah)* (Hebrew) Variant form of Hannah. Also a Spanish diminutive *(CHAH-nah)* of names ending in *-iana*. [CHANNA]

Chandelle: *(shan-DELL)* (French) "Candle." [CHANDEL]

Chandler: *(CHAN-dler)* (English) "Candlemaker." A surname in occasional use as a given name for girls as well as boys.

Chandra: *(SHAN-drah, SHAHN-drah)* (Sanskrit) "Of the moon"; Chanda means "foe of evil." [CHANDA, CHANDARA, CHANDRIA, CHANDY, CHAUNDRA]

Chanel: *(sha-NELL)* (French) "Canal, channel." Contemporary usage may be due to the influence of the famous perfume. It is also the name of a 14th-century French missionary saint. [CHANELL, CHANELLE, CHANNELLE, CHE-NELLE]

Chante: *(shawn-TAY)* (French) "To sing." [CHANTAE, CHAN-TAY, CHAUNTE]

Chantel: *(shahn-TELL)* (French) "Singer." Chantal is the name of a 17th-century French saint. See also Shantel. [CHANTAL, CHANTALLE, CHANTELL, CHANTELLE, CHAN-TRELL, CHAUNTEL]

Charis: *(KARE-iss)* (Greek) "Grace." Mythology: a reference to the three Graces, symbols of womanly beauty, charm, and inspiration. Charisma is the related English word used as a given name. See also Cherise, Karisma, and Sherisa. [CARISMA, CHARISA, CHARISE, CHARISMA, CHARISSA, CHARISSE]

Charita: *(sha-REE-tah)* (Hindi) "Good."

Charity: *(CHARE-ih-tee)* (Latin) "Benevolent goodwill and love." One of the virtue names. See also Faith and Hope.

Charla: *(SHAR-lah)* (English) Feminine form of Charles. See also Charlene and Sharlene. [CHARLEE, CHARLI, CHARLIE, CHARLY, CHARLYN, CHARLYNN]

Charlene: *(shar-LEEN)* Diminutive feminine form of Charles. *Char-* is also used as a blend prefix. See also Sharlene. [CHARLAINE, CHARLAYNE, CHARLEEN, CHAR-LEENA, CHARLEENE, CHARLENA, CHARLINE, CHARLISA, CHARLITA]

Charlotte: *(SHAR-let)* (French) Feminine form of Charles. See also Carlotta. [CHARLETTE, CHARLOTTA]

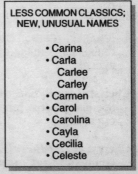

LESS COMMON CLASSICS; NEW, UNUSUAL NAMES

- Carina
- Carla
  Carlee
  Carley
- Carmen
- Carol
- Carolina
- Cayla
- Cecilia
- Celeste

Charmaine: *(shar-MAYNE)* (French) Possibly a variant form of Charmian, the name of one of Cleopatra's attendants in Shakespeare's *Antony and Cleopatra*. [CHARMAIN, CHARMAYNE, CHARMIAN, CHARMINE]

Charo: *(CHAR-oh)* (Spanish) Pet name for Rosa.

Chastity: *(CHASS-ti-tee)* (Latin) "Purity, innocence." A virtue name. Chasity *(CHASS-i-tee)* is a slurred phonetic variant. This name has been familiar since the 1970s due to Chastity Bono, daughter of singer/actress Cher and singer/actor/politician Sonny Bono. Chasida is a saint's name. [CHASIDA, CHASITY, CHASTA, CHASTINA, CHASTINE]

Chavela: *(sha-VAY-lah)* (Spanish) Variant form of Isabel. [CHAVELLE]

Chaya: *(CHYE-ah)* (Hebrew) "Life." Also a Spanish short form for names ending in *-ario*.

Chelsea: *(CHELL-see)* (English) Place name, especially in reference to the district in London. Noted name bearer: Chelsea Clinton, daughter of U.S. President Bill Clinton. [CHELSEY, CHELSIE, CHELSA, CHELSEE, CHELSI, CHELSY]

Cherie: *(sha-REE)* (French) "Dear one, darling." Contemporary variants of Cherie follow the *sha-* name pattern. Cher may be a short form of Cherie or of other names beginning with *Cher-*. Singer/actress Cher's name is a short form of Cherilyn. See also *Cha-*, Cheryl, *Sha-*, and Sherry. [CHAREE, CHER, CHERE, CHEREE, CHEREEN, CHERELL, CHERELLE, CHERI, CHERINA, CHERITA, CHERREE, CHERRELLE]

Cherise: *(sha-REESE)* (English) Blend of Cherie and Cerise. See also Charis. [CHERESE, CHERESSE, CHERICE, CHERISA, CHERISSE]

Cherry: *(CHARE-ee)* (English) Fruit-bearing tree of the rose family. [CHERRI, CHERRIE]

Cheryl: *(CHARE-el, SHARE-el)* (English) Rhyming variant of names like Meryl and Beryl, developed early in this century. Cherilyn is a further variant based on Marilyn. See also Cherie and Sheryl. [CHERILYN, CHERILYNN, CHERRELL, CHERRILL, CHERYLL]

Chessa: *(CHESS-ah)* (Slavic) "At peace." [CHESSIE]

Cheyenne: *(shy-ENN)* (Native American) Name of an Algonquian tribe of the Great Plains and of the capital city of Wyoming. [CHEYANNA, CHEYANNE, CHIANA, CHIANNA]

Chiara: *(kee-AR-ah)* (Italian) "Light." Variant form of Clare. See also Ciara.

China: (Chinese) Name of the country used as a given name. Famous name bearer: singer Chynna Phillips. [CHYNA, CHYNNA]

Chinara: *(sha-NAR-ah)* (Nigerian) "God receives."

Chiyo: *(chee-yoh)* (Japanese) "Thousand years; eternal."

Chloe: *(KLO-ee)* (Greek) "Fresh-blooming."

Christa: *(KRIS-tah)* (Greek) "Anointed one; a Christian." Chrysta's spelling may refer to the Greek word for "gold" or "golden." See also Christina, Christy, and Krysta. [CHRYSSA, CHRYSTA, CHRYSTIE, CRISTA, CRYSTA]

Christabel: *(KRIS-ta-bell)* (Latin) "Beautiful Christian." [CHRIS-TABELLA, CRISTABEL, CRISTA-BELL]

Christen: *(KRIS-ten)* (Greek) Variant form of Christian. Spanish

---

LESS COMMON CLASSICS; NEW, UNUSUAL NAMES

- Celina
- Chantel
  Chantal
- Charlene
- Chasity
- Chelsie
- Cherokee
- Christa
- Christian
- Christy

and Italian forms begin with *Cr-*. See also Christina and Kristen. [**CHRISTIN**, CHRISTAINE, CHRISTAN, CHRISTANA, CHRISTANNE, CHRYSTYN, CRISTEN, CRISTIN, CRISTYN]

Christian: *(KRIS-t'-ynn)* (Greek) "Follower of Christ." Spanish and Italian forms begin with *Cr-*. See also Christina. [CHRISTIANA, CHRISTIANE, CHRISTIANNA, CHRISTIANNE, CHRYSTIAN, CRISTIAN, CRISTIANA, CRISTIANNA, CRISTIANNE]

Christina: *(kris-TEEN-ah)* (Greek) Variant form of Christiana. See also Christa, Christabel, Christen, Christian, Christy, Crystal, Khristina, Kirsten, Krista, Kristen, Kristina, Kristine, and Krystal. [**CHRISTINE**, **CRISTINA**, CHRISTEEN, CHRISTEENA, CHRISTENA, CHRISTENE, CHRYSTINA, CRISTINE]

Christy: *(KRIS-tee)* (English) Short form of Christine. See also Krista. In the news in the 1990s: model Christie Brinkley. [**CHRISTIE**, CHRISSA, CHRISSIE, CHRISSY, CHRISTI, CRISSA, CRISSIE, CRISSY, CRISTIE, CRISTY]

Chrysantha: *(kris-ANN-thah)* (Greek) Variant form of Chrysanthus, a saint's name. Chrysandra is a contemporary blend using Sandra. See also Krisandra. [CHRISANNA, CHRISANNE, CHRYSANDRA, CRISANNA]

Ciana: *(see-AHN-ah, chee-AHN-ah)* (Italian) Feminine variant of John. Pronounced *kee-AHN-ah*, may also be a contemporary feminine variant of an Irish name meaning "ancient." [CIANDRA, CIANNA]

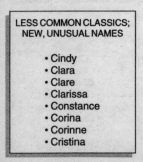

LESS COMMON CLASSICS; NEW, UNUSUAL NAMES

- Cindy
- Clara
- Clare
- Clarissa
- Constance
- Corina
- Corinne
- Cristina

Ciara: *(kee-ARR-ah, see-ARR-ah)* (Irish) "Dark." Feminine form of Ciaran, the name of two major Irish saints. See also Chiara, Kiara, and Sierra. [CEARA, CIARAN, CIARRA, CIERA, CIERRA]

Cindy: *(SIN-dee)* (English) Short form of Cynthia and Lucinda. In the news in the 1990s: model Cindy Crawford and singer Cyndi Lauper. [CINDA, CINDEL, CINDI, CINDIA, CYNDEE, CYNDI, CYNDY]

Cira: *(SEER-ah)* (Spanish) Variant of Cyril. See also Cyrah and Cyrilla. [CERI, CERIA, CIRI]

Circe: *(SIR-see)* (Latin) Mythology: a sorceress who tempted Perseus and changed his men into swine and back again.

Claire: (French) "Bright, shining." Clare of Assisi (13th century) is one of the notable saints of the medieval period. In the news in the 1990s: actress Claire Danes. See also Claribel and Clarissa. [CLAIR, CLARA, CLARE, CLARINDA, CLARITA]

Claribel: *(KLARE-a-bell)* (English) "Bright; beautiful." Blend of Clare and Bella. Literary: a name used by Shakespeare in *The Tempest*.

Clarissa: *(kla-RISS-ah)* (English) Variant of Claire or Clarice. [CLARESSA, CLARICE, CLARISA, CLARISSA, CLARISSE]

Claudia: *(KLAW-dee-ah)* (Latin) Feminine form of Claude. Biblical: a Christian woman of Rome greeted by Paul in his second letter to Timothy. [CLAUDELLE, CLAUDETTE, CLAUDINE]

Clemence: *(klem-AWNCE)* (Latin) "Clemency, mercy." [CLEMENTINA, CLEMENTINE]

Cleo: *(KLEE-oh)* (Greek) Short form of Clotilde and Cleopatra. Clio *(KLY-oh)* is the mythological muse of historical poetry. [CLEA, CLIO]

Cleone: *(klee-OWN-ee)* (Greek) "Glorious." Mythology: daughter of a river god. Cliona is an Irish form. [CLEONIE, CLIONA]

Cleopatra: *(klee-oh-PAT-rah)* (Greek) "Glory of her father."

The queen of Egypt who was immortalized by Shakespeare in *Antony and Cleopatra*. Also a fourth-century Palestinian saint. See also Cleo.

Cleta: *(KLEE-tah)* (Greek) "Illustrious." Feminine form of Cletus, the name of a first-century saint.

Cloris: *(KLOR-iss)* (Greek) "Blooming." Mythology: the goddess of flowers. Noted name bearer: actress Cloris Leachman. [CHLORIS]

Clytie: *(KLY-tee)* (Greek) Mythology: a nymph in love with Helios, god of the sun. Clytie was changed into a sunflower, which always turns its face toward the sun.

Coco: *(KO-ko)* (Spanish) Diminutive form of Soccoro. Also a French pet name. Famous name bearer: couturier Coco Chanel.

Cody: *(KO-dee)* (Irish) "Helpful." [CODI, CODIE]

Colette: *(ko-LET)* (French) "Victorious." Variant of Nicolette. Famous name bearer: the French author Colette. St. Collette (15th century) was noted for her organizational abilities. [COLETA, COLETTA, COLLETTA, COLLETTE]

Colleen: *(kah-LEEN)* (Irish) "Girl." Colene *(koh-LEEN)* is a feminine form of Cole. See also Cailin. [COLEEN, COLENE, COLLENA, COLLENE]

Concetta: *(kohn-CHET-ah)* (Latin) Italian form of Concepción, referring to the doctrine of the Immaculate Conception of Mary. [CONCEPCIÓN, CONCHITA]

Connie: *(KAH-nee)* (English) Short form of Constance.

Constance: *(KAHN-stans)* (Latin) "Constancy, steadfastness." [CONSTANCIA, CONSTANTIA, CONSTANTINA, CONSTANZA]

Consuelo: *(kohn-SWAY-loh)* (Latin) "Consolation."

Cora: *(KOR-ah)* (English) Possibly a variant of Kore: (Greek) "maiden." [CORALEE, CORALIA, CORALIE, CORALYN, CORELLA, CORETTA, CORISA, CORISSA, CORLENE, CORRISSA]

Coral: *(KOR-ul)* (English) A semiprecious natural sea growth, often deep pink to red in color. [CORALINE, CORALYN]

Corazón: *(kor-a-SOHN)* (Spanish) "Heart." [CORAZANA]

Cordelia: *(kor-DEEL-yah)* (English) "Good-hearted." Literary: in *King Lear*, Shakespeare portrays Cordelia as a woman of rare honesty. [CORDELLA]

Corina: *(kor-REE-nah)* (Latin) Variant form of Corinne. The *-een* spellings are Irish endings. [COREEN, COREENE, CORENA, CORINE, CORREEN, CORREENA, CORRINA, CORRINE]

Corinne: *(ko-RINN)* (French) Variant of Cora. [CORINNA, CORRIN, CORRYN, CORYN, CORYNN, CORYNNE]

Corinthia: *(ko-RIN-thee-ah)* (Greek) "Woman of Corinth."

Corliss: *(KOR-liss)* (English) "Carefree."

Cornelia: *(kor-NEEL-yah)* (Latin) Feminine form of Cornelius. [CORNELLA]

Cory: *(KOR-ee)* (Irish) Corrie and Corre are Scottish surnames. Cori is also used as a prefix in contemporary blended names. See also Kori. [COREY, CORI, CORIANN, CORIANNE, CORIE, CORRI, CORRIANNA, CORRIE, CORRY]

Courtney: *(KORT-nee)* (English) "Courtly; courteous." Place name and surname. Noted name bearer: actress Courteney Cox. Courtlyn is a contemporary variant. [CORTNEY, COURTENEY, COURTLYN]

Cozette: *(koh-ZETT)* (French) "Little pet." Literary: in Victor Hugo's *Les Misérables*, Cosette is Jean Valjean's beloved adopted daughter. [COSETTE]

Crecia: *(KREE-shah)* (Latin) Short form of Lucrecia, a saint's name. Cree may be a short form of Lucrecia or a use of the Native American tribal name. [CREE]

Crystal: *(KRISS-tal)* (Greek) "Ice." A transparent quartz, usually colorless, that can be cut to reflect brilliant light. *Cr-* spellings are Spanish/Italian. See also Krystal. [CRISTAL, CHRISTAL, CHRISTEL, CHRISTELLA, CHRISTELLE, CHRYSTAL, CHRYSTALANN, CRISTALLE, CRISTALYN, CRISTELLA, CRYSTALANN, CRYSTALINA, CRYSTALL, CRYSTALYN, CRYSTALYNN, CRYSTELL]

Cybele: *(si-BELL)* (Greek) Mythology: an ancient nature goddess worshipped as the Great Mother in Asia Minor. The mother of all gods, men, and wild nature, lions were her faithful companions. She was identified with Rhea by the Greeks, and with Maia and Ceres by the Romans.

Cybil: *(SIH-bul)* (Greek) Variant form of Sibyl, the name given in Greek mythology to a prophetess or fortune-teller. [CYBILL]

Cydney: *(SID-nee)* (English) Variant form of Sydney. [CIDNEY, CYDNEE]

Cynthia: *(SIN-thee-ah)* (Greek) Mythology: one of the names of Artemis, the goddess of the moon, referring to her birthplace on Mount Cynthus. Cyntia is a Spanish form. See also Cindy. [CINTHIA, CYNTIA]

Cyrah: *(SEER-ah, SYE-rah)* (Persian) "Enthroned," if Cyrah and variants are feminine forms of Cyrus. "Lady," if variants of Kyria (Greek). Greek mythology: Cyrene was a maiden-huntress loved by Apollo. See also Cira and Kyra. [CYRA, CYRENA, CYRENE, CYRINA]

Cyrilla: *(sir-ILL-ah)* (Greek) "Mistress, lady." Feminine form of Cyril. [CERELIA, CERELLA, CIRILLA]

Czarina: *(zar-EEN-ah)* (Russian) Feminine form of *czar*; the Russian equivalent of a female caesar or an empress.

D

Da- : (American) Blends of *Da-* plus various endings, with pronunciation emphasis on the second syllable. See also *De-*. [DAMESHIA, DANESSA, DANIESHA, DANILLE, DANIQUE, DANIRA, DANISHA, DASHAWNA, DASHAY, DASHEA, DAVISHA, DAVONNA, DAVONNE]

Dacia: *(DAY-sha)* (Latin) "From Dacia." May be used in reference to Dasius or Datius, saints' names from the fourth and sixth centuries. See also Deja. [DACEY, DACY, DAESHA, DAISHA, DAYSHA, DEYCI]

Dagmar: *(DAG-mar)* (Scandinavian) "Glorious."

Dahlia: *(DAL-yah)* (Swedish) "Valley." The flower was named for botanist Anders Dahl. See also Dalia. [DAHL]

Daisy: *(DAY-zee)* (English) "Day's eye." A flower name. [DAISEY, DAISI, DAISIE, DAIZY, DAYSI, DEYSI]

Dakota: *(da-KOH-tah)* (Native American) "Friend, ally." Tribal name.

Dale: *(dayl)* (English) "Small valley." Dalena and Dalenna are also short form variants of Madeline. [DAEL, DAELYN, DALENA, DALENE, DALENNA, DALINA, DALY, DAYLA, DAYLE]

Dalia: *(DAL-yah)* (Arabic) "Gentle."

QUICK REFERENCE
NAMES IN THE TOP 300

- Daisy
- Dakota
- Dana
- Danielle
- Darian
- Deanna
- Deja
- Denise

(Hebrew) "Tree branch." See also Dahlia. [DALIAH, DAL-ILA, DALIYAH]

Dallas: *(DAL-iss)* (Scottish) "From the dales, the valley meadows." Name of the Texas city used as a given name. Used more for boys than for girls. [DALLIS]

Damaris: *(DAM-a-riss)* (Latin) "Gentle." Biblical: an educated woman who heard Paul speak at Mar's Hill, the open-air supreme court of Athens. [DAMARA, DAMARESS, DAMARISS, DAMARIZ]

Damiana: *(day-mee-AHN-ah)* (Greek) "One who tames, subdues." Feminine form of Damian.

Dana: *(DAY-nah)* (English) "From Denmark." A surname also used as a variant form of Daniel. See also Danna. [DAENA, DAINA, DANAH, DANEY, DANIA, DAYNA, DAYNE]

Danae: *(DAN-ay, da-NAY)* (Greek) Mythology: the mother of Perseus by Zeus. [DANAY, DANAYE, DANEA, DANEE, DENAE, DENAY]

Danica: *(DAN-i-kah)* (Slavic) "Morning star." [DANIKA, DANNICA, DANNIKA]

Danielle: *(dan-YELL)* (French) Feminine form of Daniel. [DANIELA, DANIELE, DANIELLA, DANYELL, DANYELLE, DHANIELLE, DONEILLE]

Danna: *(DANN-ah)* (English) Feminine variant form of Daniel. Dannah is a Biblical place name. See also Dana. [DA-NELLE, DANETTE, DANI, DANIA, DANICE, DANISE, DANITA, DANITZA, DANNAH, DANNALEE, DANNEE, DANNELL, DAN-NELLE, DANNI, DANNIA, DANNON, DANTINA, DANY, DANYA]

Daphne: *(DAFF-nee)* (Greek) "The laurel tree." Mythology: virtuous Daphne was transformed into a laurel tree to protect her from Apollo. Dafne is a Swedish form. [DAFNE, DAPHNA, DAPHNEY]

Dara: *(DAR-ah)* (Hebrew) "Wise." Biblical: the name of a descendant of Judah noted for his wisdom. Also, Dara and Darra are Gaelic names meaning "oak tree." See also Derry. [DARAH, DAREEN, DARICE, DARISSA, DARRA, DARRAH]

Darby: *(DAR-bee)* (English) "Deer park."

Darcy: *(DAR-see)* (Irish) "Dark." Also a French surname. See also Dorcey. [DARCEL, DARCELL, DARCELLE, DARCEY, DARCHELLE, DARCI, DARCIA, DARCIE, D'ARCY]

Daria: *(DAR-ee-ah)* (Latin) Feminine form of Darius, a Persian royal name. Variants may also be feminine forms of names like Daryl and Darin. [DARIAN, DARIANE, DARIANNA, DARIELE, DARIELLE, DARIENNE, DARINA, DARION, DARRELLE, DARRIAN, DARYA]

Darlene: *(dar-LEEN)* (English) Contemporary form of the Old English "dearling; darling." [DARLA, DARLEEN, DARLEENA, DARLENA, DARLINA, DARLINE, DARLYN]

Darnell: *(dar-NELL)* (English) "Hidden." Place name and surname. [DARNAE, DARNELLE, DARNETTA, DARNISHA]

Daryl: *(DARE-el)* (English) Actress Daryl Hannah has probably influenced the occasional use of Daryl and variants as names for girls. [DAROLYN, DARRELLYN, DARRILL, DARRYLL, DARRYLYNN, DARYLENE, DARYLL, DARYLYN]

Daryn: *(DARE-en)* (Greek) "Gift." Contemporary feminine form of Darin. [DARYNN, DARYNNE]

Daveney: *(DAV-nee, DAV-a-nee)* (French) Name of a town and castle in Flanders. May be used as a variant of Daphne.

> QUICK REFERENCE
> NAMES IN THE TOP 300
>
> • Desirée
> • Destiny
>   Destinee
> • Devon
>   Devin
> • Diamond
> • Diana
> • Dominique

Davina: *(dah-VEE-nah)* (Scottish) "Beloved." Feminine form of David. [DAVEEN, DAVIA, DAVIANA, DAVIANNA, DAVIDA, DAVINE, DAVINIA, DAVITA, DAVY, DAVYNN]

Dawn: (English) "The first appearance of light, daybreak." [DAWNA, DAWNE, DAWNELLE, DAWNETTA, DAWNETTE, DAWNIELLE, DAWNIKA]

De-: (American) Blends of *De-* plus various name endings, with pronunciation emphasis on the second syllable. See also *Da-* and Delicia. [DEANGELA, DEJANA, DELANA, DELANDRA, DELARA, DELAREE, DELEENA, DELENA, DELINA, DELINDA, DELISA, DELOISE, DELYN, DELYNDEN, DELYSE, DEMEISHA, DENEISHA, DENELL, DENESHA, DENISHA, DENITA, DESHAY]

Deandra: *(dee-AHN-drah, dee-ANN-drah)* (American) Blend of Deanne plus variants of Andrea and Sandra. [DEANDA, DEANDREA, DEANDRIA, DEEANDRA, DIANDA, DIANDRA, DIANDRE]

Deanna: *(de-ANN-ah)* (English) Variant form of Diana. See also Dionna. [DAYANA, DEANA, DEANE, DEANN, DEANNE, DEEANA, DEEANN, DEEANNA, DEENA, DEONA, DEONDRA, DEONNA, DEONNE]

Deborah: *(DEB-er-ah)* (Hebrew) "Bee." Biblical: a prophetess who summoned Barak to battle against an invading army. The victory song she wrote after the battle is part of the Book of Judges. See also Devora. [DEBBIE, DEBRA, DEBBY, DEBORA, DEBRAH, DEBRALEE, DEBREANNA, DEBRIANA]

Dee: (English) Short form of names beginning with the letter *D*. [DEDE, DEEDEE, DIDI]

Deirdre: *(DEER-drah)* (Irish) "Melancholy." Mythology: from a Celtic legend comparable to Tristram and Isolde. The Celtic Deidre died of a broken heart. Modern name bearer: soap opera actress Deirdre Hall. [DEDRA, DEEDRA, DEIDRA, DEIDRE, DIEDRE]

Deitra: *(DEE-tra)* (Greek) Variant form of Demetria. [DEE-TRA, DETRIA]

Deja: *(DAY-hah)* (Spanish) Short form of Dejanira, from the Greek name Deianeira, the wife of Hercules. Sometimes a use of the French *déjà vu (DAY-zhah),* "remembrance." See also Dacia. [DAIJA, DAIJAH, DAJAH, DEIJA, DEIJAH, DEJAH, DEJANAE, DEJANEE, DEJANIQUE, DEJANIRA, DEYANIRA]

Delaney: *(da-LAY-nee)* (Irish) "Dark challenger." (French) "From the elder tree grove." [DELAINA, DELAINE, DELANIE, DELAYNA, DELAYNE]

Delfina: *(del-FEEN-ah)* (Latin) "Dolphin." Variant form of Delphine, the name of the 13th-century French saint. Delphi *(DEL-fye)* refers to the oracle of Delphi on Mount Parnassus. [DELPHI, DELPHIA, DELPHINE]

Delia: *(DEEL-yah)* (Greek) "From Delos." Mythology: the island of Delos was Artemis's birthplace. Delia is also used as a short form of Cordelia and Adelia.

Delicia: *(de-LEE-shah)* (Latin) "Gives pleasure." Variant forms are blends of *De-* plus various name endings. [DELICE, DELISA, DELISHA, DELISSA, DELIZA, DELYSSA]

Delilah: *(dee-LYE-lah)* (Hebrew) "Languishing." Biblical: the woman who beguiled Samson into revealing the secret of his superhuman strength. Dalila (Tanzanian) means "gentle." [DALILA, DELILA]

Della: *(DEL-ah)* (German) "Noble." Short form of Adela. [DELL]

LESS COMMON CLASSICS; NEW, UNUSUAL NAMES
• Daisha
• Dallas
• Daniela
Daniella
• Darby
• Darlene
• Dawn
• Deborah
Debra

Delma: *(DEL-mah)* (German) "Noble protector." Short form of Adelma. May also be an Irish short form of Fidelma. [DELMI, DELMIRA, DELMY]

Delores: *(da-LOR-ess)* (Latin) Variant form of Dolores. [DELORA, DELORIS]

Delta: *(DEL-tah)* (Greek) Fourth letter of the Greek alphabet. Famous name bearer: actress Delta Burke.

Demetria: *(da-MEE-tree-ah)* (Greek) "Of Demeter." Feminine form of Demetrius. Mythology: Demeter was the goddess of corn and harvest. See also Deitra and Demi. [DEMETER, DEMETRA, DEMITRA, DEMITRAS, DIMETRIA]

Demi: *(DEH-mee, deh-MEE)* (English) Short form of Demetria. Noted name bearer: actress Demi Moore. [DEMIA, DEMIANA]

Dena: *(DEE-nah)* (English) Variant form of Deana and Dina. See also Deanna and Dinah. [DENE, DENEEN, DENIA, DENICA, DENNI]

Denise: *(de-NEES)* (French) Feminine form of Denis, from the Greek name Dionysus. [DENICE, DENIECE, DENISA, DENISSA, DENISSE, DENNISE, DENYSE]

Derica: *(DARE-ih-kah)* (American) "Gifted ruler." Feminine form of Derek. [DEREKA, DERICKA, DERRICA]

LESS COMMON CLASSICS;
NEW, UNUSUAL NAMES

- Deirdre
- Delaney
- Demi
- Desirae
- Diamond
- Diane
- Donna
- Dorothy

Derry: *(DARE-ee)* (Irish) "Oak grove."

Desirée: *(DEZ-a-ray)* (French) "The one desired." Often spelled phonetically to ensure the French pronunciation. [DESARAE, DESAREE, DESIRAE, DESIRE, DESYRE, DEZIRAE, DEZIREE]

Dessa: *(DESS-ah)* (Latin) From the Greek name Odysseus, meaning "wandering."

Destiny: *(DES-tih-nee)* (English) "One's certain fortune; fate." Mythology: the Greek deity of fate. [DESTANEE, DESTINA, DESTINE, DESTINEE, DESTINEY, DESTINI, DESTINIE]

Devany: *(DEV-a-nee)* (Irish) "Dark-haired." Variants may be contemporary rhyming blends of Devon and Bethany. [DEVANEY, DEVANIE, DEVENNY, DEVINEE, DEVONY]

Devi: *(DEV-ee)* (Sanskrit) "Divine." Hindu mythology: title, especially relating to Shiva's wife, who is known by various names according to her exercise of power for good or ill. Devika means "little goddess."

Devon: *(DEV-en)* (English) The name of a county in England noted for its beautiful farmland. [DEVIN, DEVAN, DEVANA, DEVANNA, DEVONA, DEVONDRA, DEVONNA, DEVONNE, DEVYN, DEVYNN]

Devora: *(DEV-or-ah)* (Hebrew) "Bee." Variant form of Deborah. [DEVERY, DEVI, DEVORAH, DEVRA, DEVRI]

Dextra: *(DEK-stra)* (Latin) "Adroit, skillful." A feminine form of Dexter.

Dhana: *(DAHN-ah)* (Sanskrit) "Wealthy." [DHANNA]

Diamond: *(DIE-mund)* *(English)* *"Of high value; brilliant." The gemstone.* [DIAMANDA, DIAMANTE, DIAMONIQUE, DIAMONTINA]

Diana: *(dy-ANN-ah, dee-AHN-ah)* (Latin) "Divine." Mythology: Diana was an ancient Roman divinity who came to be associated with the Greek god Artemis. Noted for her beauty and fleetness, Diana is often depicted as a huntress. Popularized by the late Princess of Wales. Actresses Diahann Carroll and Dyan Cannon illustrate the potential for spelling variants of this much-favored name. See also Deanna, Diantha, and Dionna. [DIANE, DI, DIAHANN,

DIAHNA, DIAN, DIANDRA, DIANNA, DIANNAH, DIANNE, DY-
ANA, DYANN, DYANNA]

Diantha: *(di-ANN-thah)* (American) Blend of Diana and Anthea.

Dilys: *(de-LEES)* (Welsh) "Perfect; true."

Dinah: *(DYE-nah)* (Hebrew) "Judged and vindicated." Biblical: Jacob's only daughter. Dina and Dinora are Spanish
forms of Dinah. See also Dena. [DINA, DINORA, DINORAH,
DYNAH]

Dionna: *(dee-AHN-ah)* (English) "From the sacred spring."
Mythology: Dione was the wife of Zeus and the mother of
Aphrodite. Famous name bearer: singer Dionne Warwick.
See also Deanna and Diana. [DIONA, DIONDRA, DIONE,
DIONNE]

Dior: *(dee-ORR)* (French) Surname. D'Or is a French variant
meaning "golden." [D'OR]

Dita: *(DEE-tah)* (Spanish) Short form of Edith.

Divina: *(dih-VEEN-ah)* (Latin) "Divine one." [DEVINA]

Dixie: *(DIK-see)* (English) Surname and short form of Richard. The American name refers to the French word for
"ten" or to the region of the southern states below the
Mason-Dixon line. Noted name bearer: actress Dixie Carter.

Dolly: *(DAH-lee)* (English) Short form of Dorothy. Famous
name bearers include Dolly Madison and Dolly Parton.

Dolores: *(doh-LOR-iss)* (Spanish) "Sorrows." Refers to the
Virgin Mary as "Mary of the sorrows." See also Delores
and Lola.

Dominique: *(dom-ih-NEEK)* (French) "Of the Lord." Variant form of Dominic. [DOMENICA, DOMENIQUE, DOMINEE, DOMINGA, DOMINICA]

Donna: *(DAH-nah)* (Italian) "Lady." A title of respect, equivalent to Don for men. See also Madonna. [DAHNA, DAHNYA, DONA, DONELLA, DONELLE, DONETTA, DONIELLE, DONISHA, DONNALEE, DONNALYN, DONNA-MARIE, DONNI, DONNIE, DONYA]

Dora: *(DOR-ah)* (Greek) "Gift." Short form of Dorothy. Also used as a prefix in blended names. [DODI, DODIE, DORAE, DORAH, DORALEE, DORALYN, DOREEN, DOREINA, DORELIA, DORENE, DORIA, DORINA, DORINDA, DORINE, DORLISA]

Dorcas: *(DOR-kuss)* (Greek) "Gazelle." Biblical: a woman who "abounded in good deeds and gifts of mercy."

Dorcey: *(DOR-see)* (English) "Dark." Variant form of Darcy. [DORSEY]

Dorian: *(DOR-ee-an)* (Greek) "Descendant of Dorus." Variant form of Doris. [DORIANA, DORIANNA, DORIANNE, DORIENNE, DORRIAN]

Doris: *(DOR-iss)* (Greek) "Gift." Mythology: a daughter of the sea god Oceanus. See also Dorian. [DOREE, DORI, DORICE, DORIE, DORISA, DORRI, DORRIE, DORRIS, DORRY]

Dorothy: *(DOR-a-thee)* (Greek) "Gift of God." See also Dora. [DOLLIE, DOLLY, DORIT, DORO, DOROTEA, DOROTHA, DOROTHEA, DOROTHEE, DORTHA, DORTHEA, DOTTIE]

Drew: (Scottish) Short form of Andrew. Popularized by actress Drew Barrymore.

Drina: *(DREE-nah)* (Spanish) Short form of Alexandrina. [DREENA]

Drusilla: *(drew-SILL-ah)* (Latin) Feminine form of Drusus, a Roman family name. Biblical: daughter of Herod Agrippa and wife of Governor Felix. [DRU, DRUCILLA]

Duana: *(D'WAY-nah, D'WAH-nah)* (Irish) "Dark." Feminine form of Duane. [DUAYNA]

Dulce: *(DOOL-cee)* (Latin) "Sweet, sweetness." Dulcinea *(dool-see-NAY-ah)* was a name created by Cervantes's *Don Quixote* for his idealized lady. [DULCEA, DULCIA, DULCIE, DULCINA, DULCINE, DULCINEA, DULCY]

Dylan: *(DILL-en)* (Welsh) "From the sea." [DYLANA]

E

Earline: *(er-LEEN)* Feminine form of Earl. Erlina (Spanish) is from the German name Herlinde, meaning "shield." [EARLENA, EARLENE, EARLINA, ERLENE, ERLINA]

Eartha: *(ER-thah)* (German) "The earth." Noted name bearer: singer Eartha Kitt. See also Terra and Tierra. [ERTHA]

Ebony: *(EB-o-nee)* (Egyptian) "Black." [EBONEE, EBONI, EBONIQUE]

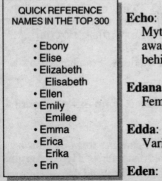

QUICK REFERENCE
NAMES IN THE TOP 300

- Ebony
- Elise
- Elizabeth
  Elisabeth
- Ellen
- Emily
  Emilee
- Emma
- Erica
  Erika
- Erin

Echo: *(EK-oh)* (Greek) "Sound." Mythology: a nymph who faded away until only her voice was left behind. [EKKO]

Edana: *(ee-DAH-na)* (Irish) "Fiery." Feminine form of Aidan.

Edda: *(ED-ah)* (German) "Strives." Variant form of Hedda or Hedwig.

Eden: *(EED-'n)* (Hebrew) "Pleasure." Biblical: the name of the gardenlike first home of Adam and Eve. [EDENIA]

Edith: *(EE-dith)* (English) "Spoils of war." See also Dita. [EDA, EDEE, EDELINA, EDIE, EDITA, EDYTHA, EDYTHE]

Edna: *(ED-nah)* (Hebrew) "Pleasure."

Edwina: *(ed-WEEN-ah)* (English) "Rich in friendship." Feminine form of Edwin. [EDWINNA]

Effie: (Greek) Short form of Euphemia, a Greek name meaning "well spoken."

Eileen: *(eye-LEEN)* (Irish) Variant form of Evelyn. See also Aileen and Ilene. [EILA, EILEENE, EILENA, EILENE]

Elaine: *(ee-LAYNE)* (French) "Shining light." Variant form of Helen. In the news in the 1990s: comedienne Elayne Boosler. [ELAINA, ELAYNA, ELLAINE, ELLAYNE]

Elana: *(ee-LANN-ah)* (Hebrew) "Oak tree." See also Ilana. [ELANAH, ELANIE, ELANNA]

Eldora: *(el-DOR-ah)* (Greek) "Gift of the sun." Variant form of Heliodorus, the name of many saints. [ELEADORA, ELDA]

Eleanor: *(EL-a-nor)* (Greek) "Shining light." Variant form of Helen. History: Eleanor of Aquitaine (12th century) was heiress to a large portion of France, wife of two kings and mother of two more (Richard the Lionhearted and John). Her powerful personality, intelligence, and inexhaustible energy made her unique in her time. Literary: Jane Austen's Elinor Dashwood in *Sense and Sensibility*. Notable name bearer:

LESS COMMON CLASSICS; NEW, UNUSUAL NAMES
• Eden
• Edith
• Eileen
• Elaine
Elaina
• Eleanor
• Elena
• Elisa
• Eliza

actress Elinor Donahue. See also Ella, Elnora, Leonora, and Nelly. [ELEANORA, ELENI, ELINOR, ELEONORA, ELEONORE]

Elektra: *(ee-LEK-trah)* (Greek) "The fiery sun." Mythology: the daughter of Agamemnon. Literary: a central character in three Greek tragedies. Also the inspiration for Lavinia in Eugene O'Neill's trilogy of plays, *Mourning Becomes Electra.* [ELECTRA]

Elena: *(eh-LAYN-ah)* (Spanish) Variant form of Helen. [ELEENA, ELENI, ELINA]

Elfrida: *(el-FREE-dah)* (German) "Peaceful ruler." Variant form of Frieda. See also Frederica.

Eliana: *(el-ee-AH-nah)* (Hebrew) "The Lord answers." See also Liana. [ELEANA, ELI, ELIA, ELIANE, ELIANNA, ELIANNE]

Elisa: *(el-LEES-uh)* (Latin) Short form of Elisabeth. See also Elissa and Ellyce. [ELICIA, ELISAMARIE, ELISE, ELISHA, ELISHIA]

Elissa: *(eh-LIS-sah)* (Greek) "From the blessed isles." Mythology: another name for Dido, Queen of Carthage. Variants may also be intended as forms of Elise and Elisabeth. [ELISIA, ELISSE, ELYSA, ELYSE, ELYSHA, ELYSIA, ELYSSA, ELYSSE]

Elita: *(ee-LEE-tah)* (Latin) "Chosen one." Also a short form of names like Carmelita.

Elizabeth: *(ee-LIZ-a-beth)* (Hebrew) "My God is bountiful; God of plenty." Biblical: the mother of John the Baptist. Since the reign of Queen Elizabeth I, Elizabeth has been one of the most frequently used names, with variants and short forms still being created today. See also Beth, Betty, Elisa, Elissa, Elsa, Elspeth, Ilse, Isabel, Libby, Liesl, Lilibeth, Lisa, Liza, Lizbeth, and Lizette. [ELISABETH, ELISABET, ELISABETTA, ELIZA, ELIZABEL, ELIZABET, ELYZA]

Elke: *(EL-kah)* (German) "Noble." Variant form of Alice. Noted name bearer: actress Elke Sommer.

Ella: *(EL-ah)* (English) Short form of Eleanor and Ellen. Also a French medieval given name meaning "all." Famous name bearer: singer Ella Fitzgerald. Elle *(el)* is a variant made familiar by supermodel Elle MacPherson. [ELLE, EL-LEE, ELLESSE, ELLI, ELLIA, ELLIE, ELLY]

Ellen: *(EL-en)* (English) Variant form of Helen. [ELIN, EL-LEEN, ELLENA, ELLENE, ELLYN, ELYNN]

Ellyce: *(el-EECE)* (English) Variant form of Elias, the Greek form of Elijah. See also Elisa. [ELLECIA, ELLICE, ELLISHA, ELLISON, ELYCE]

Elma: *(EL-mah)* (German) "God's protection."

Elnora: *(el-NOR-ah)* (English) Variant form of Eleanor.

Eloisa: *(el-o-WEE-sah)* (Latin) Variant form of Louise. See also Heloise. [ELOISE, ELOIZA]

Elsa: *(EL-sah)* (German) Short form of Elisabeth. See also Ilse. [ELSE, ELSIE, ELSY, ELZA]

Elspeth: *(ELS-peth)* (Scottish) Variant form of Elisabeth. [ELSBETH]

Elvia: *(EL-vee-ah)* (Irish) "Elfin." [ELVA, ELVIE, ELVINA, EL-VINIA]

Elvira: *(el-VYE-rah, el-VEER-ah)* (Latin) "Truth." [ELVERA, ELVITA]

Emily: *(EM-i-lee)* (Latin) "Industrious, striving." See also Amelia. [EMELIA, EMILEE, EMILIA, EMILIE]

Emma: *(EM-ah)* (German) "Whole, complete." Literary: title character of the Jane Austen novel *Emma*. Noted name bearers: actress/writer Emma Thompson, singer Emmylou Harris. [EMMAJEAN, EMMALEE, EMMY]

Emmaline: *(EM-a-leen)* (French) Variant form of Emma. [EMELINA, EMELINE, EMMALYN, EMMELINE]

Enid: *(EE-nid)* (Welsh) "Life."

Enrica: *(ahn-REE-kah)* (Spanish) "Rules her household." Feminine form of Henry.

Erica: *(AIR-a-ka)* (Scandinavian) "Ever kingly." Feminine form of Eric. [ERIKA, ERICKA, ERIKKA, ERYKA]

Eriko: *(air-ee-koh)* (Japanese) "Child with a collar." The suffix *-ko,* meaning "child," is frequently used as an ending for Japanese girls' names.

Erin: *(AIR-en)* (Gaelic) Poetic name for Ireland. [ERIENNE, ERINA, ERINN, ERINNA, ERINNE, ERYN, ERYNN]

Erma: *(ER-mah)* (German) "Complete." Famous name bearer: writer/humorist Erma Bombeck. See also Irma.

Ernestina: *(er-ness-TEEN-ah)* (German) "Serious; determined." Feminine form of Ernest. [ERNA, ERNESHA, ERNESTA, ERNESTINE]

Esme: *(es-MAY)* (French) "Esteemed."

Esmeralda: *(ez-mer-AHL-dah)* (Spanish) Variant form of *emerald*, the prized green gemstone. [EMERALD, EZMERALDA]

Esperanza: *(ess-per-AHN-zah)* (Spanish) "Hope."

Essence: *(ESS-ens)* (American) "Perfume." Literally, the distilled elements of a thought, speech, or substance.

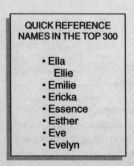

QUICK REFERENCE
NAMES IN THE TOP 300

- Ella
  Ellie
- Emilie
- Ericka
- Essence
- Esther
- Eve
- Evelyn

Estefany: *(ess-STEFF-a-nee)* (Spanish) Feminine form of Stephan. [ESTEFANI, ESTEFANIA, ESTEPHANIE]

Estella: *(ess-STEL-ah)* (Latin) "Star." The French variant Estée *(ess-TAY)* is familiar due to Estée Lauder, co-founder of the cosmetic company. [ESTÉE, ESTELA, ESTELITA, ESTELLE, ESTRELLA, ESTRELLITA]

Esther: *(ESS-ter)* (Persian) "Myrtle leaf." Biblical: a young Hebrew woman who became the wife of the Persian ruler Ahasuerus and risked her life to save her people. Ester is a Spanish form. See also Hester. [ESTER]

Ethel: *(ETH-el)* (German) "Noble."

Etta: *(ETT-ah)* (English) Short form of names ending in *-ette* and *-etta,* especially Henrietta and Harriet. [ETTIE, ETTY]

Eugenia: *(yoo-JEEN-yah)* (Greek) "Well-born." Feminine form of Eugene. [EUGENA, EUGENIE, EUGINA]

Eulalie: *(yoo-LAY-lee)* (Greek) "Sweet-spoken." Eulalia (fourth century) was a celebrated Spanish saint. [EULA, EULAH, EULALIA, EULIA]

Eunice: *(YOO-niss)* (Greek) "She conquers." Biblical: a woman who was noted for being "without hypocrisy."

Eustacia: *(yoo-STAY-shah)* (Greek) "Productive." Feminine form of Eustace.

Eva: *(AY-vah, EE-vah)* (Hebrew) "Living one." Variant form of Eve, used much more frequently than the original name. Biblical: Adam's wife, the first woman. Famous name bearer: Evita ("Little Eva") Perón, much venerated wife of the Argentinian dictator, Juan Perón. See also Ava. [EVE, EVETTA, EVETTE, EVIA, EVIANA, EVIE, EVITA]

Evangelina: *(ee-van-ja-LEEN-ah)* (Greek) "Brings good news." [EVANGELA, EVANGELIA, EVANGELINE, EVANGELYN]

Evania: *(ee-VAHN-yah)* Possibly a variant form of the Greek name Evadne meaning "goodness" or a feminine form of Evan. See also Ivana. [EVANA, EVANNA]

Evelyn: *(EV-a-lin, EEV-lin)* (English) Meaning uncertain; an English male surname of French and German origin used in this century as a given name for girls. [EVALEEN, EV-ALINA, EVALINE, EVALYN, EVELIN, EVELINA, EVELINE, EV-ELYNE, EVELYNN, EVELYNNE]

Evonne: *(ee-VAHN)* (French) Variant form of Yvonne, from Yves. See Yvonne and Ivonne. [EVON, EVONNA, EVONY]

F

Fabiola: *(fah-bee-OH-lah)* (Latin) Feminine variant of Fabian, from the Roman family clan name Fabius. St. Fabiola (fourth century) was an energetic Roman matron who organized the first hospice for sick and needy travelers. [FA-BIA, FABIANNA, FABIANNE, FABIENNE, FABRA, FAVIANNA, FAVIOLA]

Faith: (English) "Confidence, trust; belief." See also Faye. [FAYTHE]

Fallon: *(FAL-en)* (Irish) "In charge." [FALINE, FALLYN]

Fanny *(FAN-ee)* (English) Pet name; variant form of Frances. [FANCEEN, FANNI, FANNIA, FANNIE, FANTINE]

Farrah: *(FARE-ah)* (English) "Fair-haired." (Arabic) "Happy." Noted name bearer: actress Farrah Fawcett. [FARAH]

Farren: *(FARE-en)* (English) "Adventurous." [FAREN, FARIN, FARRAN, FARRIN, FARRON, FARRYN, FARYN, FERRAN, FERRYN]

Fatima: *(FAH-tee-mah)* (Arabic) The name of a daughter of the prophet Mohammed; one of the four "perfect women" mentioned in the Koran. See also Aisha, Khadijah, and Mary. [FATIMAH]

Faustine: *(foss-TEEN)* (Latin) "Fortunate one." Feminine form of Faustus, the name of many saints.

Fawn: (English) Literally, "young deer." Greek mythology: Fauna, a deity of fertility and nature, was famous for her chastity. [FAUNA, FAWNA, FAWNE]

Faye: *(fay)* (English) Variant form of Faith. [FAE, FAY, FAYANNA]

Felicia: *(feh-LEE-shah)* (Latin) "Happy." Feminine form of Felix. See also Felicity and Phylicia. [FALISHA, FELICE, FELICIONA, FELISA, FELISHA]

Felicity: *(fa-LISS-a-tee)* (English) "Happiness." One of the "virtue" names. [FELICITA, FELICITAS]

Fern: (English) A green shade-loving plant. A name from nature. [FERNE]

Fernanda: *(fer-NAHN-dah)* (German) "Adventurous." Feminine form of Fernando.

Fiala: *(fee-AH-lah)* (Czech) "Violet."

Fidelia: *(fee-DAYL-yah)* (Latin) "Faithful." [FIDELINA, FIDELMA, FIDESSA]

QUICK REFERENCE NAMES IN THE TOP 300

- Faith
- Felicia

LESS COMMON CLASSICS; NEW, UNUSUAL NAMES

- Felicity
- Fiona
- Frances
- Francesca

Filomena: *(fee-lo-MAY-nah)* (Italian) "Beloved." Variant form of Philomena.

Fiona: *(fee-OWN-ah)* (Gaelic) "Fair." [FIONNA]

Fiora: *(fee-OR-ah)* (Gaelic) A variant of Fiona, created by A. E. Maxwell for a lead character in the *Fiddler* series of mystery novels.

Flavia: *(FLAH-vee-ah)* (Latin) "Yellow-haired." Feminine form of Flavius, a Roman clan name.

Flor: (Latin) "Flower." Mythology: the Roman goddess of flowers. Flora (ninth century) was a Spanish martyr-saint. Florian is the patron saint of firefighters. [FLEUR, FLORA, FLORESSA, FLORETTA, FLORI, FLORIA, FLORIANA, FLORIDA, FLORINDA, FLORITA, FLORRIE]

Florence: (Latin) "Flowering." [FLORENCIA, FLORENTINA, FLORENZA]

Fontanne: *(fawn-TAN)* (French) "Fountain spring." [FONTAINE]

Fortuna: *(for-TOO-nah)* (Latin) "Fortune, fortunate." Mythology: the Roman goddess of fortune and chance. Also a saint's name.

Frances: *(FRAN-siss)* (Latin) "From France." Feminine spelling of Francis. See also Francesca and Francine. [FRAN, FRANCE, FRANCI, FRANCIA, FRANCIE, FRANÇOISE, FRANKI, FRANKIE]

Francesca: *(fran-CHESS-kah)* (Italian) Variant form of Frances. [FRANCESKA, FRANCHESA, FRANCHESCA, FRANCISCA]

Francine: *(fran-SEEN)* (French) Variant form of Frances. [FRANCENA, FRANCENE, FRANCILLE, FRANCINA]

Frederica: *(fred-er-EE-kah)* (German) "Peaceful ruler." Feminine form of Frederick. [FREDDI, FREDERIKA, FREDRIKA]

Freya: *(FREE-yah, FRAY-ah)* (Scandinavian) Mythology: Freya, wife of Odin, was the goddess of love and fertility.

Frieda: *(FREE-dah)* (German) "Lady." [FREDA, FREDDA, FRIDA]

Fritzi: *(FRIT-zee)* (German) Nickname of Frederica. [FRITZIE]

G

Gabriela: *(gab-ree-ELL-ah)* (Hebrew) "God's able-bodied one." Feminine form of Gabriel. [GABRIELLA, GABRIELLE, GABI, GABRIELE, GABRIELL, GABY, GAVRIELLA, GAVRIELLE]

Gaea: *(GYE-ah)* (Greek) "The earth." Mythology: the womanly personification of the earth; mother of the Titans. St. Gaiana (fourth century) is an Armenian saint. [GAIA, GAIANA]

Gail: *(gayl)* (English) "Joyful." Short form of Abigail. Gael is a term for descendants of the ancient Celts, especially in Scotland, Ireland and the Isle of Man. See also Gayle. [GAEL, GALE, GALIA, GAYLENE]

Galatea: *(gal-ah-TEE-ah)* (Greek) Mythology: Galatea was a statue loved by the sculptor Pygmalion. She was brought to life for him by Aphrodite.

Galiana: *(gah-lee-AHN-ah)* (Arabic) The name of a Moorish princess for whom a splendid palace was built in Spain.

Galina: *(ga-LEEN-ah)* (Russian) Variant form of Helen.

Gardenia: *(gar-DEEN-yah)* (English) The flower; a name from nature.

Garnet: *(GAR-net)* A dark red gemstone named for the pomegranate that the garnet crystals resemble. Also a surname.

Gavina: *(gah-VEE-nah)* (Latin) "From Gabio." Variant form of Gabinus, a saint's name. May also be used as a feminine form of Gavin.

Gayle: *(gayl)* (English) Variant form of Gail. Gala literally means "festive party." Gay has declined in usage as a given name due to its general appropriation as a term denoting homosexuality. [GALA, GALEA, GALEN, GALENA, GAY, GAYLA, GAYLEN]

Geena: *(JEE-nah)* (American) Variant form of Gina made popular by actress Geena Davis.

Gemma: *(JEM-ah)* (Latin) "Gem, jewel." See also Jemma. [GEM, GEMMALYN, GEMMALYNN]

Genesis: *(JEN-eh-siss)* (Hebrew) "Origin, birth." Biblical: name of the first book in the Bible. In Catholic tradition, Genisia, Virgin Mary of Turin, is invoked as a protectress against drought. [GENESSA, GENISA, GENISIA, GENISIS]

Genevieve: *(JEN-a-veev)* (French) "Of the race of women." [GENEVA, GENEVE, GENEVIE, GENIVEE]

Genna: *(JEN-ah)* (English) Rhyming variant of Jenna. See also Jenna and Jenny. [GENAE, GENAYA, GENNY]

Georgia: *(JOR-jah)* (Greek) "Farmer." Feminine form of George.

Georgina: *(jor-JEE-nah)* (Latin) Diminutive form of Georgia. [GEORGEANNE, GEORGETTE, GEORGIANA, GEORGIANNA, GEORGINE, GEORJETTE]

Geraldine: *(jare-ul-DEEN)* (German) "Rules by the spear." Feminine form of Gerald. [GERALDINA, GERALYN, GERA-LYNN]

Geri: *(JER-ee)* (English) Feminine form of Gerry. Variant forms listed here are blends of Geri plus Erica and Marilyn. [GERALYN, GERALYNN, GERICA, GERICKA, GERIKA, GERRI, GERRILYN]

Germaine: *(jer-MAYNE)* (Latin) Feminine form of Germain, from a Roman name meaning "brother." St. Germaine (16th century) was a French shepherdess.

Gertrude: *(GER-trood)* (German) "Spear's strength." [GERTIE]

Gianna: *(jee-AHN-ah)* (Italian) Feminine form of Jane, from John. [GEONNA, GIA, GIANA, GIANARA, GIANINA, GIANELLA, GIANNINA, GIONNA]

Gigi: *(JEE-jee, zhee-ZHEE)* (French) Pet form of names like Georgine. Literary: the name of a young girl in a French novel by Colette, later made into an award-winning stage play and movie musical.

Gilana: *(je-LAHN-ah)* (Hebrew) "Joy." [GILAH]

Gilda: *(JILL-dah, GILL-dah, GEEL-dah)* (English) "Golden." Also a short form of Teutonic names containing "gilde." Familiar since the 1940s due to the movie *Gilda* starring Rita Hayworth. Notable in the 1980s: comedienne Gilda Radner.

Gillian: *(GILL-ee-an, JILL-ee-an)* (Latin) Variant form of Juliana. Notable in the 1990s: actress Gillian Anderson. See also Jillian.

Gina: *(GEE-nah)* Short form of names ending in *-gina*. Also used as a prefix to form new variants. See also

QUICK REFERENCE
NAMES IN THE TOP 300

• Gabriela
  Gabriella
  Gabrielle
• Gina
• Grace

Geena. [GENA, GEANA, GEANNDRA, GENALYN, GENEENE, GENELLE, GENETTE, GENIE, GENINA, GINAMARIA, GINEEN, GINELLE]

Ginevra: *(je-NEV-rah)* (Italian) "Fair one." Variant form of Jennifer. [GENEVRA]

Ginger: *(JIN-jer)* (English) Nickname for Virginia. Literally, "pep, liveliness," referring to the pungent root used as a spice. Noted name bearer: actress Ginger Rogers.

Ginny: *(JIN-ee)* (English) Short form, usually of Virginia. [GENNY, GINNA, GINNELLE, GINNETTE, GINNIE, GINNILEE]

Giordana: *(jor-DAHN-ah)* (Italian) Feminine form of Jordan. Refers to the Jordan River. See also Jordan.

Giovanna: *(jo-VAHN-ah)* (Italian) Feminine form of John. [GEOVANA, GEOVANNA, GIAVANNA, GIOVANA]

Giselle: *(je-ZELL)* (French) "Pledge." [GISELA, GISELDA, GISELE, GISELLA, GIZELLE]

Giuliana: *(joo-lee-AHN-nah)* (Italian) Variant form of Juliana. [GIULIA]

Gladys: *(GLAD-iss)* (Welsh) Variant form of Claudia. [GLADIS]

Glenda: *(GLEN-dah)* (Welsh) "Fair; good." Literary: Glinda was the name of the good witch in Frank Baum's *The Wizard of Oz*. See also Glynnis. [GLINDA, GLYNDA]

Glenna: *(GLEN-ah)* (Gaelic) "Valley." Glenn is occasionally used as a girl's name due to actress Glenn Close. [GLENN, GLENNE, GLYN, GLYNN]

LESS COMMON CLASSICS;
NEW, UNUSUAL NAMES

• Genevieve
• Georgia
• Gianna
• Giselle
• Gloria
• Gretchen

Gloria: *(GLOR-ee-ah)* (Latin) "Glory." [GLORIANA, GLO-RIANNA, GLORIANNE, GLORIBEL, GLORIBELL, GLORY]

Glynnis: *(GLEN-iss)* (Welsh) Variant form of Glenna. Made familiar in America in the 1950s–1960s due to Welsh actress Glynis Johns. [GLENNIS, GLENYS, GLYNAE, GLYNICE, GLYNIS]

Goldie: *(GOHL-dee)* (English) The precious metal. Famous name bearer: actress Goldie Hawn. Golda is a variant made prominent by Golda Meir, the late prime minister of Israel. [GOLDA]

Grace: *(grayce)* (Latin) "Favor; blessing." A virtue name referring to God's grace. Greek mythology: the Three Graces were goddesses of nature: Aglaia (brilliance), Thalia (flowering), and Euphrosyne (joy). [GRACELLA, GRACELYNN, GRACELYNNE, GRACIA, GRACIE, GRACIELA, GRACIELLE]

Greer: (Scottish) "Watchful." Surname. Variant form of Gregory. Notable in the 1940s and 1950s due to actress Greer Garson.

Greta: *(GREH-tah)* (German) "Pearl." Noted name bearer: actress Greta Garbo. Short form of Margaret. [GRETEL, GRETTA]

Gretchen: *(GREH-chen)* (German) Variant form of Margaret.

Griselda: *(gri-ZELL-dah)* (Latin) "Gray, gray-haired." Italian author Giovanni Boccaccio's use of the name in a tale about an exceptionally patient wife has made the expression *patience of Griselda* proverbial. [GRICELDA, GRISELLA, GRI-SELLE, GRIZELDA]

Guadalupe: *(gwah-da-LOO-pay)* (Spanish) "Wolf valley." Refers to Mary as Mexico's "Our Lady of Guadalupe."

Guinevere: *(GWIN-a-veer)* (Welsh) "Fair one." An early form of Jennifer. Mythology: King Arthur's queen. See also Ginevra. [GUENEVERE, GWENEVERE]

Gwen: *(gwyn)* (Welsh) "Fair; blessed." The variant Gwyneth is gaining attention in the 1990s due to actress Gwyneth Paltrow. [GWENDA, GWENDI, GWENETH, GWENNA, GWENYTH, GWINN, GWYN, GWYNETH, GWYNN, GWYNNE]

Gwendolyn: *(GWYN-doh-lin)* (Welsh) "Fair, blessed." [GWENDALYN, GWENDOLYNN, GWYNDOLYN]

H

Hadara: *(ha-DAR-ah)* (Hebrew) "Adorned with beauty." [HADARAH]

Hadassah: *(ha-DAHS-sah)* (Hebrew) "Myrtle tree." Biblical: the Persian Queen Esther's Hebrew name.

Hadley: *(HAD-lee)* (English) "Field of heather." Surname. It was the name of Hemingway's first wife.

Haidee: *(HAY-dee)* (Greek) "Well-behaved." [HAYDEE]

Haley: *(HAY-lee)* (English) "Field of hay." The surnames listed here as variants undoubtedly came into popular use as girls' names due to actress Hayley Mills. The Haley spelling is more frequently used in the 1990s. [HAILEY, HAYLEY, HAILEE, HALEIGH, HAYLEE, HAYLIE]

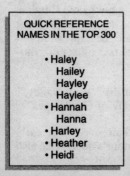

QUICK REFERENCE
NAMES IN THE TOP 300

- Haley
  Hailey
  Hayley
  Haylee
- Hannah
  Hanna
- Harley
- Heather
- Heidi

Halia: *(ha-LEE-ah)* (Hawaiian paraphrase) "Remembrance of a loved one."

Halima: *(ha-LEE-mah)* (Swahili) "Gentle."

Hallie: *(HAL-lee)* "From the hall." Halle (Scandinavian) is familiar in the 1990s due to actress Halle Berry. [HALLE, HALLEY, HALLI]

Hana: *(HAH-nah)* (Spanish) Variant form of Hannah. (Arabic) "Happiness." (Japanese) "Flower." (Hawaiian) "Work." (Slavic) Variant form of Johanna. See also Hannah.

Hanako: *(hah-nah-koh)* (Japanese) "Flower child."

Hannah: *(HAN-ah)* (Hebrew) "Favor; grace." Biblical: mother of the prophet Samuel. See also Hana. [HANNA, HANAH, HANALEE, HANALISE]

Harley: *(HAR-lee)* (English) "Meadow of the hares." Notable in the 1990s as a female name due to actress Harley Jane Kozak. [HARLEE, HARLEEN, HARLENE, HARLIE]

Harmony: *(HAR-mon-ee)* (English) "Unity, concord; musically in tune." Greek mythology: Harmonia was the daughter of Aphrodite. [HARMONEE, HARMONI, HARMONIA, HARMONIE]

Harriet: *(HARE-ee-et)* (French) "Rules her household." Feminine form of Harry, from Henry. See also Etta. [HARRIETT, HATTIE]

Hasina: *(hah-SEE-nah)* (Swahili) "Good." (Hindi) "Beautiful."

Hayley: *(HAY-lee)* (English) Surname. See Haley.

Hazel: *(HAY-zel)* "The hazel tree." A name from nature. [HAZELL]

Heather: *(HEH-ther)* (English) An evergreen flowering plant that thrives on peaty barren lands, as in Scotland.

Hedda: *(HED-ah)* (German) "Strives." Variant form of Hedwig. Both are saints' names. Hedy *(HED-ee)* was made familiar in the 1940s and 1950s by actress Hedy LaMarr. [HEDY]

Heidi: *(HYE-dee)* (German) "Little miss." Short form of Adelheid. Literary: the name of a girl of the Swiss Alps in Johanna Spyri's beloved children's novel *Heidi*. [HEIDE]

Helen: *(HEL-en)* (Greek) "Shining light." Mythology: the abduction of Zeus's mortal daughter, Helen, resulted in the Trojan War. Helene *(hel-LANE)* is a French form; Halina is Polish. See also Alana, Elaine, Eleanor, Elena, Ellen, Elnora, Galina, Ilona, Jelena, and Leonora. [HELENE, HALINA, HELAINA, HELAINE, HELANA, HELEENA, HELENA, HELENNA, HELLEN]

Helga: *(HEL-gah)* (Scandinavian) "Holy, devout."

Heloise: *(HEL-oh-ees)* (French) "Renowned fighter." Variant form of Eloise, a feminine form of Louis. See also Eloisa.

Henrietta: *(hen-ree-ET-ah)* (French) "Rules her household." Feminine form of Henry. See also Etta. [HETTA, HETTIE]

Hera: *(HARE-ah)* (Greek) Mythology: Hera (Juno to the Romans) was the Greek Queen of Heaven, wife of Zeus. Dealing with her husband's infidelities resulted in her also being called the goddess of marriages.

Herminia: *(air-MEEN-ee-ah)* (Latin) Feminine form of Herman. A saint's name. [HERMINE]

QUICK REFERENCE
NAMES IN THE TOP 300

• Helen
• Holly
• Hope
• Hunter

• Isabel
   Isabella

Hermione: *(her-MY-oh-nee)* (Greek) "Messenger." Feminine form of Hermes.

Hesper: *(HESS-per)* (Greek) "Evening star."

Hester: *(HESS-ter)* (English) Variant of Esther. Literary: Hester Prynne is the much put-upon heroine of Nathaniel Hawthorne's novel *The Scarlet Letter*.

Hilda: *(HILL-dah)* (German) "Battle." Scandinavian mythology: Hildegard was a Valkyrie, sent by Odin to escort battle heroes to Valhalla. St. Hilda (seventh century) was a much-esteemed abbess of her time in England. [HILDAGARDE, HILDE, HILDEGARD, HULDA, HYLDA]

Hillary: *(HILL-a-ree)* (Latin) "Joyful, glad." Hilaire *(ee-LARE)* is a French form. [**HILARY**, HILAIRE]

Holly: *(HAH-lee)* (English) "The holly tree." Often given to daughters born on or near Christmas. Hollis is a surname. [HOLLEE, HOLLI, HOLLIE, HOLLIS, HOLLYANN]

Honey: *(HUN-ee)* (English) "Nectar." Nickname and name of endearment.

Honor: *(AHN-er)* (Latin) Literally, one's good name and integrity. A virtue name. See also Annora and Nora. [HONORIA, HONOUR]

Hope: (English) "Expectation; belief." One of three names/qualities (Faith, Hope, Charity) described in the Bible at 1 Corinthians 13:13; was favored for sisters by Puritans and Catholics alike. A legendary trio with the names were the daughters of St. Sophia, whose name means "wisdom."

Hortencia: *(or-TEN-see-ah)* (Spanish) "Garden." The English form Hortense is rare. [HORTENSE, HORTENSIA]

Hosanna: *(ho-ZAN-ah)* (Hebrew) A prayer of acclamation and praise for salvation.

Hunter: *(HUN-ter)* (English) Occupational surname used as a given name. Made familiar by actress Hunter Tylo.

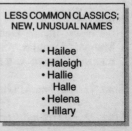

LESS COMMON CLASSICS;
NEW, UNUSUAL NAMES

• Hailee
• Haleigh
• Hallie
  Halle
• Helena
• Hillary

Hyacinth: *(HYE-a-cinth)* (Greek) "Alas." Name of a flower and a color that ranges from sapphire to violet. A saint's name. See also Jacinda.

I

Ianthe: *(eye-AN-thee)* (Greek) "Violet flower." Mythology: a sea nymph, daughter of Oceanus. [IANTHA]

Ida: (German, Greek) "Diligent." Mythology: a Greek nymph who cared for the infant Zeus on Mount Ida. [IDANIA, IDETTE]

Idalia: *(eye-DAYL-yah)* (Greek) "Behold the sun."

Idelle: *(eye-DELL)* (Welsh) "Bountiful." [IDELISA, IDELLA]

Igrayne: *(ee-grayne)* (English) Mythology: in Arthurian legend, the mother of Arthur. [IGRAINE, YGRAINE]

Ilana: *(ee-LAHN-ah)* (Hebrew) "Tree." See also Elana. [ILANE, ILANIA]

Ilene: *(eye-LEEN)* (English) Variant form of Eileen. [ILA, ILEEN, ILEENE, ILENA]

Iliana: *(ee-lee-AHN-ah)* (Spanish) Variant form of Elena. In the news: Illeana Douglas, actress, granddaughter of actor Melvyn Douglas. See also Liana. [ILEANA, ILEANE, ILEANNA, ILIANNA, ILLIONA]

Ilima: *(ee-LEE-mah)* (Hawaiian) "The flower of Oahu."

Ilona: *(eye-LOH-nah)* (Hungarian) Variant form of Helen.

Ilse: *(ILL-sah)* (German) Short form of Elisabeth. [ILISA, ILSA]

Iman: *(ee-MAHN)* (Arabic) "Believes." Made familiar in the 1990s by supermodel Iman. [IMANI]

Imelda: *(ee-MEL-dah)* (Latin) "Powerful fighter." The name of a 14th-century Spanish saint.

Imogene: *(EYE-ma-jeen)* (Latin) "Blameless, innocent."

Ina: *(EYE-nah, EE-nah)* Diminutive ending of many names, used as an independent name.

India: *(IN-dee-ah)* (English) The name of the country. [INDA, INDEE, INDIANA]

Indira: *(in-DEER-ah)* (Sanskrit) "Splendid." Hindu mythology: the wife of Vishnu. Made familiar by Indira Gandhi, former prime minister of India.

Inez: *(ee-NEZ)* (Spanish) "Chaste." Variant form of Agnes. See also Ynez. [INES, INESSA, INETTA]

Inga: *(ING-ah)* (Scandinavian) "Ing's abundance." Feminine form of Ing. See also Ingrid. [INGE, INGER]

Ingrid: *(ING-rid)* (Scandinavian) "Ing rides." Norse mythology: Ing, god of earth's fertility, rides the land each year to prepare it for spring planting.

Iola: *(eye-OH-lah)* (Greek) "Violet-colored dawn."

Iolana: *(ee-oh-LAH-nah)* (Hawaiian) "To soar like the hawk."

Ione: *(eye-OHN)* (Greek) "Violet." Iona is the name of an island in the Hebrides where St. Columba (sixth century) founded a monastery of the Celtic Church. [IONA]

LESS COMMON CLASSICS; NEW, UNUSUAL NAMES
• Imani
• India
• Ingrid
• Irene
• Iris
• Isabelle
• Ivy

Irene: *(eye-REEN, eye-REE-nee)* (Greek) "Peace." The three-syllable pronunciation is mostly British. Mythology: Greek goddess of peace. St. Irene (fourth century) was one of three sisters martyred for their faith in Macedonia. See also Rena. [IRAYNA, IRENA, IRENEE, IRIANA, IRINA]

Iris: *(EYE-riss)* (Greek) "Rainbow." A flower name. Mythology: Iris was a messenger-goddess who rode rainbows between heaven and earth to deliver messages from Olympus. [IRISA, IRISHA]

Irma: *(IR-ma)* (German) "Complete." Short form of names like Ermintrude. See also Erma.

Isabel: *(iz-a-bel)* (Latin) Variant form of Elizabeth. See also Bella, Chavela, Sabelle, and Ysabel. [ISABEAU, ISABELA, ISABELITA, ISABELL, ISABELLA, ISABELLE, ISOBEL, IZABEL, IZABELLA, IZABELLE]

Isadora: *(iz-a-DOR-ah)* (Greek) "Gift of Iris." Feminine form of Isadore. Notable name bearer: Isadora Duncan, acclaimed American dancer in the 1920s.

Isha: *(ee-SHAH)* (Hebrew) "Woman." See also Aisha. [IESHA, IESHIA]

Ishara: *(ee-SHAR-ah)* (Hindi) "Rich." [ISHANI]

Isis: *(EYE-siss)* (Egyptian) Mythology: the most powerful of all the female goddesses; sister to Osiris.

Ivana: *(ee-VAH-nah)* (Czech) Feminine form of Ivan, from John. See also Evania. [IVANIA, IVANNA, IVANYA]

Ivette: *(ee-VET)* (French) Variant form of Yvette. [IVETTA]

Ivonne: *(ee-VON)* (French) Variant form of Yvonne. See also Evonne. [IVON, IVONNA]

Ivory: *(EYE-vree)* (English) Literally, a reference to the creamy-white color, or to the hard tusk used for carving fine art and jewelry. [IVORIE, IVORINE]

Ivy: *(EYE-vee)* (English) Name from nature; an evergreen climbing ornamental plant. Iva is a feminine form of Ivo, a saint's name. [IVA, IVALYN, IVEY, IVIE, IVYANNE]

J

Ja- : (American) Blends of *Ja-* plus various endings, with pronunciation emphasis on the second syllable. The second syllable may or may not begin with a capital. See also Jae, Janae, Janessa, *Je-*, and *Jo-*. [JACODI, JACONDA, JAKAYLA, JAKEISHA, JAKIRA, JAKISHA, JAKIYA, JALAINA, JALAINE, JALAYNA, JALEA, JALEESA, JALEESE, JALENA, JALESSA, JALICIA, JALISA, JALISSA, JALIYAH, JALYN, JAMAINE, JAMARI, JAMEISHA, JAMEKA, JAMESHA, JAMIESHA, JAMIKA, JAMISHA, JANECIA, JANEESA, JANEESE, JANEILLE, JANIEL, JANIELLE, JANIKA, JANIQUE, JANISA, JANISHA, JANORA, JARAE, JARAI, JAVONA, JAZELLE]

Jacey: *(JAY-cee)* (American) Phonetic variant based on the initials J.C. or a short form of Jacinda. [JACEE, JACELYN, JACI, JACINE, JACY, JAICEE, JAYCEE, JAYCIE]

Jacinda: *(ja-SIN-dah)* (Greek) "Hyacinth." [JACENIA, JACINTA, JACINTHE]

Jackie: *(JAK-ee)* (English) Short form of Jacqueline. [JACKEE, JACKI, JACQUE, JACQUETTA, JACQUI, JACQUIE]

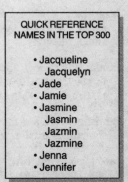

QUICK REFERENCE NAMES IN THE TOP 300

- Jacqueline
  Jacquelyn
- Jade
- Jamie
- Jasmine
  Jasmin
  Jazmin
  Jazmine
- Jenna
- Jennifer

Jaclyn: *(JAK-lin)* (American) Two-syllable phonetic form of Jacqueline made familiar by actress Jaclyn Smith. [JACK-LYN, JACKLEEN, JACKLYNN, JACLYNN, JAKLEEN, JAKLYN]

Jacqueline: *(JAK-kwa-lin, jak-LEEN, zhak-LEEN, ZHAK-ah-leen, JAK-ah-lin, JAK-lin)* (French) Feminine form of Jacques, from James and Jacob. Famous name bearer: Jacquline Kennedy Onassis, popularly called "Jackie." See also Jackie and Jaclyn. [JACQUELYN, JACALYN, JACALYNN, JACQUALINE, JACQUALYN, JACQUELEEN, JACQUELIN, JAC-QUELINA, JACQUELYNE, JACQUELYNN, JACQUELYNNE, JAK-LEEN, JAKLYN, JAQUELIN, JAQUELINE, JAQUELYN, JAQUELYNN]

Jada: *(JAY-dah)* (Arabic) "Goodness." Jade (English) refers to the gemstone and the color green. Made familiar in the 1990s by actress Jada Pinkett. [JADE, JADEANA, JADEE, JADEN, JADINE, JADIRA, JADRIAN, JADRIENNE, JADY, JADYN, JAEDA, JAIDA, JAIDE, JAIDRA, JAYDA, JAYDE, JAYDEE, JAY-DEN, JAYDRA]

Jae: *(jay)* (American) Feminine variant form of Jay. Also used as a prefix in blended names. See also Jaya. [JAELANA, JAELEAH, JAELEEN, JAELYN, JAENA, JAENELLE, JAENETTE, JAYLEE, JAYLEEN, JAYLENE, JAYLYNN]

Jamaica: *(ja-MAY-kah)* The name of the West Indies island.

Jameelah: *(ja-MEE-lah)* (Arabic) "Beautiful." [JAMEELA, JA-MELA, JAMELIA, JAMILA, JAMILAH, JAMILIA, JAMILLA, JA-MILLE, JEMILA]

Jamie: *(JAY-mee)* (Scottish) Pet form of James. [JAIME, JAIMA, JAIMEE, JAIMELYNN, JAIMI, JAIMIE, JAMEE, JAMEY, JAMI, JAMIA, JAMIELEE, JAMILYN, JAYME, JAYMEE, JAYMIE]

Jamison: *(JAY-ma-son)* (Scottish) "James's son." Surname sometimes used as a girl's name.

Jan: *(jann)* (English) As a girl's name, a short form of Janet and Janice. [JANN, JANNE]

Jana: *(YAH-nah, JAN-ah)* (Slavic) Feminine form of John, with contemporary variant forms. Roman mythology: Jana *(JAY-nah)* was the wife of Janus. [JANAH, JANALEE, JANALYN, JANALYNN, JANCEENA, JANICA, JANNA, JANNAH, JANNALEE, JANNIE, JANNY]

Janae: *(ja-NAY)* (American) An especially favored contemporary variant of Jane or Jean. Janai is a Biblical male name with the meaning "God has answered." [JANAI, JANAIS, JANAY, JANAYA, JANAYE, JANNAE, JEANAE, JEANAY, JENAE, JENAI, JENAY, JENEE, JENNAE, JENNAY]

Jane: *(jayn)* (English) Variant form of Joan, from John. A longtime popular girl's name, from the 16th century's Lady Jane Grey, to the Victorian *Jane Eyre*, to the 1990s, as represented by actresses Jane Seymour and Jane Fonda. Often used as a middle name, Jane is also the basis of many variants. See also Gianna, Giovanna, Ivana, Jan, Jana, Janae, Janelle, Janessa, Janet, Janice, Janine, Jean, Jeanelle, Jeanette, Jeannine, Jenny, Jiana, Joan, Johanna, Johnna, Juanita, Seana, Sheena, Siana, Sinead, and Siobhan. [JAYNE, JAINA, JANEE, JANEY, JANIE, JAYNA, JAYNI, JAYNIE]

Janelle: *(ja-NELL)* (English) Variant form of Jane. See also Jeanelle. [JANEL, JANELL, JANELLA, JANNELLE]

Janessa: *(ja-NESS-ah)* (American) Blend of Jan or Jane and Vanessa. See also *Ja-*. [JANESSE, JANISSA, JANNESSA]

Janet: *(JAN-et)* (Scottish) Variant form of Jane, from the French Jeanette. [JANETTE, JANETH, JANETT, JANETTA, JANNET, JANNETH, JANNETTE]

Janice: *(JAN-iss)* (English) Variant form of Jane. [JANEECE, JANICIA, JANIECE, JANIS, JANISE, JANNICE, JANNIS]

QUICK REFERENCE
NAMES IN THE TOP 300

- Jessica
  Jessie
- Jillian
- Joanna
- Jordan
  Jordyn
- Joscelyn
- Josie
- Julie
  Julia
- Justice

Janine: *(ja-NEEN)* (English) Variant form of Jeannine. See also Jeannine. [JANEEN, JANENE, JANINA, JANNINA, JANNINE]

Jasmine: *(JAZ-min, jaz-MEEN)* (French) A flower name, from the earlier form Jessamine. Notable in the 1990s: actress Jasmine Guy. See also Jazzlyn and Yasmin. [JASMIN, JAZMIN, JAZMINE, JASMEEN, JASMINA, JASMYN, JASMYNE, JAZMYN, JAZMYNE, JAZZMIN, JAZZMINE, JAZZMYN, JESSAMINE, JESSAMYN]

Javiera: *(ha-vee-AIR-ah)* (Spanish) "Bright." Feminine form of Xavier.

Jaxine: *(jax-EEN)* (American) Variant form of Jacinta. May also be a contemporary blend of Jack and Maxine.

Jaya: *(JAY-ah)* (Hindi) "Victorious." Mythology: a Buddhist female deity and one of the names of the wife of Shiva.

Jazzlyn: *(JAZ-lin)* (American) Variant form of Jasmine, influenced by Jocelyn and the musical term jazz. *Jaz-* is also used as a prefix in other blended names. See also Jasmine. [JASLEEN, JASLYN, JASLYNN, JASMAINE, JASMINIQUE, JAZETTE, JAZLYN, JAZLYNN, JAZMA, JAZMAINE, JAZMINA, JAZZALYN, JAZZY]

Je-: (American) Blends of *Je-* plus various endings, with pronunciation emphasis on the second syllable. The second syllable may or may not begin with a capital. See also *Ja-* and *Jo-*. [JELANI, JELISA, JELISSA, JEMELLE, JENESSA, JEONDRA, JERAE, JERAINE, JEREE, JERESSA, JERONA]

Jean: *(jeen)* (French) Variant form of John. See also Sheena.

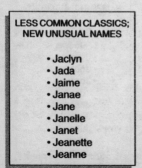

LESS COMMON CLASSICS;
NEW UNUSUAL NAMES

- Jaclyn
- Jada
- Jaime
- Janae
- Jane
- Janelle
- Janet
- Jeanette
- Jeanne

[JEANNE, JEANA, JEANE, JEANEE, JEANICE, JEANIE, JEANNA, JEANNIE, JEENA]

Jeanelle: *(ja-NELL)* (English) Diminutive form of Jeanne. See also Janelle. [JEANNELL, JEANNELLE, JENELL, JENELLA, JENELLE, JENNEIL, JENNELLE]

Jeanette: *(je-NET)* (French) Diminutive form of Jeanne. A favorite name in France and Scotland. See also Janet. [JEANETTA, JEANNETTE, JENETTE, JENNET]

Jeannine: *(ja-NEEN)* (French) Diminutive form of Jane or Jeanne. See also Janine. [JEANINA, JEANINE, JENINA, JENINE, JENNINE, JINEEN]

Jelena: *(ya-LAY-nah, je-LEE-nah)* (Russian) "Shining light." Variant form of Helena. [JALAINA, JALAINE, JALAYNA, JALENA, JELINA]

Jemima: *(je-MYE-mah)* (Hebrew) "Little dove." Biblical: one of the three daughters of Job (see also Keren and Keziah), renowned as the most beautiful women of their time. [JEMIMAH]

Jemma: *(JEM-ah)* (English) Variant form of Gemma.

Jenevieve: *(JEN-nah-veeve)* (French) Phonetic variant form of Genevieve. [JENAVIEVE, JENEVA, JENNAVIEVE, JENNEVA]

Jenna: *(JEN-ah)* (English) Variant form of Jenny and Jennifer. Jenna is also used for blends and compound names. See also Genna and Jenny. [JENA, JENNABEL, JENNAH, JENNALEE, JENNALYN, JENNARAE, JENNASEE]

Jennifer: (Welsh) "Fair one." Variant form of Guinevere. Mythology: in Arthurian tales, Guinevere was Arthur's queen. Jenifer is a spelling variant used especially in Cornwall. See also Ginevra and Jenna. [JENIFER]

Jenny: *(JEN-ee)* (English) Diminutive of Jane and Jennifer.

Also used for blends and compound names. In the news: dancer Jennita Russo. See also Jenna. [JEN, JENALEE, JENALYNN, JENARAE, JENEEN, JENENE, JENETTA, JENI, JENICA, JENICE, JENIECE, JENIKA, JENISE, JENITA, JENNESSA, JENNI, JENNIE, JENNIKA, JENNILEE, JENNILYN, JENNIS, JENNITA, JENNYANN, JENNYLEE, JINNI, JINNY]

Jeorjia: *(JOR-jah)* (American) Phonetic variant form of Georgia. [JORJA]

Jeovanna: *(joh-VAH-nah)* (Latin) Feminine form of Giovanni or variant of Jovana. [JEOVANA]

Jeraldine: *(JARE-al-deen)* (English) Variant spelling of Geraldine.

Jeralyn: *(JARE-a-lin)* (American) Blend of Jerry and Marilyn. [JERELYN, JERILYN, JERILYNN, JERRALYN, JERRILYN]

Jeri: *(JARE-ee)* (American) Feminine form of Jerry. [JERALEE, JERRI]

Jerica: *(JARE-a-kah)* (American) "Strong; gifted ruler." Blend of Jeri and Erica. Author Jean Auel used Jerika as the name of the hero's sister in the *Clan of the Cave Bear* series. [JERIKA, JERRICA, JERRIKA]

Jerusha: *(je-ROO-shah)* (Hebrew) "He has taken possesion." A Biblical name that James Michener used for the missionary heroine in his novel *Hawaii*.

LESS COMMON CLASSICS; NEW UNUSUAL NAMES

- Jenny
- Jerrica
- Jill
- Jodi
  Jody
- Johanna
- Josephine
- Joy
- Joyce

Jessenia: *(jes-SEE-nee-ah)* (Spanish) Variant of Llesenia, originally made popular by the Gypsy title character of a 1970s Spanish soap opera. See also Llesenia and Yessenia. [JASENIA, JESENIA]

Jessica: *(JESS-a-kah)* (Hebrew) Feminine form of Jesse. For *The Merchant of Venice*, Shakespeare is said to have devised this name for Shylock's daughter, a young Jewish woman who elopes with Lorenzo and converts to Christianity. See also Jessie. [JESSIKA]

Jessie: *(JESS-ee)* (English) Short form of Jessica. Also a spelling variant of the male name Jesse. *Jess-* is a popular prefix in contemporary girls' names, especially in blends that sound like Jocelyn. Famous name bearer: opera diva Jessye Norman. [JESIRAE, JESLYN, JESSA, JESSALYN, JESSALYNN, JESSAMAE, JESSANA, JESSANDRA, JESSELYN, JESSI, JESSILYN, JESSINA, JESSLYN, JESSLYNN, JESSYE, JEZIREE]

Jestina: *(jess-TEEN-ah)* (Welsh) Feminine form of Justin. [JESSTINA, JESTINE]

Jetta: *(JET-ah)* (English) Refers to jet, an intensely black, shiny gemstone. [JETT, JETTE]

Jewel: *(JEW-al)* (French) "Playful." Literally, a precious gem. Notable in the 1990s: pop singer Jewel. [JEWELENE, JEWELISA, JEWELL, JEWELLE, JEWELYN, JUELLINE]

Jezebel: *(JEZ-a-bel)* (Hebrew) "Where is the prince?" Biblical: a queen of Israel condemned by God.

Jiana: *(jee-AHN-ah)* (American) Phonetic form of Gianna, an Italian form of Jane. [JIANNA]

Jill: (English) Short form of Jillian. See also Gillian. [JILLY, JYL, JYLL]

Jillian: *(JIL-ee-an)* (English) "Jove's child." Variant form of Gillian, from Julian. See also Gillian and Jill. [JILIAN, JILLAINE, JILLANNE, JILLAYNE, JILLENE, JILLESA, JILLIANE, JILLIANN, JILLIANNA, JILLIANNE, JYLLINA]

Jina: *(JEEN-ah)* (Swahili) "Named child." See also Gina.

Jiselle: *(ji-ZELL)* (American) "Pledge." Phonetic spelling of Giselle. [JISELA, JIZELLE, JOSELLE, JOZELLE]

Jo and **Jo-** : (American) Jo is an independent name and short form of names like Joanna and Josephine, frequently used as a prefix in blends and compound names. See also *Ja-*, *Je-*, Jodelle, and Jolene. [JOBELLE, JOBETH, JODEAN, JOETTA, JOETTE, JOLANA, JOLEESA, JOLINDA, JOLISA, JO-LISE, JOLISSA, JOLYN, JOLYNN, JO-MARIE, JONELL, JONELLE, JONESSA, JONETIA, JONIECE, JONIQUE, JONISA, JOQUISE, JO-RENE, JOSANNA, JOSANNE, JOVELLE, JOZETTE]

Joan: *(jone)* (English) Feminine form of John. Famous name bearer: Joan of Arc, the Maid of Orleans. See also Jane, Joanna, and Siobhan.

Joanna: *(joh-AN-ah)* (English) Variant form of Joan. Biblical: the name of several women who were disciples of Christ. See also Jane, Joan, and Johanna. [**JOANNE**, JOANA, JOANIE, JOANN, JOEANNA, JOEANNE]

Joaquina: *(wah-KEE-nah)* (Spanish) Feminine form of Joaquin.

Jocelyn: *(JOSS-lin, JOSS-sa-lyn)* (French) "Merry." Medieval male name adopted as a feminine name. Josalind is a contemporary blend of Jocelyn and Rosalind. [**JOCELYNE**, JOCELIN, JOCELINA, JOCELINE, JOCELYNN, JOCELYNNE, JOS-ALIND, JOSALYN, JOSALYNN, JOSCELYN, JOSILYN, JOSLIN, JOSLYN, JOZLYN]

LESS COMMON CLASSICS;
NEW, UNUSUAL NAMES

- Judith
  Judy
- Juliana
  Julianne
- Juliette
- Justine

Jodelle: *(joh-DELL)* (French) Surname used as a given name. [JO-DELL, JO DELL]

Jodi: *(JOH-dee)* (English) Feminine form of nicknames for Joseph and Jude. Biblical: Joda (Hebrew) is the name of an ancestor of Christ. [JODA, JODEE, JODIE, JODY]

Joelle: *(joh-EL)* (French) "Jehovah is God." Feminine form of Joel. In the news: actress Joely Fisher. [JOELL, JOELLA, JOELLEN, JOELLYN, JOELY]

Johanna: *(yoh-HAHN-ah)* (Latin) Feminine form of John. See also Joan and Joanna. [JOHANA, JOHANNAH, JOHANNE]

Johnna: *(JAH-nah)* (English) Feminine form of John and Jon. [JOHNELLE, JOHNETTA, JOHNETTE, JOHNNAE, JOHNNIE, JONAE, JONALYN, JONALYNN, JONAY, JONELL, JONETTA, JONETTE, JONI, JONITA, JONNA, JONNAE, JONNELLE, JONNI, JONNIE]

Jolene: *(joh-LEEN)* (English) A feminine variant of Joseph or a blend using *Jo-* as a prefix. [JOELINE, JOLAINE, JOLEEN, JOLENA, JOLINA, JOLINE, JOLLEEN, JOLLENE]

Jolie: *(zhoh-LEE)* (French) "Cheerful, pretty." [JOLEE, JOLEIGH, JOLI]

Jonina: *(yoh-NEE-nah, joh-NEE-nah)* (Israeli) "Little dove."

Jordan: *(JOR-dan)* (Hebrew) "Down-flowing." The river in Palestine where Jesus was baptized, used as a given name since the time of the Crusades. [JORDYN, JORDAINE, JORDANA, JORDANE, JORDANN, JORDANNA, JORDANNE, JORDYNN, JORI, JORRY, JOURDAN]

Jorgina: *(jor-JEEN-ah)* (Latin) Variant form of Georgina. [JORGEANNE, JORGELINA, JORJANA]

Josephine: *(JOH-sa-feen)* (French) Feminine form of Joseph. See also Josie. [JOSEFA, JOSEFINA, JOSEPHINA]

Josie: *(JOH-see)* (English) Diminutive form of Josephine. [JOSETTE, JOSINA, JOZETTE]

Jovana: *(hoh-VAH-nah, joh-VAH-nah)* (Spanish) Feminine form of Jovian, from Jove, the Roman Jupiter, "father of the sky." A saint's name. See also Jeovanna. [JOVANNA, JOVENA, JOVINA, JOVITA]

Joy: (English, French) "Rejoicing." Joya and Joie *(zhoh-EE, z'wah)* are French. [JOI, JOIA, JOIE, JOYA, JOYANN, JOY-ANNA, JOYANNE, JOYELLE]

Joyce: (English) "Cheerful, merry." [JOYCEANNE, JOYCELYN, JOYCELYNN]

Juanita: *(wah-NEE-tah)* (Spanish) Diminutive form of Juana, from John. [JUANA, JUANETTA, JUANISHA]

Judith: *(JOO-dith)* (Hebrew) "From Judea." [JUDY, JU-DEANA, JUDEENA, JUDI, JUDIE, JUDITHA]

Juliana: *(joo-lee-AH-nah)* (Latin) "Jove's child." Feminine form of Julius. St. Juliana of Florence (14th century). See also Gillian, Giuliana, Jillian, Julie, and Juliette. [JU-LIANNA, JULIANNE, JULIANE, JULIANN, JULIEANN, JU-LIEANNA, JULIEANNE]

Julie: *(JOO-lee, ZHOO-lee)* (French) Feminine form of Julian. Noted name bearers: Chef Julia Child and actress Julia Roberts. See also Juliana and Juliette. [JULIA, JULAINE, JU-LAYNA, JULEE, JULEEN, JULENA, JULI, JULINA, JULITA]

Juliette: *(joo-lee-ET)* (French) Variant form of Julia. Shake-speare used the name Juliet twice, in *Romeo and Juliet* and in *Measure for Measure*. [JULIET, JULIETA, JULIETTA]

Julissa: *(joo-LISS-ah)* (American) Contemporary blend of Julie and Alissa. [JULISA, JULISHA, JULYSSA]

June: *(joon)* (Latin) "Young." Roman mythology: Juno was the protectress of women and of marriage; hence June is known as the bridal month. [JUNAE, JUNEL, JUNELLE, JU-NETTE, JUNITA, JUNO]

Justice: *(JUSS-tus)* (English) "Right, just." The word used as a given name. [JUSTYCE]

Justine: *(juss-TEEN)* (French) "Just, upright." Feminine form of Justin. According to legend, St. Justina (fourth century) was a Christian maiden who converted Cyprian, a powerful sorcerer. Noted name bearer: Justine Bateman. [JUSTINA, JUSTEEN, JUSTEENE, JUSTENE, JUSTYNE]

K

Ka-: (American) Blends of *Ka-* plus various endings, with pronunciation emphasis on the second syllable. [KALEESHA, KALISA, KALISHA, KALISSA, KALYSSA, KAMARA, KAMARI, KAMESHA, KANEISHA, KANISHA, KARAINA, KARISHA, KA-SAUNDRA, KASHANA, KASHONNA, KATANA, KATASHA, KA-TESSA, KATISHA, KATIYA, KATRICE, KATRISA, KAVONNA]

Kacie: *(KAY-see)* (American) Kacie and its variants are probably phonetic forms of the initials K.C. or variants of the Irish name Casey, meaning "alert, vigorous." See also Kasey. [KACEE, KACEY, KACI, KACIA, KACY, KAYCE, KAYCEE, KAYCI, KAYCIE, K.C.]

Kady: *(KAY-dee)* (American) Variant of Katy or Cady. [KADEE, KADI, KADIA, KADIAN, KADIE, KADIENNE, KAEDEE, KAIDEE]

Kai: *(kye)* (Hawaiian) "The sea." See also Kay. [KAIA]

Kaila: *(KYE-lah, KAY-lah)* (Hebrew) "The laurel crown." Also a Ha-

---

QUICK REFERENCE NAMES IN THE TOP 300

- Kaitlyn
  Kaitlin
- Kali
- Kara
- Karen
- Karina
- Karla
- Kasey
- Kassandra

waiian name *(kye-EE-lah)* meaning "style." See also Cayla and Kayla. [KAELA, KAELAH, KAILAH, KAYLAH, KAYLE]

Kaitlyn: *(KAYT-len)* (English) Phonetic form of Caitlin, from Catherine. See also Caitlin, Katelyn, and Katherine. [KAITLIN, KAITLAN, KAITLEEN, KAITLYNN, KAITLYNNE]

Kalani: *(kah-LAH-nee)* (Hawaiian paraphrase) "The sky; chieftain." Kailani *(kye-LAH-nee)* means "sea and sky." See also Keilani. [KAILANI, KALANA, KALANIE, KALONI]

Kalei: *(kah-LAY-ee)* (Hawaiian) "The flower wreath; the beloved." [KALEA, KALEAH, KALIA]

Kali: *(KAH-lee)* (Hawaiian) "Hesitation." Mythology: Kali, wife of Shiva, is a Hindu goddess symbolizing the essence of destruction. See also Kallie.

Kalifa: *(kah-LEE-fah)* (Somali) "Chaste; holy."

Kalilah: *(kah-LEE-lah)* (Arabic) "Darling, sweetheart." [KALEILA]

Kalina: *(kah-LEE-nah)* (Slavic) A flower name and place name. Kalena is the Hawaiian equivalent of Karen. [KALEEN, KALEENA, KALENA, KALENE]

Kalinda: *(ka-LEEN-dah)* (Hindi) "The sun." Hindu mythology: a reference to the mountains of Kalinda or the sacred Kalindi river. [KALINDI, KALYNDA]

Kallan: *(KAL-en)* (Scandinavian) "Flowing water." See also Callan.

Kallie: *(KAL-ee)* (Greek) Variant form of Callie. Kalle is a Finnish form of Carol. See also Callie and Kali. [KAHLI, KALLE, KALLI, KALLITA, KALLY]

Kallista: *(kah-LISS-tah)* (Greek) "Beautiful." See also Calista.

Kambria: *(KAM-bree-ah)* (Latin) Spelling variant of Cambria, referring to Wales.

Kamea: *(ka-MAY-ah)* (Hawaiian) "The one (and only)." See also Cameo. [KAMEO]

Kamelia: *(ka-MEEL-yah)* See Camelia. [KAMELLA]

Kameron: *(KAM-ren)* (American) Variant form of Cameron. [KAMREN, KAMRIN, KAMRON, KAMRYN]

Kami: *(KAH-mee)* (Japanese) "Lord." Variants probably are short forms of names like Kamelia and Kamille, or are rhyming variants of Tammy. [KAMLYN, KAMMI, KAMMIE]

Kamilah: *(KAH-mee-lah, kah-MEE-lah)* (Arabic) "Perfection." Kamille is a variant form of Camille. [KAMILA, KAMILLA, KAMILLE, KAMILLIA]

Kanani: *(kah-NAH-nee)* (Hawaiian) "The beautiful one."

Kandace: *(KAN-diss)* Alternate spelling of Candace. [KANDEE, KANDI, KANDICE, KANDIS, KANDISS, KANDY, KANDYCE]

Kani: *(KAH-nee)* (Hawaiian) "Sound." Also the Hawaiian equivalent of Sandy. Kaneeta *(ka-NEE-tah)* is a phonetic form of Kanidtha, a Thai name. [KANEETA]

Kapri: *(ka-PREE)* (American) Alternate form of Capri. See also Caprice. [KAPRICE, KAPRICIA, KAPRISHA]

Kara: *(KARE-ah)* (Scandinavian) Short form of Katherine. See also Cara, Carrie, and Kerry. [KARI, KAIRA, KARAH, KARALEE, KARALIE,

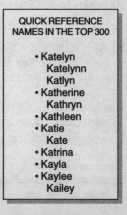

QUICK REFERENCE
NAMES IN THE TOP 300

• Katelyn
  Katelynn
  Katlyn
• Katherine
  Kathryn
• Kathleen
• Katie
  Kate
• Katrina
• Kayla
• Kaylee
  Kailey

KARALYN, KARALYNN, KAREE, KARIANA, KARIANN, KAR-
IANNA, KARIANNE, KARIE, KARIELLE, KARRAH, KARRI, KAR-
RIE, KARY]

Karen: *(KARE-en)* (Danish) Short form of Katherine. See also
Caryn, Karina, and Keren. [KARAN, KARIN, KARON, KAR-
REN, KARRIN, KARYN]

Karida: *(KAH-ree-dah)* (Arabic) "Virgin."

Karima: *(ka-REE-mah)* (Arabic) "Generous; a friend." Feminine form of Karim. [KAREEMA]

Karina: *(ka-REE-nah)* (Scandinavian) Variant form of Kath-
erine. See also Carina and Karen. [KAREEN, KAREENA, KAR-
EINA, KARENA, KARENAH, KARENE, KARINE, KARINNA,
KARINNE, KARYNA]

Karis: *(KARE-iss)* (Greek) "Grace." Phonetic variant of
Charis.

Karisma: *(ka-RIZ-mah)* (Greek) "Favor; gift." See also
Charis.

Karissa: *(ka-RISS-ah)* (Greek) "Very dear." See also Carissa.
[KARESS, KARESSA, KARISA, KARYSA, KARYSSA]

Karla: *(KAR-lah)* (German) "Womanly; strength." Feminine
form of Karl. See also Carla. [**KARLEE, KARLY,** KARLEIGH,
KARLESHA, KARLEY, KARLI, KARLIE]

Karleen: *(kar-LEEN)* (English) Diminutive form of Karla. See
also Carla. [KARLEN, KARLENE, KARLIN, KARLINA, KAR-
LINE, KARLYN]

Karma: *(KAR-mah)* (Sanskrit) "Actions are fate." In Bud-
dhism and Hinduism, karma is the inevitable effect of actions during life.

Karmel: *(kar-MEL)* (Latin) "Fruitful orchard." See also Carmela. [KARMELLE]

Karmen: *(KAR-men)* (Scandinavian) Variant form of Carmen. [KARMINA]

Karol: *(KARE-el)* (Hungarian) Variant form of Carol. [KAROLE, KAROLINA, KAROLINE, KAROLYNE]

Kasey: *(KAY-see)* (American) "Alert; vigorous." Alternate form of Casey. See also Casey and Kacie. [KASIE]

Kashmir: *(KAZH-meer)* (Sanskrit) The name of a state in India. [KASHA, KASMIRA, KAZHMIR]

Kassandra: *(ka-SAN-drah)* (Greek) "Unheeded prophetess." Contemporary variants are based on some of the preferred pronunciations of Sandra. See also Cassandra and Kassie. [KASANDRA, KASAUNDRA, KASONDRA, KASSONDRA]

Kassia: *(kah-SEE-ah)* (Polish) Short form of Katherine. Also a variant form of Cassia.

Kassidy: *(KASS-a-dee)* (American) "Curly-headed." Alternate form of Cassidy.

Kassie: *(KASS-ee)* (American) Short form of names like Kassandra and Kassidy. See also Cassie. [KASSI, KASSIE, KASSY]

Katelyn: *(KAYT-len)* (English) Alternate form of Caitlin, an Irish form of Katherine. Kateline is a medieval English form. See also Caitlin and Kaitlyn. [KATELIN, KATELINE, KATELINN, KATELYNN, KATLIN, KATLYN, KATLYNN, KATLYNNE, KITLYN]

QUICK REFERENCE
NAMES IN THE TOP 300

• Kelly
  Kelli
  Kellie
• Kelsey
  Kelsie
• Kendall
• Kendra
• Kennedy
• Kiana
• Kiara
  Kierra

Katherine: *(KATH-rin, KATH-er-in)* (Greek) "Pure." A name in use since at least the third century A.D. The early Latin forms Katerina and Caterina became Katharine and Catherine. The French Cateline and English Catlyn came into wider use during the medieval period, and variant spellings and forms multiplied. Preference in modern times is for the *K-* spelling, which is closest to the original Greek versions. See also Caitlin, Catherine, Cathy, Kaitlyn, Kara, Karen, Karina, Kassia, Katelyn, Kathleen, Kathy, Katie, Katrina, Kay, Kayla, Kaylee, Kaylin, Kitty, and Kolina. [KATHARINE, KATHRYN, KATALINA, KATARINA, KATENA, KATERINA, KATHARYN, KATHERINA, KATHERYN, KATHRINA, KATHRINE, KATHRYNE, KATHRYNN, KATINA, KATRIA, KA-TRIANA, KATRIANE, KATRYA]

Kathleen: *(kath-LEEN)* (Irish) Variant form of Caitlin, from Katherine. [KATHLEENA, KATHLENA, KATHLENE, KATHLYN, KATHLYNN]

Kathy: *(kath-EE)* (English) Short form of Katherine. [KATHIE, KATHE, KATHI, KATHIA, KATHYA]

Katie: *(KAY-tee)* (English) The most popular English short form of Katherine. In the news: film director Katt Shea Rubin. See also Kady. [KATE, KATY, KAT, KATA, KATEE, KATEY, KATI, KATIA, KATIANNE, KATILYN, KATINKA, KA-TIYA, KATT, KATYA, KAYDEE, KAYDI]

Katriel: *(ka-tree-ELL)* (Hebrew) "My crown is God."

Katrina: *(ka-TREE-nah)* (German) Variant short form of Katherine. [KATRIN, KATRINE]

Kay: (English) "Keeper of the keys." Though Kay is most often used as a short form of Katherine and its variants, it is also a surname and independent given name. Sir Kay was one of King Arthur's knights. See also Kai, Kayla, Kaylee, and Kaylin. [KAYANA, KAYANN, KAYE]

Kaya: *(KAH-yah)* (Japanese) "Adds a place of resting." Also a Ghanaian/African name meaning "don't go back" (don't die).

Kayla: *(KAY-la)* (English) Variant form of Kay. Initial popularity of the name is attributable to the character named Kayla on the daytime TV drama *Days of Our Lives*. See also Cayla, Kaila, Kaylee, and Kaylin. [KAELA, KAELAH, KAYLAH, KAYLE]

Kaylee: *(KAY-lee)* (English) Variant form of Kay and Kayla, much favored in spelling variants. See also Cayla, Kayla, and Kaylin. [KAELEE, KAELEIGH, KAELEY, KAELI, KAELIE, KAILEE, KAILEY, KALEE, KALEIGH, KALEY, KALIE, KAYLEA, KAYLEEN, KAYLEI, KAYLEIGH, KAYLENE, KAYLEY, KAYLI, KAYLIE]

Kaylin: *(KAY-lin)* (American) Variant form of Kay and Kayla. See also Cailin. [KAYLYN, KAELENE, KAELIN, KAELYN, KAELYNN, KAILAN, KAILEEN, KAILENE, KAILIN, KAILYN, KAILYNNE, KALAN, KALEN, KALIN, KALYN, KALYNN, KAYLAN, KAYLEEN, KAYLEENA, KAYLEN, KAYLYN, KAYLYNN]

Keala: *(kay-AH-lah)* (Hawaiian) "The pathway."

Keandra: *(kee-AHN-drah)* (American) A blend of *Ke-* and Andrea, or a further development of Kendra. [KEANDRIA, KEAUNDRA, KIANDRA, KIANDRIA]

Keely: *(KEE-lee)* (Irish) "Lively, aggressive." Variant form of Kelly. [KEELIE, KEELEY, KEELYN, KEILA, KEILAH]

Keena: *(KEE-na)* (Irish) Possibly a feminine variant form of Keane, meaning "ancient." See also Kiana. [KEANA, KEEANA]

QUICK REFERENCE
NAMES IN THE TOP 300

- Kimberly
- Kirsten
- Krista
- Kristen
  Kristin
- Kristina
- Krystal
- Kylie
  Kyla
- Kyra

Keiki: *(kay-EE-kee)* (Hawaiian) "Child."

Keiko: *(KAY-koh)* (Japanese) "Be glad; rejoicing child." [KIKO]

Keilani: *(kay-ee-LAH-nee)* (Hawaiian) "Glorious chief." Keilana: "glory; calmness." See also Kalani. [KEILANA]

Keisha: *(KEE-sha)* (American) Short form of Lakeisha. Kesia is an African name meaning "favorite." In the news: actress Keshia Knight Pulliam. See also Lakeisha. [KECIA, KEESHA, KESHA, KESHIA, KESIA, KIESHA, KISHA]

Keitha: *(KEE-thah)* (English) "Woodland." Feminine form of Keith.

Kelby: *(KEL-bee)* (Gaelic) "Place by the fountain; spring."

Kellen: *(KEL-en)* (Gaelic) "Slender; fair." [KELLAN, KELLYN]

Kelly: *(KEL-ee)* (Irish) "Lively; aggressive." [KELLEY, KELLI, KELLIE, KELIANNE, KELLEE, KELLEEN, KELLEIGH, KELLYANN, KELLYANNE, KELLYE]

Kelsey: *(KEL-see)* (English) "Brave." Popular preference for Kelsey and its variants may be influenced by names like Chelsea and Casey. [KELSIE, KELCEY, KELCIE, KELCY, KELLSEY, KELLSIE, KELSA, KELSEA, KELSEE, KELSI, KELSY]

LESS COMMON CLASSICS; NEW, UNUSUAL NAMES

- Kacie
  Kaycee
- Kaleigh
- Kaley
- Kallie
- Kari
- Karissa
- Karla
  Karlee
  Karly
  Karlie

Kendall: *(KEN-dal)* (English) "Royal valley." Surname referring to Kent, England. [KENDAHL, KENDAL, KENDYL, KINDALL, KYNDAL, KYNDALL]

Kendra: (American) Blend of Ken and Sandra or Andrea. See also Keandra. [KENDRIA, KENNDREA, KINDRA, KYNDRA]

Kenisha: *(ken-NEE-shah)* (American) Possibly a prefix name or a feminine variant form of Ken. [KENNESHA]

Kenna: *(KEN-ah)* (American) Feminine form of Kenneth, probably influenced by Jenna. [KENNIA]

Kennedy: *(KEN-a-dee)* (Irish) "Armored." Surname used as a given name.

Kenya: *(KEEN-yah)* (African) The name of the country used as a given name. [KENIA]

Kenzie: *(KEN-zee)* (Scottish) "The fair one." Short form of McKenzie. [KENZA, KENZY, KINZIE]

Keren: *(KARE-en)* (Hebrew) "Beauty." Short form of Kerenhappuch. Biblical: one of the three daughters of Job. See also Karen. [KERRIN, KERYN]

Kerry: *(KARE-ee)* (Irish) "Dusky, dark." See also Kara. In the news: Kerri Strug, Olympic gymnast. [KERA, KERI, KERIANA, KERIANN, KERIANNA, KERIANNE, KERILYN, KERRA, KERRI, KERRIANNE, KERRIE]

Ketifa: *(ke-TEE-fah)* (Arabic) "Flowering."

Keturah: *(ke-TOO-rah)* (Hebrew) "Sacrifice." Biblical: the second wife of Abraham and mother of six of his sons, who became ancestors of various Arabian peoples.

Kevina: *(ke-VEEN-ah, KEV-i-nah)* (American) "Beautiful child." Feminine form of Kevin. [KEVA, KEVIA]

Keziah: *(ke-ZYE-ah)* (Hebrew) "Cassia; sweet-scented spice." Biblical: one of the three fair daughters of Job. [KEZIA]

Khadijah: *(kah-DEE-jah)* (Arabic) Mohammed's first wife, named in the Koran as one of the four perfect women. (The others were Fatima, Mary, and Aisha.) Familiar in the

1990s due to the character Khadijah on the TV show *Living Single*. [**KHADIJA**, KADEEJA, KADEJAH, KADESHA, KADISHA]

Khristina: *(kriss-TEEN-ah)* (Russian) Variant form of Kristina, a Scandinavian form of Christina. See also Christina, Kirsten, and Kristina. [KHRISTEEN, KHRISTEN, KHRISTIN, KHRISTINE, KHRISTYANA, KHRISTYNA, KHRYSTINA, KHRYSTYN, KHRYSTYNA, KHRYSTYNE]

Kia: *(KEE-uh)* (American) Short form of Kiana and Kiara. [KIAH]

Kiana: *(kee-AHN-ah)* (American) May be a favored prefix name or a variant form of Kian, an Irish name meaning "ancient." Kiana is especially favored in Hawaii, perhaps as a rhyming variant of the popular Keanu, a boy's name made familiar by actor Keanu Reeves. See also Ciana and Keena. [KEANNA, KEIANA, KEONA, KEONNA, KIAHNA, KIANI, KIANNA, KIANNI, KIAUNA, KIONA, KIONAH, KIONI, KIONNA]

Kiara: *(kee-AR-ah)* (Irish) "Dusky; dark-haired." Feminine form of Kiaran or Kieran. See also Ciara. [KEIRA, KIARRA, KIERA, KIERRA]

Kiki: *(KEE-kee)* (Spanish) Pet form of Enriqueta, from Henrietta.

LESS COMMON CLASSICS; NEW, UNUSUAL NAMES
• Kassidy
• Katharine
• Kathy
• Katy
• Kayleigh
• Kaylene
• Kaylie
• Kaylin
Kaelyn
Kaylyn

Kiley: *(KYE-lee)* (Irish) "Near the church (or the wood)." See also Kylie. [KILEE]

Kim: *(kim)* (English) An independent name and short form of Kimberly. Also a Vietnamese name meaning "precious metal, gold." [KYM]

Kimberly: *(KIM-ber-lee)* (English)

"King's wood." Place name and surname. [**KIMBERLEY,** **KIMBERLEE, KIMBERLEIGH, KIMBERLI, KIMBERLIN, KIMBER-LYN, KYMBERLEE, KYMBERLIE, KYMBERLY**]

Kimi: *(kee-mee)* (Japanese) "Upright, righteous." Kimiko *(KEE-mee-koh)* means "righteous child." In the 1990s, the trend is to drop the *-ko* diminutive ending on many Japanese girls' names [KIMIKO]

Kina: *(KEE-nah)* (Hawaiian) "China." Also the Hawaiian equivalent of Tina.

Kioko: *(kee-OH-koh)* (Japanese) "Child born with happiness."

Kira: *(KEER-ah)* (Russian) "Lady." Made familiar by the character Major Kira on the TV series *Star Trek: Deep Space Nine*. Kiri *(KEER-ee)* notable name bearer: Kiri te Kanawa, Maori opera diva from New Zealand. See also Kyra. [KIRI, KIRIANA, KIRRA]

Kirby: *(KER-bee)* (English) "Church farm." Place name and surname.

Kirsten: *(KERS-ten)* (Scandinavian) Variant form of Christine. [**KIRSTIN,** KERSTIN, KIERSTEN, KIERSTIN, KIRSTINE, KIRSTYN, KYRSTIN]

Kirsty: *(KERS-tee)* (Scottish) Short form of Kristine. Kirsty is made familiar by supermodel Kirsty Hume. Actress Kirstie Alley uses the *-ie* ending. [KIRSTEE, KIRSTI, KIRSTIE]

Kishi: *(kee-shee)* (Japanese) "Happiness to the earth."

Kitra: *(KIT-trah)* (Hebrew) "Crowned one."

Kitty: *(KIH-tee)* (English) Pet name for Katherine. [KITLYN]

Klarissa: *(klare-ISS-ah)* (German) "Bright, shining, and gentle." Variant form of Klara. See also Clarissa. [KLAIRE, KLARA]

Kodi: *(KO-dee)* (American) "Helpful." See also Cody. [KO-DEE, KODIE]

Koemi: *(ko-AY-mee)* (Japanese) "A little smile."

Kolina: *(ko-LEEN-ah)* (Swedish) Variant form of Katherine.

Kora: *(KOR-ah)* (Greek) "Maiden." See also Cora. [KORAL, KORALISE; KOREEN, KOREN, KORENA, KORESSA, KORISSA]

Kori: *(KOR-ee)* (Greek) Variant form of Cory. [KOREE, KOR-EY, KORIE, KORRI, KORRIE, KORRY, KORY]

Korina: *(kor-EEN-ah)* (Greek) "Maiden." Variant form of Corrine. [KOREENA, KORINE, KORINNA, KORINNE, KORRIN, KORRINA, KORRINE, KORYN, KORYNN, KORYNNE]

Kourtney: *(KORT-nee)* (English) Variant form of Courtney. [KORTNEY]

Krisandra: *(kriss-ANN-drah, kriss-AHN-drah)* (Greek) Variant form of Chrysandra. [KRISANNE]

Krista: *(KRISS-tah)* (Czech) Variant form of Christine. Also a variant spelling of Christa. See also Christa and Christy. [**KRISTI, KRISTY,** KHRIS, KHRISTIE, KHRISTY, KHRYSTA, KRIS, KRISSA, KRISSIE, KRISSY, KRISTIE, KRYSSA, KRYSTA, KRYSTI, KRYSTIE]

LESS COMMON CLASSICS; NEW, UNUSUAL NAMES

- Keisha
- Kelley
- Kelsi
- Kenya
- Kenzie
- Kerry
- Khadijah
- Kiera
- Kiersten
- Kiley

Kristen: *(KRISS-ten)* (Scandinavian) Variant form of Christian. See also Christen and Kirsten. [**KRISTIN,** KRISTAN, KRISTIAN, KRISTYN, KRYSTEN, KRYSTIN, KRYSTYN, KRYSTYNN]

Kristina: *(kriss-TEEN-ah)* (Scandinavian, Czech) Variant form of

Christina. See also Khristina and Kristine. [KRISTEENA, KRISTENA, KRISTIANA, KRISTIANE, KRISTIANNA, KRISTIANNE, KRISTYNA, KRYSTEENA, KRYSTIANA, KRYSTIANNA, KRYSTINA, KRYSTYNA]

Kristine: *(kriss-TEEN)* (English) Variant form of Christine. See also Christine, Kirsten, Krista, Kristen, and Kristina. [KRISTEEN, KRISTIAN, KRISTYNE, KRYSTINE]

Krysanthe: *(kriss-ANN-tha)* (Greek) "Golden flower." See also Chrysantha.

Krystal: *(KRISS-tel)* (English) Variant spelling of Crystal. The *K-* spelling reflects the Greek spelling, *krystallos.* See also Crystal. [KRISTAL, KHRISTAL, KHRYSTAL, KRISTABELLE, KRISTALENA, KRISTEL, KRISTELL, KRISTELLA, KRYSTABELLE, KRYSTEL, KRYSTELLE]

Krystalyn: *(KRISS-ta-lin)* (English) "Like crystal." A contemporary variant of Krystal. [KRISTALYN, KRYSTALLINE]

Kumiko: *(KOO-mee-koh)* (Japanese) "Companion child; drawing together."

Kylie: *(KYE-lee)* (Gaelic) Feminine form of Kyle. See also Kiley. [KYLA, KYLEE, KYLAH, KYLEA, KYLEEN, KYLEIGH, KYLENE, KYLEY, KYLI, KYLIANNE, KYLIN]

Kyoko: *(kee-OH-koh)* (Japanese) "Mirror."

Kyra: *(KEER-ah)* (Greek) "Lady." May also be a Russian name meaning "beloved." In the news: actress Kyra Sedgwick. See also Cyrah and Kira. [KYRIA, KYRIE, KYRENE]

LESS COMMON CLASSICS; NEW, UNUSUAL NAMES

- Kira
- Kori
- Kourtney
- Kristy
- Kristian
- Kristine
- Krysta
- Kylee

L

La-: (American) Blends of *La-* plus various endings, with pronunciation emphasis on the second syllable, which may or may not begin with a capital. Lakeisha, Latasha, Latifah, Latisha, and LaToya are listed separately. [LACACIA, LACHELLE, LACINDA, LACOYA, LADAY, LADONYA, LAJUANA, LAKENDRA, LAKIA, LANAE, LANAI, LANELLE, LANESHA, LANESSA, LANIECE, LANIKA, LANISHA, LANITA, LAPORSHA, LAQUANA, LAQUANDA, LAQUESHA, LAQUITA, LARAE, LARAY, LAREE, LARHONDA, LARISHA, LARONDA, LASANDRA, LASHAE, LASHANDA, LASHAWN, LASHAWNDA, LATANYA, LATAVIA, LATINA, LATONIA, LATONYA, LATORIA, LATREECE, LATRICE, LATRICIA, LATRISHA, LAVETTE, LAVONDA, LAVONNA, LAVONNE, LAWANDA]

Lacey: *(LAY-see)* (French) Nobleman's surname carried to England and Ireland after the Norman conquest. Lacey and its variants may also be used in reference to lace, the delicate fabric made of netted thread. [LACY, LACE, LACEE, LACENE, LACI, LACIANN, LACIE, LACINA, LACYANN, LAYCIE]

Ladonna: *(la-DAH-nah)* (Latin) "The lady."

Lael: *(LAY-el)* (Hebrew) "Belonging to God." A Biblical male name occasionally used for girls.

Laila: *(LAY-lah)* (Arabic) "Born at night." Variant form of Leila. See also Leila and Lyla. [LAYLA, LAYLAH]

Laine: *(layn)* (English) "Path, roadway." Variant form of the surname Lane, or a short form of names like Marlaine and Melanie. [LAINA, LANEY, LANIE, LAYNE]

Lakeisha: *(lah-KEE-shah)* (American) Lakeisha and its variant forms are rhyming variants of Leticia. See also Keisha. [LAKESHA, LAKESHIA, LAKIESHA, LAKISHA, LAQUISHA]

Lalia: *(LAH-lee-ah)* (Spanish) Short form of Eulalie. Lala is the Hawaiian equivalent of Lara. [LALA, LALI, LALLA]

Lalita: *(la-LEE-tah)* (Sanskrit) "Playful." Hindu mythology: the mistress-playmate of the young Krishna.

Lana: *(LAN-ah, LAHN-ah)* (English) "Fair, good-looking." (Hawaiian) "Afloat; calm as still waters." Short form of Alana. [LANICE, LANNA]

Landra: *(LAHN-drah)* (Latin) "Counselor." Short form of Landrada, a saint's name.

Lanetta: *(lah-NET-ah)* (American) Variant form of Lynette. [LANETTE]

Lani: *(LAH-nee)* (Hawaiian) "The sky; heavenly; royal." See also Loni.

Lara: *(LAR-ah)* (Latin) "Protection." From *Lares*, referring to the individual gods of Roman households, the protectors of home and fields. Lara is popular in Russia; it is also a Spanish surname and place name. Literary: name of a central character in Boris Pasternak's novel *Doctor Zhivago*. See also Larissa. [LARALAINE, LARAMAE, LARINA, LARINDA, LARITA]

Laraine: *(la-RAYN)* (English) Variant form of Loraine. [LARAYNE, LARRAINE]

Lareina: *(la-RAY-nah)* (Spanish) "The queen." [LAREINE, LARENA]

Larissa: *(la-RISS-ah)* (Russian) Variant form of Lara. [LARI, LARISA, LARYSSA]

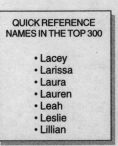

QUICK REFERENCE
NAMES IN THE TOP 300

- Lacey
- Larissa
- Laura
- Lauren
- Leah
- Leslie
- Lillian

Latasha: *(la-TAH-shah)* (American) A *La-* name based on Natasha, ''birthday.'' See also Natasha and Tasha.

Latifah: *(la-TEE-fah)* (American) Rhyming variant of Ketifa (Arabic), ''flowering.'' In the news due to rap singer Queen Latifah.

Latisha: *(la-TEE-shah)* (American) A modern variant of the medieval name Letitia. See also Leticia and Tisha. [LATEISHA, LATESHA, LATICIA, LETITIA]

LaToya: *(la-TOY-ah)* (Spanish) ''Victorious one.'' Derived from a short form of Victoria. Made familiar in the 1990s by LaToya Jackson, sister of singer Michael Jackson. See also Toya. [LATORIA, LATORYA]

Laura: *(LAW-rah, LOR-ah)* (Latin) ''The laurel tree.'' In use for at least eight centuries, Laura has many variant forms. See also Laurel, Lauren, Liora, Lora, Loren, Lorena, Lorenza, Loretta, and Lori. [LAURAINE, LAURALEE, LARALYN, LAURANA, LAUREEN, LAURENA, LAURENE, LAURETTA, LAURETTE, LAURIE, LAURINDA, LAURITA]

Laurel: *(LAWR-el)* (English) Literally, the laurel tree, also called the sweet bay tree; symbolic of honor and victory. [LAURAL, LAURELLE, LAURIEL]

Lauren: *(LAWR-en)* (English) ''From Laurentium, the place of the laurel trees.'' Feminine form of Lawrence. The earliest feminine form of the name was Laurentia, dating from the time of the early Romans; Lauren has come into use only in the 20th century. See also Loren and Lorna. [LAURENNE, LAURYN]

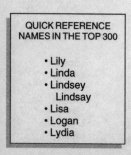

QUICK REFERENCE
NAMES IN THE TOP 300

• Lily
• Linda
• Lindsey
  Lindsay
• Lisa
• Logan
• Lydia

Laverne: *(la-VERN)* (French) ''Woodland.'' [LAVERN]

Lavina: *(la-VEEN-ah)* (Spanish)

From Levinia, a Roman given name of uncertain meaning. [LAVINIA, LEVINA, LUVENIA, LUVINA]

Lea: *(LAY-ah, LEE-ah)* (Hawaiian) Mythology: the goddess of canoe makers. Also a Spanish form of Leah. Notable name bearer: actress Lea Thompson. See also Leah, Leilani, and Lia.

Leah: *(LEE-ah)* (Hebrew) Biblical: Jacob's first wife, the mother of Dinah and six of Jacob's twelve sons. See also Lea.

Leala: *(lee-AL-ah)* (French) "Loyal, faithful." [LEOLA]

Leandra: *(lee-AN-drah)* (Greek) "Lioness." Feminine form of Leander. Leanza is a variant made familiar by Leanza Cornett, the 1993 Miss America. [LEANDRE, LEANDRIA]

Leanna: *(lee-ANN-ah)* (English) Possibly derived from an Irish Gaelic form of Helen; most likely a blend of Lee and Anna. In the news: country-western singer LeAnn Rimes. See also Liana. [LEANNE, LEANA, LEANN, LEEANN, LEEANNE]

Leatrice: *(LEE-a-triss)* (English) A rhyming variant of Beatrice. [LEETRISS]

Lecia: *(LEE-shah)* (Latin) Short form of names like Alicia and Felicia, used as an independent name. [LISHA]

Leda: *(LEE-dah)* (Greek) Mythology: queen of Sparta, mother of Helen of Troy. [LETA, LEYDA, LYDA]

Lee: (English) "Meadow." Surname. Lee is often chosen as a middle name. [LEIGH]

Leila: *(LEE-lah, LAY-lah, LYE-lah)* (Arabic) "Born at night." Lela (French) refers to loyalty. See also Laila and Lyla. [LEELA, LEILAH, LELA, LELAH, LELIA, LEYLA]

Leilani: *(lay-LAH-nee)* (Hawaiian) "Child of heaven; heavenly flowers." The fictional Princess Leia of *Star Wars* fame has made Leia *(LAY-ah)* familiar as a given name. [LALANI, LEIA]

Lena: *(LEE-nah)* (German, Scandinavian) Originally a name ending. Also an Irish name meaning "wet meadow." See also Lina. [LEENA, LEYNA]

Leonie: *(LAY-o-nee, LEE-oh-nee, lay-OH-nee)* (French) "Lion, lioness." Feminine form of Leon. See also Loni. [LEONA, LEONDA, LEONDRA, LEONDREA, LEONELA]

Leonora: *(lee-a-NOR-ah)* (Italian) "Shining light." Variant of Eleanor. Literary: Lenore was the lady lost forever in Edgar Allen Poe's poem *The Raven*. [LANORA, LEANORA, LENORA, LENORE, LEONOR, LEONORE, LEORA]

Leontyne: *(LEE-'n-teen, LAY-'n-teen)* (French) Feminine form of Leon made familiar by operatic star Leontyne Price. [LEONTINA, LEONTINE]

Leorah: *(lee-OR-ah)* (Israeli) "Light to me." [LEORA]

Leslie: *(LESS-lee, LEZ-lee)* (Scottish) Name of a prominent Scottish clan. Used mainly for boys in England and Scotland. In America, Leslie is used almost exclusively for girls. The Lezlie spelling preserves the original Scottish pronunciation. [**LESLEY, LESLY**, LESLEE, LEZLIE]

LESS COMMON CLASSICS;
NEW, UNUSUAL NAMES

- Lacy
- Lacie
- Lakeisha
- Lara
- Laurel
- Leanna
- Leilani
- Lena
- Leticia

Leticia: *(le-TEE-shah)* (Latin) "Great joy." Variant of Letitia. See also Latisha. [LAETITIA, LETISHA, LETITIA, LETTY]

Levana: *(le-VAHN-ah)* (Latin) "Raise up." Mythology: Levana was the Roman goddess/protectress of the newborn. [LIVANA, LIVAUN]

Lexie: *(LEK-see)* (Greek) Short form of Alexis and Alexandra. [LEXA, LEXANDRA, LEXANN, LEXI, LEXINE, LEXUS]

Lia: *(LEE-ah)* (Latin) Short form of names like Amelia and Rosalia. See also Lea and Leah.

Liana: *(lee-AHN-ah)* (Latin) A short form of names like Liliana and Juliana, or a variant of Eliana. See also Leanna. [LIANE, LIANN, LIANNA]

Libby: *(LIB-ee)* (English) Diminutive of Elizabeth.

Liberty: *(LIH-ber-tee)* (English) Literally, freedom.

Licia: *(LEE-shah)* (Latin) Short form of Alicia. [LEESHA]

Lida: *(LEE-dah, LYE-dah)* (Russian) Originally a diminutive name ending. Variant form of Lydia.

Liesl: *(LEES-ul, LEE-zul)* (German) Short form of Elizabeth. [LIEZEL, LIEZL]

Liliana: *(lil-ee-AH-nah)* (Latin) Variant of Lillian, from Lily, the flower name. [LILIAN, LILIANNA, LILLIAN, LILLIANA, LILLIANE, LILLIANN, LILLIANNA]

Lilibeth: *(LIL-a-beth)* (English) Blend of Lily and Elizabeth. [LILIBET, LILYBETH, LILYBELL]

Lily: *(LIL-ee)* (English) A flower name; the lily is a symbol of innocence and purity as well as beauty. See also Liliana. [LILI, LILLIA, LILLI, LILLIE, LILLY]

Lin: *(lin)* (Chinese) Family name. (English) Short form for names like Linden and Linette.

Lina: *(LEE-nah)* (Latin) Originally an ending of names like Carolina. (Arabic) "Palm tree." See also Lena. [LYNA]

Linda: *(LIN-dah)* (English) "Lime tree; linden tree." Originally derived from *linde*, a Germanic name element refer-

ring to the lime tree, today Linda is associated by most
parents with the Spanish word meaning "beautiful." See
also Lynda. [LINDALEE, LINDEE, LINDI, LINDY]

Linden: *(LIN-den)* (English) "The linden tree."

Lindsey: *(LIN-zee)* (Scottish, English) May refer to a lake or
to a place of linden trees. Lindsay is a surname of some of
the major Scottish and English noble families. Notable
name bearer in the 1980s and 1990s: actress Lindsay Wag-
ner. See also Lyndsey. [**LINDSAY**, LINSEY]

Linnea: *(le-NEE-ah, le-NAY)* (Scandinavian) A small blue
flower. [LENAE, LINNA, LINNAE, LYNAE, LYNNAE]

Linnet: *(LIN-et)* (English) "Songbird." See also Lynette.
[LINNETTE]

Liora: *(lee-OR-ah)* (Israeli) "Light."

Lisa: *(LEE-sah)* (English) Short form of Elisabeth. See also
Liza. [LISE]

Lisandra: *(lih-SAN-drah, lih-SAHN-drah)* (Greek) "Liberator." Feminine form of Lysander. Lissandra is an Italian
variant form of Alexandra; Lizandra is a contemporary
blend of Liz and Alexandra; Lizann is a blend of Liz and
Ann. [LISSANDRA, LIZANDRA, LIZANN]

Lissa: *(LISS-ah)* (English) Short form of names like Melissa,
Lissandra, and Alyssa. [LYSSA]

Lita: *(LEE-tah)* (Latin) Originally a diminutive ending. [LETA]

Liv: *(liv, leev)* (Scandinavian) "Life." Made familiar by actress
Liv Ullman. Livia is an ancient Roman name as well as being a
short form of Olivia. [LIVIA, LY-VIA]

LESS COMMON CLASSICS;
NEW, UNUSUAL NAMES

- Lexie
  Lexi
  Lexus
- Lia
- Liliana
- Liza
- Lizbeth
- Lizette

Liza: *(LYE-za, LEE-zah)* (English) Short form of Elizabeth and Eliza. See also Lisa. [LEEZA, LIZ, LIZZIE, LYZA]

Lizbeth: *(LIZ-beth)* (English) Short form of Elizabeth. [LISABET, LISABETH, LISBET, LIZABETH, LIZBET, LYZBETH]

Lizette: *(liz-ZET)* (American) Variant of Elizabeth. [LISETTE, LISSETTE, LIZETH, LYZETTE]

Llesenia: *(yeh-SEE-nee-ah)* (Spanish) Meaning uncertain, probably created for the gypsy female lead in a 1970s Spanish soap opera. See also Jessenia and Yessenia.

Logan: *(LOH-gan)* (Scottish) "Low meadow." The use of this surname as a girl's first name became familiar due to the popular character Brooke Logan on the TV show *The Bold and the Beautiful*. She was called by her last name rather than her first by her love interest on the show, and the name caught on with parents.

Loida: *(LOY-dah)* (Latin) Variant form of Leda. [LOYDA]

Lois: *(LOH-iss)* (Greek) "Pleasing." Biblical: a first-century Christian, the grandmother of Timothy.

Lola: *(LOH-lah)* (Spanish) Short form of Dolores. [LOLITA]

Loni: *(LAH-nee)* Variant form of Alona or Leona. Modern usage is probaly due to actress Loni Anderson. See also Lani. [LONA, LONNA, LONNI, LONNIE]

Lora: *(LOR-ah)* (French) Variant form of Laura. See also Lori and Loretta. [LORAH, LORANNA, LOREANNA, LOREE, LORINDA, LORITA, LORRAE]

Lorelei: *(LOR-a-lye)* (German) A

LESS COMMON CLASSICS; NEW, UNUSUAL NAMES
• Lora
• Loren
• Lorena
• Lori
• Lucy
Lucia
• Lyndsey
• Lynn
• Lyric

rocky cliff on the Rhine river, dangerous to boat passage, has been poetically personified as the Lorelei, whose singing lures men to destruction. [LORALEI]

Loren: *(LOR-en)* (English) Variant of Lawrence, from the Latin Laurentius, meaning "from Laurentium." See also Lauren and Lorna. [LORIN, LORREN, LORRIN, LORRYN, LORYN]

Lorena: *(lor-EEN-ah, lor-AY-nah)* Variant form of Laura or Lora. See also Lorraine. [LOREEN, LOREENE, LORENE, LORENIA, LORENNA, LORRINA]

Lorenza: *(lo-REN-zah)* (Italian) Feminine form of Lorenzo, from Lawrence.

Loretta: *(lor-RET-ah)* (Latin) Diminutive form of Laura or Lora. Loreta is a saint's name. [LORETA, LORETTE]

Lori: *(LOR-ee)* (English) Variant of Laurie and Lora. [LORIA, LORIAN, LORIANA, LORIANN, LORIANNE, LORIEL, LORILEE, LORILYNN, LORINDA, LORIS]

Lorna: *(LOR-nah)* (Scottish) Feminine form of Lorne, from Loren, made familiar by the heroine of Blackmore's novel *Lorna Doone*.

Lorraine: *(lor-AYN)* (French) Name of the province in France and a family name of French royalty. See also Laraine and Lorena. [LORAINA, LORAINE, LORAYNE, LORRAINA]

Louise: *(loo-EEZ)* "Renowned fighter." Feminine form of Louis. St. Louise (16th century) was co-founder with St. Vincent de Paul of the nursing order Daughters of Charity. See also Luisa. [LOUISA, LOUELLA, LUELLA]

Lourdes: *(LOOR-des, LOORDZ)* (Basque) Place name. Miracles of healing are attributed to the site in France where the Virgin Mary reportedly appeared to a young girl. In the news: actress-singer Madonna chose the name for her first-born daughter. See also Bernadette.

Luana: *(loo-AHN-ah)* (Hawaiian) "Content, happy." Also contemporary blends based on Lou and Ann or Anna. [LOUANN, LUANDA, LUANN, LUANNA, LUANNE]

Lucille: *(loo-SEEL)* (French) Diminutive form of Lucia. [LU-CIELA, LUCIENNE, LUCILA, LUCILE, LUCILIA, LUCILLA]

Lucine: *(loo-SEEN)* (Latin) "Illumination." Mythology: the Roman goddess of childbirth, giver of first light to the newborn. Also a reference to Mary as the Lady of the Light. See also Lucia and Luz. [LUCENA, LUCINA, LUCINDA, LU-CINNA, LUSINE]

Lucretia: *(loo-KREE-shah)* (Latin) The name of a Roman matron who committed suicide in public protest against dishonor. During the Renaissance, darker associations were added to the name through Lucrezia Borgia, sister to Cesare Borgia. See also Crecia. [LACRETIA, LUCRECE, LUCRECIA, LUCREZIA]

Lucy: *(LOO-see)* (Latin) "Light, illumination." Feminine form of Lucius. The feast day of St. Lucy (fourth century) is called the Festival of Light in Sweden. See also Lucille and Lucine. [LUCIA, LUCETTE, LUCI, LUCIANA, LUCIANNA, LUCIE, LUCIENNE, LUCITA]

Luisa: *(loo-EE-sah)* (Spanish) Feminine form of Louis. See also Louise. [LUISANA, LUIZA]

Lulu: *(LOO-loo)* (Swahili) "Precious." (Tanzanian) "Pearl." (Hawaiian) "Calm, peaceful; protected." Also a pet form of names like Louise and Louella.

Lumina: *(loo-MEEN-ah)* (Latin) "Brilliant, illuminated."

Luna: *(LOO-nah)* (Latin) "The moon." Mythology: one of the names of Artemis, goddess of the moon.

Lupita: *(loo-PEE-tah)* (Spanish) Short form of Guadalupe. [LUPE]

Luz: *(looz)* "Almond tree." Biblical: an early name of the town of Bethel. Also a reference to Mary as "Our Lady of Light." [LUZELENA, LUZETTE, LUZIANA]

Lydia: *(LID-ee-ah)* (Greek) "From Lydia." Biblical: a Christian woman called a "seller of purple." One of the rare descriptions of a woman of business, probably affluent, in Biblical times. [LIDIA]

Lyla: *(LYE-lah)* (English) Possibly a feminine form of Lyle, or a variant short form of Delilah. See also Leila. [LILA, LILAH]

Lynda: *(LIN-dah)* (English) Variant form of Linda. [LYNDALL, LYNDEE, LYNDI]

Lyndsey: *(LIND-zee)* (English) Variant form of Lindsey. [LYNDSAY, LYNDSIE, LYNSEY, LYNZEE, LYNZIE]

Lynette: *(le-NET)* (Welsh) Variant of an ancient Welsh given name. In the Arthurian tales, Lynette accompanied Sir Gareth on a knightly quest. See also Linnet and Lynn. [LYNELLE, LYNESSA, LYNNET, LYNNETTE]

Lynn: *(lin)* (English) Possibly a short form of Lynette, or a variant form of *lann*, an Irish Gaelic word meaning "house; church." Used especially as a middle name and as a feminine beginning or ending in many name blends, like Kaylyn and Lynlee. [LYNNE, LYN, LYNLEE, LYNLEY, LYNNA]

Lyric: *(LEER-ick)* (French) "Of the lyre." Literally, the words of a song. [LYRA, LYRICA]

M

Mabel: *(MAY-bel)* (English) "Lovable." Short form of Amabel. [MABELLE, MABLE, MAYBELL]

Machiko: *(MAH-chee-koh)* (Japanese) "Child who learns truth; beautiful child." Machiko is the name of the current Empress of Japan.

Mackenzie: *(ma-KEN-zee)* (Scottish) "Son of Kenzie; fair, favored one." See also Kenzie, *Mc-* names, and McKenzie.

Macy: *(MAY-see)* (French) From a medieval male name, possibly a form of Matthew. [MACEE, MACEY, MACI, MACIE]

Madeline: *(MAD-a-linn)* (French) "Woman from Magdala." Variant form of Madeleine. See Magdalena. [MADELEINE, MADELYN, MADALENA, MADALENE, MADALYN, MADALYNN, MADDELENA, MADDIE, MADDY, MADELAINE, MADELNA, MADELENE, MADELINA, MADELON, MADELYNE, MADELYNN, MADELYNNE, MADENA, MADILYN, MADINA, MALENA]

Madison: *(MAD-a-son)* (English) Surname derived from Matthew, "gift of Jehovah," or Matilda, "strong fighter." The mermaid heroine Madison in the hit film *Splash* probably influenced the adoption of the surname as a girl's name. [MADDISON, MADISYN, MADYSON]

Madonna: *(ma-DAH-nah)* (Italian) "My lady." A form of respectful address, like the French *madame*. Also used to signify the Virgin Mary, or a work of art depicting her as a mother. Twentieth-century name bearer: singer/actress Madonna. See also Donna and Mona.

Maeko: *(MYE-ee-koh)* (Japanese) ''Truth child.''

Maemi: *(mah-AY-mee)* (Japanese) ''Smile of truth.''

Maeve: *(mah-EEVE)* (Irish) ''Joy.'' Maeve, the legendary warrior queen of ancient Connacht, is described in the *Tain*, the Celtic equivalent of the *Iliad*, as ''tall, fair . . . carrying an iron sword.'' Famous name bearer: author Maeve Binchy.

Magda: *(MAG-dah)* (Slavic, German) Short form of Magdalena.

Magdalena: *(mag-da-LEE-nah)* (Greek) ''Woman from Magdala.'' Biblical: Mary Magdalene came from the Magdala area near the sea of Galilee. [MAGDALEN, MAGDALENE, MAGDELENA, MAGDELINE]

Maggie: *(MAG-ee)* (English) Short form of Margaret; usage as an independent name has risen due to a revival of interest in ''old-fashioned'' names. [MAGGI, MAGGY]

Magnolia: *(mag-NOL-yah)* A name from nature; the magnolia flower.

Mahala: *(ma-HAH-lah)* (Native American) ''Woman.''

Mahalia: *(ma-HAL-yah, ma-HAYL-yah)* (Hebrew) ''Praise is God.'' Famous name bearer: singer Mahalia Jackson. [MAHALEE, MAHALI]

Mahina: *(mah-HEE-nah)* (Hawaiian) ''Moon, moon-light.'' The Hawaiian equivalent of Diana, goddess of the moon.

Mai: *(mye)* (French) ''May.'' Roman mythology: Maia (source of the name May for the calendar month)

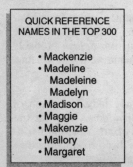

QUICK REFERENCE
NAMES IN THE TOP 300

- Mackenzie
- Madeline
    Madeleine
    Madelyn
- Madison
- Maggie
- Makenzie
- Mallory
- Margaret

was the goddess of spring growth. Maiya *(MY-ah)* is a Japanese surname meaning "rice valley."[2] See also May and Maya. [MAIA, MAIYA, MAIYAH]

Maida: *(MAY-dah)* (English) "Maiden; virgin."

Maira: *(MAY-rah)* (Irish) Variant form of Mary. See also Mayra.

Maisie: *(MAY-zee)* (English) Nickname for Margaret or Marjorie. [MAISEE]

Majesta: *(ma-JESS-tah)* (Latin) "Royal bearing, dignity." Mythology: Majestas was the Roman goddess of honor. [MAJESTY]

Majida: *(MA-jee-dah)* (Arabic) "Glorious." [MAJI]

Malana: *(ma-LAH-nah)* (Hawaiian) "Buoyant, light." Malina means "calming, soothing." [MALINA]

Malia: *(ma-LEE-ah)* (Hawaiian) Variant of Mary. Also a Spanish variant of Maria. [MALEA, MALEAH, MALEIA]

Mallory: *(MAL-or-ee)* (French) Surname that came into favor as a girl's name during the 1980s, initially due to the character Mallory on the TV series *Family Ties*. [MALORI, MALORIE, MALLORI, MALLORIE]

Mamie: *(MAY-mee)* Short form of Mary and Miriam. See also Mimi. [MAYME]

Mandisa: *(man-DEE-sah)* (African) "Sweetness."

Mandy: *(MAN-dee)* (English) Short form of Amanda. [MANDA, MANDI, MANDIE]

Manon: *(man-awn)* (French) Diminutive form of Marie.

Manuela: *(mahn-WAY-lah)* (Spanish) "With us is God." Variant form of Manuel.

Mara: *(MAHR-ah)* (Hebrew) "Bitter." Biblical: Naomi, mother-in-law of Ruth, claimed the name Mara as an expression of grief after the deaths of her husband and sons. May also be used as a variant form of Mary and as a short form of Tamara. See also Mary and Tamara. [MARAH, MAR-ALINDA]

Marcella: *(mar-SELL-ah)* (Latin) "Of Mars." Feminine form of Marcellus. Mythology: Mars, the Roman god of fertility, for whom the spring calendar month March was named, came to be identified with the Greek god Ares, god of war. St. Marcella (fourth century) was a cultivated woman of ability who was killed during the sack of Rome. See also Marcia and Maricela. [MARCELA, MARCELINA, MARCE-LINDA, MARCELINE, MARCELLE, MARCELLINA, MARCELLINE, MARCELYN, MARCHELLE]

Marcia: *(MAR-shah)* (Latin) "Of Mars." Feminine form of Marcus. See also Marcella and Marsha. [MARCENA, MARCI, MARCIANA, MARCIANNE, MARCIE, MARCILA, MARCINE, MARCY]

Margaret: *(MAR-gret)* (Greek) "Pearl." A saint's name. Historical: the name of nine queens of England, Scotland, France, and Austria. See also Greta, Gretchen, Maggie, Maisie, Margo, Marjorie, Megan, Peggy, and Rita. [MARGA-RITA, MADGE, MARGARETA, MAR-GARETE, MARGARETTE, MARGEEN, MARGETTE, MARGIE, MARGIT, MAR-GITA, MARGRET, MARGRETE, MAR-GRIT, MARGUERITE, MARKETA, MEG, MEGGIE]

QUICK REFERENCE
NAMES IN THE TOP 300

- Maria
 Mariah
 Marie
- Marina
- Marisa
 Marissa
- Mary
- Maya
- McKayla
- McKenna

Margo: *(MAR-go)* (French) Variant of Margaret. Margaux was the name of Ernest Hemingway's granddaughter, an actress. [MAR-GOT, MARGAUX, MARGEAUX]

Mari: *(MAH-ree)* (Welsh) Variant of Mary; also a favored prefix for blending with other names, such as Marisol (Latin), "Mary alone" and Maricruz, "Mary of the cross." See also Maria and Maribel. [MARIBETH, MARIDEL, MARI-LEE, MARILENA, MARILENE, MARILISA, MARILOU, MARILU, MARITA, MARYCRUZ]

Maria: *(mah-REE-ah)* (Latin) Variant of Mary, popular with both Spanish and non-Spanish cultures. Marie, the French variant, was the preferred form of Mary in England until about the time of the Reformation. Mariah *(ma-RYE-ah)* has greatly increased in popularity, probably due to singer Mariah Carey. Maria and Marie are very often blended with other names and suffixes. See also Manon, Mari, Maribel, Marisa, Mary, Mia, and Ria. [MARIAH, MARIE, MAREE, MARIALENA, MARIALINDA, MARIALISA, MARIEANNE, MA-RIELENA, MARIETTA, MARIETTE, MARIKA, MARYA]

Mariana: *(mar-ee-AHN-ah)* (Latin) A blend of Mary and Ana. Shakespeare gave the name Mariana to a woman noted for her loyalty in *Measure for Measure*. The short form Marian is memorable due to *Robin Hood*'s Maid Marian. See also Mary, Maryann, and Miriam. [MARIAN, MARIAM, MAR-IANDA, MARIANE, MARIANN, MARIANNA, MARIANNE, MAR-IEN, MARYAM, MARYAN]

Maribel: *(mare-a-BEL)* (Latin) "Beautiful Marie." Blend of Mari and Belle. See also Mary. [MARIBELL, MARIBELLA, MARIBELLE]

Maricela: *(mar-a-SEE-lah)* (Spanish) Variant of Marcella. [MARISELA, MARICEL, MARICELLA]

Mariela: *(mar-ee-ELL-ah)* (Latin) Diminutive form of Maria. Notable name bearer: actress Mariel Hemingway. See also Meriel. [MARIEL, MARIELE, MARIELLA, MARIELLE]

Marigold: *(MARE-a-gold)* (English) "Mary's gold," a reference to the flower and to the mother of Jesus.

Mariko: *(MAH-ree-koh)* (Japanese) "Ball, circle."

Marilla: *(ma-RILL-ah)* "Shining sea." Variant of Muriel. Marilis is a short form of Amaryllis. [MARELLA, MARILIS]

Marilyn: *(MARE-a-lin)* (English) Blend of Marie or Mary and Lyn. Notable name bearer: actress Marilyn Monroe. [MARALYN, MARILYNN, MARLYN, MARYLIN, MARYLYN, MARYLYNN]

Marina: *(mah-REE-nah)* (Latin) "Of the sea." A saint's name. Shakespeare gave the name to Pericles' daughter in his play *Pericles, Prince of Tyre*. See also Marni. [MAREEN, MAREENA, MARENA, MARIN, MARINDA, MARINELLA, MARINELLE, MARINNA, MARYN]

Marisa: *(ma-REES-ah)* (Latin) Variant of Maria. Notable name bearer: actress Marisa Tomei. [MARESSA, MARISE, MARYSA, MARYSE]

Marise: *(MAH-ree-say)* (Japanese) "Infinite, endless."

Marissa: *(ma-RISS-ah)* (Latin) "Of the sea." Also a variant of Marie and Mary. [MARESSA, MARICIA, MARIS, MARISABEL, MARISHA, MARITZA, MARIZA, MARYSSA, MERIS, MERISSA]

QUICK REFERENCE
NAMES IN THE TOP 300

- McKenzie
- Megan
  Meagan
  Meghan
- Melanie
- Melissa
- Mercedes
- Meredith
- Mia
- Michelle

Marjan: *(mar-YAN, mar-jan)* (Polish) Variant form of Mary. [MARJANNE, MARJON]

Marjorie: *(MAR-jor-ee)* (English) Variant of the French Margerie, from Margaret. Marjo may be used as a blend of Mary and Joseph. [MARGERIE, MARGERY, MARGIE, MARJA, MARJI, MARJO]

Marketa: *(mar-KEE-tah)* (Czech) Variant form of Margaret. [MARKEDA, MARKEE, MARKEETA, MARKIA, MARKIE, MARKITA, MARQUITA, MARQUETA]

Markeisha: *(mar-KEE-shah)* (American) A contemporary blend of *Mar-* and Keisha, possibly a further development of the favored sound of Marquise *(mar-KEESE)*. [MARKESHA, MARKIESHA, MARKISHA]

Marla: *(MAR-lah)* (Latin) Variant form of Marlene or Marlo. Marlo became familiar in the 1970s due to actress Marlo Thomas. See also Marlee. [MARLETTE, MARLO, MARLOWE]

Marlee: *(MAR-lee)* (English) "Marshy meadow." May also be used as a variant of Marlene. Notable name bearer: actress Marlee Matlin. See also Marla. [MARLEIGH, MARLEY, MARLIE]

Marlen: *(MAR-len)* (English) Feminine form of Marlon or variant of Marlene. [MARLYN, MARLENNE, MARLIN, MARLYNN]

Marlene: *(mar-LEEN, mar-LAYNE, mar-LAY-nah)* (German) Variant of Madeline. Some contemporary names are spelled phonetically to ensure the desired pronunciation. See also Marla, Marlee, and Marlen. [MARLENA, MARLAINA, MARLANA, MARLAYNA, MARLAYNE, MARLEEN, MARLEENA, MARLEENE, MARLEINA, MARLENI, MARLINA, MARLINE]

Marlisa: *(mar-LEE-sah)* (Latin) A blend of Mary and Lisa. Marlise *(mar-LEESE)* is a German form. [MARLISE, MARLISHA, MARLISS, MARLISSA, MARLYS, MARLYSE, MARLYSSA]

Marni: *(MAR-nee)* (Hebrew) "Rejoicing." Marnie is a variant of Marina. [MARNEE, MARNELL, MARNIE, MARNINA, MARNISHA]

QUICK REFERENCE
NAMES IN THE TOP 300

- Michaela
  McKayla
  Mikaela
  Mikayla
- Miranda
- Molly
- Monica
  Monique
- Morgan

Marquise: *(mar-KEES)* (French) The feminine equivalent of the French title *marquis*. [MARQUESA, MARQUI, MARQUISA, MARQUISHA]

Marsha: *(MAR-sha)* (English) Variant form of Marcia.

Martha: *(MAR-tha)* (Aramaic) "Lady." Biblical: the sister of Mary and Lazarus. [MARTA]

Martina: *(mar-TEEN-ah)* (Latin) Feminine form of Martin. Martinique (French) is a West Indies island. [MARTEENA, MARTINE, MARTINIQUE]

Marvell: *(mar-VELL)* (Latin) "Wonderful, extraordinary." [MARVELA, MARVELLA, MARVELYN]

Marvina: *(mar-VEEN-ah)* (English) "Renowned friend." Feminine form of Marvin. [MARVA, MARVADENE]

Mary: *(MARE-ee)* (Hebrew) "Bitter." Variant form of Miriam. Biblical: the virgin mother of Christ. Mary became the object of great veneration in the Catholic Church. Through the centuries, names like Dolores and Mercedes have been created to express aspects of Mary's life and worship. Mary is also frequently used in blends and compound names. See also Maira, Malia, Mamie, Manon, Mara, Mari, Maria, Mariana, Maribel, Mariela, Marigold, Marilyn, Marisa, Marissa, Marjan, Maryann, Maureen, May, Mayra, Mia, Mimi, Miriam, Mitzi, Moira, and Molly. [MARYBEL, MARY-BELL, MARYBETH, MARYJO, MARYLEE, MARYLOU, MARYLU]

Maryann: *(mare-ee-ANN)* (English) An 18th-century blend of Mary and Ann, perhaps meant to signify that "bitterness" of spirit is comforted by "grace and favor." See also Mariana. [MARYANNA, MARYANNE]

Matilda: *(muh-TIL-dah)* (German) "Strength for battle." Once a favored name due to William the Conqueror's

Queen Matilda (11th century), now very rarely used. A saint's name. See also Maude. [MATILDE, MATTIE]

Matsuko: *(MAHT-soo-koh)* (Japanese) "Pine tree child."

Maude: *(mawd)* (French) Variant form of Matilda. Like Matilda, now very rarely used. [MAUD]

Maureen: *(maw-REEN)* (Irish) Variant form of Moira and Mary. Maurissa and Maurisa may also be feminine forms of Maurice. See also Mara, Moreen, and Morisa. [MAURA, MAURIANNE, MAURISA, MAURISSA]

Mavis: *(MAY-viss)* (English) "Song-thrush."

Maxine: *(mak-SEEN)* (English) "The greatest." Feminine form of Max. [MAXI, MAXIE, MAXIMINA]

May: (Latin) "Maia; the month of May." Also used as a short form of Mary. See also Mai. [MAE, MAELEE, MAELYNN, MAYLEEN, MAYLENE]

Maya: *(MYE-ah)* (Spanish) Short form of Amalia. (Hindi) "One of a kind." (Russian) A form of Mary. A star constellation. See also Mai.

Mayda: *(MAY-dah)* (English) "Maiden." See also Maida.

Mayra: *(MAY-rah, MYE-rah)* (Irish) Variant of Maire, a Gaelic form of Mary; also a Spanish form of Maria. See also Moira and Myra. [MAIRA, MAIRE, MAIRI]

Maysa: *(MAY-sah)* (Arabic) "Graceful."

McKayla: *(ma-KAY-lah)* (American) "Fiery." Blend of the Irish

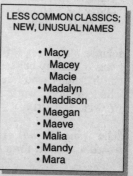

LESS COMMON CLASSICS; NEW, UNUSUAL NAMES

- Macy
  Macey
  Macie
- Madalyn
- Maddison
- Maegan
- Maeve
- Malia
- Mandy
- Mara

and Scottish surname McKay with Kayla, resulting in a variant of Michaela. [MCKAY, MCKAYLEE]

McKenna: *(ma-KEN-ah)* (Scottish) Popular usage of this surname as a given name is undoubtedly influenced by the similar use of McKenzie.

McKenzie: *(ma-KEN-zee)* (Scottish) "The fair one." See also Kenzie and Mackenzie.

Medina: *(ma-DEEN-ah)* (Arabic) "City of the Prophet." The city where Mohammed began his campaign to establish Islam.

Medora: *(meh-DOR-ah)* (English) A literary creation; Medora is a romantic heroine in Lord Byron's narrative poem *The Corsair*.

Meena: *(MEEN-ah)* (Sanskrit) "Fish." Astrological name, Pisces. Hindu mythology: a name of the wife of Shiva.

Meera: *(MEER-ah)* (Israeli) "Light." (Hindi) "Saintly woman." See also Mira. [MEIRA]

Megan: *(MEG-an, MEE-gan, MAY-gan)* (Welsh) Variant form of Margaret, based on the short form Meg. Phonetic spellings of Megan are used to ensure one of the three pronunciations. Meegan (Gaelic) means "soft, gentle." [MEAGAN, MEGHAN, MAEGAN, MAYGAN, MEAGHAN, MEEGAN, MEEGHAN, MEGGAN]

Melanie: *(MEL-a-nee)* (Greek) "Dark." Religion: St. Melania was a wealthy heiress and philanthropist of the fourth and fifth century who freed thousands of slaves and engaged in lifelong good works. [MELAINA, MELAINE, MELANA, MELANEE, MELANIA]

Melia: *(ma-LEE-ah)* (Hawaiian) "Plumeria." Occasionally used as a short form of Amelia *(MEEL-yah)*.

Melina: *(ma-LEEN-ah)* (Greek) "Honey." [MELENE]

Melinda: *(ma-LIN-dah)* (English) Blend of Melissa and Linda. [MALINDA, MELYNDA]

Melisande: *(MEL-a-sahnd)* (French) "Strength; determination." Variant of Millicent. [MELISANDRA]

Melissa: *(ma-LISS-ah)* (Greek) "Bee." Mythology: the name of a princess of Crete who was changed into a bee after she learned how to collect honey. [MELISA, MELISE, MELISHA, MELISSE, MELIZA, MISSY]

Melita: *(ma-LEE-tah)* (Spanish) Short form of Carmelita. May also be a feminine variant of Mellitus, a saint's name. Malita is a variant of Maria. [MALITA]

Melody: *(MEL-a-dee)* (Greek) "Music, song." [MELODEE, MELODI, MELODIE]

Melva: *(MEL-vah)* (English) Feminine form of Melvin. [MELVINA]

Meralda: *(mer-AHL-dah)* (Latin) "Emerald." Short form of Esmeralda.

Mercedes: *(mer-SAY-dees)* (Latin) "Mercies." Used in reference to Mary as "Our Lady of Mercies." Literary: the name of the lost love of Edmond Dantes in Dumas's *The Count of Monte Cristo*. See also Mercy. [MERCEDEZ]

Mercer: *(MER-ser)* (English) "Merchant."

Mercy: *(MER-see)* (English) "Compassion, forebearance." See also Mercedes. [MERCIA, MERCIE, MERCILLA, MERCINA]

LESS COMMON CLASSICS;
NEW, UNUSUAL NAMES

- Mariana
- Marilyn
- Marlene
- Marley
- Martha
- Maura
- Maureen
- Mayra
- Meaghan

Meredith: *(MARE-a-dith)* (Welsh) "Great one." In America, Meredith is now used almost entirely as a girl's name.

Meriel: *(MARE-ee-al)* (English) "Shining sea." Variant of Muriel. See also Mariel and Muriel.

Merry: *(MARE-ee)* (English) "Mirthful, joyous." Merryn was the name of a seventh-century Irish saint. [MERRI, MERRIE, MERRILEE, MERRYN]

Meryl: *(MARE-el)* (French) "Blackbird." Feminine form of Merle. Well-known today due to actress Meryl Streep. [MARYL, MERLA, MERLYN, MERRYL, MIRLA, MYRLA]

Mia: *(MEE-ah)* (Israeli) Feminine short form of Michal. (Latin, Scandinavian) A short form of Maria. See also Miya.

Micah: *(MYE-cah)* (Hebrew) "Who is like God?" A short form of Michael. Biblical: a prophet and writer of the book of Micah. Micaiah *(mih-KYE-ah)* "Who is like Jehovah?" was the wife of a king of Judah. [MICAIAH]

Michaela: *(mih-KAY-lah)* (English) Feminine form of Michael. One of the most frequently misspelled names. Care should be taken with phonetic spelling variants. See also McKayla, Michal, and Michelle. [MAKAYLA, MICAELA, MIKAELA, MIKAYLA, MIKELLA, MIKELLE, MYCHAELA]

Michal: *(MYE-kal)* (Hebrew) "Who is like God?" Feminine form of Michael. Biblical: Michal was King Saul's daughter, the first wife of David. [MICAL, MICHAELINE, MICHAELYN, MICHALA, MICOLE, MYCHAL]

Michelle: *(mee-SHELL)* (French) Feminine form of Michael. In the news: singer Me'Shell N'Degé Ocello. See also Michaela and Michal. [MICHELE, ME'SHELL, MICHELA, MICHELLA, MYCHELE, MYCHELLE]

Michiko: *(MEE-chee-koh)* (Japanese) "Child of beauty."

Midori: *(mee-DOR-ee)* (Japanese) "Green."

Miki: *(MEE-kee)* (Japanese) "Three trees together." (Hawaiian) "Quick, nimble." Mikki is sometimes used as a short form of names like Michaela. [MIKA, MIKKI, MIKKO]

Mildred: *(MIL-dred)* (English) "Gentle strength." An apt name for St. Mildred (eighth century), an abbess from a royal household noted for her gentleness and kindness.

Milena: *(mi-LEE-nah)* (Czech, Latin) "Favored." [MILA, MILEENA]

Miliani: *(mee-lee-AH-nee)* (Hawaiian) "Gentle caress." Miliana is a Latin feminine form of Emeliano. [MILANA, MILIANA]

Millicent: *(MIL-a-sent)* (French) "Strength; determination." See also Melisande. [MILLIE]

Mimi: *(MEE-mee)* (French) Pet name for Miriam or Marie. Also used as a Spanish pet name for Mira, Maria, and Noemi.

Mina: *(MEE-nah)* (German) "Love." Name endings (*-mina* and *-mena*) used as independent names. Min and Meena are Irish Gaelic names meaning "smooth, fine, small." See also Meena. [MEENA, MENA, MIN, MINETTE, MINNA, MINNETTE, MINNIE]

Mindy: *(MIN-dee)* (English) Short form of Melinda. [MINDA, MINDEE, MINDI, MINDIE]

Minerva: *(mi-NER-vah)* (Latin) Mythology: name of the Roman goddess of wisdom.

LESS COMMON CLASSICS;
NEW, UNUSUAL NAMES

- Melinda
- Melody
- Micaela
- Michele
- Miriam
- Misty
- Mollie
- Montana
- Moriah

Mira: *(MEER-ah)* (Slavic) Variant of Myra and Miranda. Noted name bearer: actress Mira Sorvino. See also Meera. [MIRANA, MIRI, MIRIANA]

Mirabel: *(MEER-a-bel)* (Latin) "Wonderful." [MIRABELL, MIRABELLA, MIRABELLE]

Miranda: *(mer-ANN-dah)* (Latin) "Worthy of admiration." In Shakespeare's *The Tempest*, Miranda is an innocent girl raised and educated on an isolated island by her magician father. [MYRANDA]

Mirella: *(mer-ELL-ah)* (Latin) Feminine variant form of Mireya, from the Hebrew male name Amariah, meaning "Jehovah has said." [MIREILLE, MIRELL, MIREYA, MYRELLE]

Miriam: *(MEER-ee-em)* (Hebrew) An older version of the name Mary. Biblical: the sister of Moses, who saved his life as a baby when she hid him in a basket among the rushes at the river's edge for Pharaoh's daughter to find. [MARYAM, MYRIAM]

Misty: *(MISS-tee)* (English) Literally, "misty." A name from nature. See also Mystique. [MISTI, MISTIE, MYSTEE, MYSTI]

Mitzi: *(MIT-zee)* (German) Pet name for Mary and Marie. [MITZY]

Miya: *(MEE-yah)* (Japanese) "Temple." See also Mia.

Modesty: *(MAH-dess-tee)* (Latin) "Without conceit; modest." [MODESTA, MODESTINE]

Mohala: *(mo-HAH-lah)* (Hawaiian) "Petals unfolding; shining forth."

Moira: *(MOY-rah)* (Scottish) Variant of the Irish Maire, from Mary. See also Mayra and Myra. [MOYRA]

Molly: *(MAH-lee)* (Irish) From the Gaelic Maili, a pet form of Mary. In use since the late Middle Ages; recently revived in popular usage, probably in part due to actress Molly Ringwald. [MOLLEE, MOLLEY, MOLLI, MOLLIE]

Mona: *(MOH-nah)* (Irish) "Noble." Mona is also an Italian short form of Madonna. Famous name bearer: the *Mona Lisa*, a portrait painted by Leonardo da Vinci, which has itself inspired name blends. See also Madonna and Monica. [MONALISA, MONALISSA]

Monica: *(MAH-ni-kah)* (English, Latin) Possibly a variant of Mona. A saint's name. Notable in the 1990s: fictional character Monica Geller on the TV sitcom *Friends*. [MONIQUE, MONIKA]

Monisha: *(moh-NEE-shah)* (Hindi) "Intelligent woman."

Monserrat: *(mohn-sare-AHT)* (Latin) "Jagged mountain." The name of a mountain in Spain (Montserrat), a monastery and a celebrated image of the Virgin Mary. Famous name bearer: opera diva Montserrat Caballe. [MONTSERRAT]

Montana: *(mon-TAN-ah)* (Latin) "Mountain." The name of the western state used as a given name. May also be used as a form of Montanus, a saint's name. [MONTANNA, MONTEENE, MONTINA]

Moreen: *(mor-EEN)* (Irish) "Great." See also Maureen. [MORELLA]

Morena: *(moh-RAY-nah)* (Spanish) "Brown, brown-haired."

Morgan: *(MOR-gen)* (Welsh) "Bright sea." Usage for girls increased sharply during the 1980s, probably due to actress Morgan Fairchild. Morgaine and Morgayne are medieval Irish forms. [MORGAINE, MORGANA, MORGANN, MORGANNE, MORGAYNE]

Moriah: *(moh-RYE-ah)* (Hebrew) Biblical: the name of the

Mount of the Temple of Solomon in Jerusalem. See Maria for the similar-sounding name Mariah.

Morisa: *(mor-EES-ah)* (Spanish) Feminine form of Maurice. See also Maureen. [MORISSA]

Morna: *(MOR-nah)* (Irish) "Affection." See also Myrna.

Morwenna: *(mor-WEN-ah)* (Welsh) "Ocean waves."

Muriel: *(MYUR-ee-el)* (Irish) "Shining sea." See also Meriel and Marilla.

Myisha: *(mye-EE-shah)* (Arabic) "Woman; life." Variant of Aisha. [MYEISHA, MYESHA, MYESHIA, MYIESHA]

Myla: *(MYE-lah)* (English) "Merciful." Feminine form of Myles. [MYLEEN, MYLENE]

Myra: *(MYE-rah)* (English) Poetic invention, possibly a variant of Mayra. See also Moira. [MYRAH, MYRIAH]

Myrna: *(MIR-nah)* (Irish) "Beloved." Made familiar in the 1930s and 1940s by actress Myrna Loy. See also Morna. [MIRNA, MURNA]

Myrta: *(MER-tah)* (Latin) A variant of Myrtle, a nature name based on the evergreen shrub that was sacred to Venus as a symbol of love. Myrtle is very rarely used today. [MYRTLE]

Mystique: *(miss-TEEK)* (French) "Air of mystery." The use of Mystique as a contemporary name for girls is probably an outgrowth of the popularity of the name Misty. [MYSTICA, MISTIQUE]

N

Na-: (American) Blends of *Na-* plus various endings, with pronunciation emphasis on the second syllable. [NAKEISHA, NAKIA, NAKISHA, NAKITA, NALANI, NAQUITA, NAREESHA, NATAHNEE, NATAVIA, NATISHA, NATOSHA, NATOYA]

Nadia: *(NAH-d'-yah)* (French, Slavic) "Hope." See also Nadine. [NADJA, NADYA]

Nadine: *(nay-DEEN)* (French) Variant of Nadia. [NADEEN]

Nana: *(NAH-nah)* (Hawaiian) Name of a spring month and the name of a star. The Spanish Nana is a pet form of Ana.

Nancy: *(NAN-cee)* (English) Variant of Anne. [NAN, NANCEY, NANCI, NANCIE, NANN]

Nanette: *(nan-NET)* (French) "Favor; grace." Variant form of Anne. [NANINE, NANNETTE]

Naomi: *(nay-OH-mee)* (Hebrew) "Pleasantness." Biblical: an ancestress of Jesus and mother-in-law to Ruth. Noemi *(no-AY-mee)* is the Spanish form. [**NOEMI**, NEOMA, NEOMI, NOEMIE]

Nariko: *(NAH-ree-koh)* (Japanese) "Gentle child." [NARI]

Natalie: *(NAT-a-lee)* (Latin) "Birthday," especially referring to the birthday of Christ. The *h* is silent in the French form Nathalie; some American variants (like Nathalee)

QUICK REFERENCE
NAMES IN THE TOP 300

• Nancy
• Naomi
• Natalie
• Natasha
• Nicole
  Nichole
• Nikki

are phonetically spelled to retain the *h* sound. See also Natasha. [**NATALIA, NATHALIE,** NATALEE, NATALYA, NATHALEE, NATHALIA, NATHALY]

Natasha: *(na-TAH-shah)* (Russian) Variant of Natalie. Noted name bearer: actress Natasha Richardson. See also Tasha. [NATASCHA, NATASHIA, NATASIA]

Nazneen: *(nahz-NEEN)* (Farsi) "Exquisitely beautiful; charming." The name is meant to convey the superlative sense of the charm of a beloved woman or child.

Nedda: *(NED-dah)* (English) Feminine form of Ned, the equivalent of Edda. [NEDRA]

Neema: *(NEE-mah)* (Swahili) "Born in prosperity."

Neila: *(NEE-lah)* (Irish) Feminine form of Neil. [NEELIE, NEELY]

Neiva: *(NEE-vah)* (Spanish) "Snow." Feminine variant of the Spanish word *nieve*. Neva is the name of a river in Russia. [NEIVES, NEVA, NEYVA]

Nelly: *(NEL-ee)* (English) Short form of Eleanor. [NELIDA, NELL, NELLA, NELLIE]

Nereida: *(ne-RAY-dah)* (Greek) "Sea nymph; daughter of Nereus." Greek mythology: the Nereids were deities of the seas, mermaids. May also be used in reference to St. Nerus (first or second century), a Roman soldier who became a Christian. [NEREYDA, NERIDA, NERISSA]

Nesta: *(NESS-tah)* (Welsh) Variant form of Agnes. Also used as a short form of Ernesta. [NESSIE]

Nettie: *(NEH-tee)* (English) Name ending used as an independent name. [NETTA, NETTY]

Nia: *(NEE-ah)* (American) Short form of names with the *-nia* ending, used as an independent name after the fashion of Mia. Made familiar by actresses Nia Peeples and Nia Long.

Nichelle: *(nee-SHEL)* (American) Blend of Nichole and Michelle. First popularized by actress Nichelle Nichols, *Star Trek*'s Lt. Uhura. [NACHELL, NICHELE]

Nicole: *(ni-KOHL)* (French) Feminine form of Nicholas. (See historical note in boys' index.) During the Middle Ages names that seem feminine today, like Nicolet and Nicol, were actually male names. See also Colette, Nikita, and Nikki. [NICHOLE, NICCOLE, NICHOL, NICHOLLE, NICKOLE, NICOLA, NIKKOLE, NIKOLE, NYCOLE]

Nicolette: *(nee-ko-LET)* (French) Diminutive form of Nicole. See also Nikita and Nikki. [NICOLETTA, NICOLLETTE]

Nidia: *(NEE-dee-ah)* (Latin) "Nest." Literary: in Edward Bulwer-Lytton's novel *The Last Days of Pompeii*, Nydia *(NIH-dee-ah)* was a blind flower-seller who saved her beloved at the cost of her own life. [NYDIA]

Nikita: *(nih-KEE-tah)* (Russian) "Victorious." A diminutive form of Nicole. In Russia, also a male name.

Nikki: (English) Short form of Nicole. *Nic-* and *Nik-* variants are used in many cultures. Greek mythology: Nike *(NYE-kee)* was the name of the goddess of victory. Nikki *(NEE-kee)* is also a Japanese surname with the potential meaning "two trees." [NICCI, NICKI, NICKIE, NIKA, NIKE, NIKI, NIKIA, NIKITA, NIKKIE]

Nina: *(NEE-nah, NYNE-ah)* (Latin) A short form of Antonina. Diminutive name ending used as an independent name, especially in Russia. Neena is a Hindi name meaning "pretty eyes." [NEENA, NEENAH, NENA]

LESS COMMON CLASSICS; NEW, UNUSUAL NAMES

- Nadia
- Natalia
- Nathalie
- Nia
- Nicolette
- Nina
- Noelle
- Nora
- Norma

Ninon: *(nan-ahn)* (French) Variant of Anne. Ninon de Lenclos was a 17th-century aristocrat famous for her wit and beauty. [NINETTE, NYNETTE]

Nisha: *(NEE-shah)* (Hindi) "Night." [NEESHA, NIESHA, NYSSA]

Nita: *(NEE-tah)* (Spanish) Diminutive ending used as an independent name.

Noelani: *(no-ah-LAH-nee)* (Hawaiian) "Mist of heaven." Noe *(noh-AY)*: "Mist, misty rain." [NOE]

Noelle: *(noe-ELL)* (French) "Birthday." Feminine form of Noel. Commonly used in reference to Christ's birth and the Christmas festival. [NOEL, NOELE, NOELL, NOELLA]

Nola: *(NO-lah)* (Irish) Feminine form of Nolan or a variant short form of Fenella, from Fiona. [NOLANA, NOLENE]

Nona: *(NOH-nah)* (Latin) "Nine."

Nora: *(NOR-ah)* (English) Short form of names like Eleanora and Honora. [NORAH, NORISSA]

Noreen: *(nor-EEN)* (Irish) Variant of Nora. [NOREENA, NORENE, NORINE]

Norell: *(no-RELL)* (Scandinavian) "From the north." Occasional usage of this surname as a given name may be due to the perfume. The variant Narelle is especially popular in Australia. [NARELLE]

Noriko: *(NOR-ee-koh)* (Japanese) "Law, order."

Norma: *(NOR-mah)* (Latin) "From the north." Feminine form of Norman. In Bellini's tragic opera *Norma*, Norma is a druidess at the time of the Roman occupation of England.

Nova: *(NOH-vah)* (Latin) "New." Astronomy: a nova is a star that suddenly releases a tremendous burst of energy, increasing its brightness many thousandfold.

Nura: *(NOOR-ah)* (Arabic) "Light."

Nyla: *(NYE-lah)* (English) Feminine form of Nyles, from Neil. [NILA, NYLAH]

Nyree: *(ny-REE)* (Maori) "Sea." Made familiar in the 1960s–1970s by New Zealand actress Nyree Dawn Porter.

Oceana: *(oh-shee-AH-nah)* (Greek) "Ocean." Feminine form of Oceanus. Greek mythology: Oceanus was a Titan, the father of rivers and water nymphs.

Octavia: *(ock-TAHV-yah, ock-TAY-vee-ah)* (Latin) "Eighth." Feminine form of Octavius. A clan name of Roman emperors. See also Tavia. [OCTAVIANA]

Odelia: *(oh-DEEL-yah)* (French) "Wealthy." Odilia was an eighth-century French saint. [ODELLA, ODETTE, ODILA, ODILE, ODILIA, OTTILIE]

Odessa: *(oh-DESS-ah)* (Greek) "Wandering; quest." Variant form of Odysseus.

Ola: *(OH-lah)* (Hawaiian) "Life; well-being." (Nigerian) "Precious."

Oletha: *(oh-LEE-tha)* (Scandinavian) "Light; nimble."

Olexa: *(oh-LEKS-ah)* (Czech) Feminine form of Alexander.

Olga: *(OL-gah)* (Russian) "Blessed."

Olida: *(oh-LEE-dah)* (Latin) Variant form of Olivia. [OLETA]

Olina: *(oh-LEE-nah)* (Hawaiian) "Joyous." [OLEEN, OLINE]

Olinda: *(oh-LIN-dah)* (Latin) A poetic name created in the 16th century. [OLYNDA]

Olivia: *(oh-LIV-ee-ah)* (Latin) "The olive tree." Feminine form of Oliver. Biblical: the olive tree is a symbol of fruitfulness, beauty, and dignity. Today, "extending an olive branch" traditionally signifies an offer of peace. See also Olida.

Olympia: *(oh-LIM-pee-ah)* (Greek) "From Olympus." One of the many saints' names with origins in mythology. Mount Olympus was the home of the ancient Greek gods. [OLIMPIA]

Omega: *(oh-MAY-gah)* (Greek) "Large." The last letter in the Greek alphabet.

Ondrea: *(ON-dree-ah)* (Czech) Variant of Andrea. [ONDRA]

Oonagh: *(OO-nah)* (Irish) "Lamb." See also Una. Playwright Eugene O'Neill gave this name to his daughter. Though very unusual, Oonagh is still occasionally used in America. [OONA]

Opal: *(OH-pel)* (Sanskrit) "Gemstone, jewel." A uniquely colorful iridescent gemstone.

QUICK REFERENCE
NAMES IN THE TOP 300

• Olivia

• Paige
• Patricia
• Payton
  Peyton

Ophelia: *(oh-FEEL-yah)* (Greek) "Help." Name of the unfortunate maiden who loved Hamlet in Shakespeare's play *Hamlet*. [OFELIA]

Ophrah: *(OHF-rah)* (Hebrew) "Young deer; place of dust." A biblical place name. Oprah Winfrey, actress and TV talk show hostess, has made this very rare name familiar, although by accident. A clerical error changed the intended Orpah to Oprah on her birth certificate. Ofra is an Israeli variant. [OFRA, OPHRA, OPRAH]

Orah: *(OR-ah)* (Hebrew) "Light." [ORIA]

Oralia: *(oh-RAYL-yah)* (Latin) "Golden." Variant form of Aurelia. [ORELIA]

Oriana: *(or-ee-AHN-ah)* (Latin) "Dawning." [OREANA, ORI-ANE, ORIANNA]

Orinda: *(or-RIN-dah)* (Latin) A 17th-century poetic name.

Orla: (Irish) "Golden lady."

Osanna: (Latin) Short form of the Latin *hosannah*, a chanted prayer meaning "save, we pray."

P

Pagan: *(PAY-gan)* "Country dweller." Once a common medieval given name, Pagan fell out of favor when it became a term used for an irreligious person or someone who believed in more than one god.

Paige: *(page)* (English) "Young attendant." A page in medieval households was usually a young boy whose service was the first step in his training as a knight. [PAGE, PAGETT]

Paisley: *(PAYS-lee)* (Scottish) The name of a patterned fabric that was at one time the principal product manufactured in Paisley, Scotland.

Paloma: *(pa-LOH-mah)* (Spanish) "Dove." Famous name bearer: Paloma Picasso.

Pamela: *(PAM-eh-lah)* (Greek) "Honey; all sweetness." A poetic invention from the 16th century. [PAM, PAMELLA]

Pandora: *(pan-DOR-ah)* (Greek) "All gifted." Greek mythology: Pandora was gifted with all powers and desirable attributes from all the gods, then given charge of a mysterious box she was forbidden to open. When she opened the box, every kind of humankind's ills flew out, followed by the one counteragent, Hope.

Paris: *(PARE-iss)* The name of the French capital. Mythology: see boys' index. [PARISA, PARISSA, PARRIS, PARRISH]

Patience: *(PAY-shuns)* (English) "Enduring, forebearing." A virtue name.

Patricia: *(pa-TRISH-ah)* (Latin) "Noble; a patrician." The Romans once were divided socially and politically into two major classes, the plebeians and the patricians. To be patrician meant one was highly ranked, an aristocrat. See also Trisha. [**PATRICE**, PATRINA, PATRISHA, PATRISSE, PATRIZIA, PATRYCE, PATSY, PATTI, PATTY]

Paula: *(PAW-lah)* (Latin) "Little." Feminine form of Paul. A saint's name. [**PAOLA**, PAULETTA, PAULETTE, PAULI, PAULITA, PAVLA]

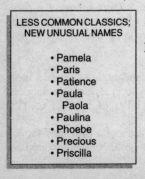

LESS COMMON CLASSICS;
NEW UNUSUAL NAMES

- Pamela
- Paris
- Patience
- Paula
    Paola
- Paulina
- Phoebe
- Precious
- Priscilla

Paulina: *(pawl-EEN-ah)* (Latin) A feminine diminutive form of Paul in use for nearly 2,000 years. Pauline is the French form. Pavlina is a Slavic form; Paolina is Italian. Notable in the 1990s: model Paulina Porizkova. [**PAULINE**, PAOLINA, PAULENE, PAVLINA]

Payton: *(PAYT-en)* (Irish) Variant form of Patrick. [PEYTON]

Paz: *(pahz)* (Spanish) "Peace," from the Latin word *pax*. In Catholic use, a reference to "Our Lady of Peace."

Pearl: *(perl)* (English) A jewel name. [PEARLA, PEARLIE, PEARLINE, PERLA, PERLE, PERLITA]

Peggy: *(PEH-gee)* (English) Rhyming pet name from medieval times, based on Margaret (Meggy). Molly to Polly is another example.

Penny: *(PEN-nee)* (Greek) "Weaver's tool." Short form of Penelope *(pen-NELL-a-pee)*. Mythology: Penelope, wife of Ulysses, fended off suitors by weaving during the day and unraveling at night a tapestry she said had to be completed before she would wed another husband. The name has come to signify a loyal, capable, and clever woman. [PENELOPE, PENNIE]

Peony: *(PAY-uh-nee)* (Greek) "Praisegiving." A flower name. As a Chinese name motif, the peony signifies riches and honor.

Perdita: *(per-DEE-tah, PER-di-tah)* (Latin) "Lost." Shakespeare created this name for a young heroine in *The Winter's Tale*.

Peri: *(PARE-ee)* (Greek) In Greek mythology, an *oread*, nymph of mountains and caves. In Persian fable, a fallen angel. Pera and Perita are Spanish short forms of Esperanza. Perah is an Israeli name meaning "flower." [PERA, PERAH, PERITA]

Perri: *(PARE-ee)* (English) Feminine variant of Peter. See also Petra. [PERRIANNE, PERRIN, PERRINE, PERRIS]

Persis: *(PER-sees, PER-siss)* (Greek) "Woman of Persia." Biblical: a first-century Christian woman commended by

Paul. Familiar since the late 1970s due to actress Persis Khambatta.

Petra: *(PEH-trah)* (Latin) Feminine variant form of Peter. Pier is recognized as a girl's name due to the 1950s actress Pier Angeli. Peta is a Dutch form. [PETA, PETRINA, PETRONELLA, PIER, PIERETTE]

Phaedra: *(FAY-drah)* (Greek) "Shining." Phaedra is derived from Phoebus, another name for Apollo. [FEDRA, PHADRA, PHEDRE]

Phillipa: *(FIL-lip-ah, fil-LIP-ah)* (English) "Fond of horses." Feminine form of Philip. [PHILANA, PHILINA, PIPPA]

Phoebe: *(FEE-bee)* (Greek) "Bright, radiant." Biblical: a Christian woman who aided Paul and others. Greek mythology: a reference to Apollo, the god of light. Familiar in the 1990s due to the fictional character Phoebe Buffay on the *Friends* TV series. [PHEBE]

Phylicia: *(fa-LEE-shah)* (American) Blend of Felicia and Phyllis, made familiar today by actress Phylicia Rashad. [PHILICIA]

Phyllis: *(FILL-iss)* (Greek) "Green branch." [PHILLIDA, PHY-LISS]

Pia: *(PEE-ah)* (Latin) "Pious, reverent."

Pilar: *(pee-LAR)* (Latin) "Pillar." In Catholic tradition, a reference to a marble pillar connected with an appearance of the Virgin Mary.

Pola: *(POH-lah)* (Arabic) "Poppy." Short form of Amapola.

Polly: *(PAH-lee)* (English, Irish) A medieval rhyming nickname based on Mary (Molly). Eleanor Porter's novel *Pollyanna* made the name proverbial for one who sees the bright side of every situation. [POLLYANNA]

Portia: *(POR-shah)* (Latin) Feminine form of a Roman clan name. Portia was used by Shakespeare as the name of a clever, determined young heroine in *The Merchant of Venice*. Today, the similar sounding name Porsche is also used, though probably more in reference to the sports car than to Portia. [PORCHA, PORSCHA, PORSCHE, PORSCHIA, PORSHA]

Precious: *(PRESH-us)* (English) "Of great value; highly esteemed." A name of endearment. In Catholic tradition, also a reference to the "precious blood of Christ." [PRECIA, PRECIOSA]

Prima: *(PREE-mah)* (Latin) "First."

Princess: *(PRIN-sess)* (English) A title name. [PRINCESA, PRINCESSA]

Priscilla: *(pris-SILL-ah)* (Latin) "Of ancient times." Biblical: a first-century Christian missionary. Priscilla was a favored name with the Puritans of England. Longfellow gave the name to the heroine of his poem, *The Courtship of Miles Standish*.

Prudence: *(PROO-dens)* (English) "The exercise of caution and wisdom." A virtue name. [PRUE]

Queena: *(KWEE-nah)* (English) Variant of the title used as a given name. [QUEEN, QUEENIE, QUENNA]

Querida: *(kare-EE-dah)* (Spanish) "Beloved, darling."

Quiana: *(kee-AHN-ah)* (American) "Silky." A use of the 1970s fabric brand name Qiana as a given name for girls.

Quiana possibly led to the Kiana variants. See also Kiana. [QIANA, QUIANNA]

Queta: *(KAY-tah)* (Spanish) Short form of names like Enriqueta.

Quinn: *(kwin)* (Gaelic) "Counsel." A Scottish and Irish surname occasionally used for girls. [QUINCY]

R

Rachana: *(ra-SHA-nah)* (Hindi) "Creation." See also Roshan. [RACHANNA, RASHANA, RASHANDA]

Rachel: *(RAY-chel)* (Hebrew) "Ewe." Biblical: Jacob's wife, described as being "beautiful in form and countenance." Rachelle *(ra-SHELL)* is a variant pronounciation. See also Raquel, Richelle, and Rochelle. [**RACHAEL, RACHELLE,** RACHELANNE, RACHELE, RACHELL, RAECHEL, RASHELLE, RAYCHEL]

Rae: *(ray)* (English) Short form of Rachel or a feminine form of Ray. Also used as a prefix in blended and compound names. See also Rayann. [RAEANN, RAEANNA, RAEANNE, RAEDELL, RAEDINE, RAELANI, RAELEE, RAELEEN, RAELENA, RAELENE, RAELINA, RAELLA, RAELYN, RAELYNN, RAELYNNE, RAENISHA]

QUICK REFERENCE
NAMES IN THE TOP 300

• Rachel
  Rachael
• Raquel
• Raven
• Rebecca
  Rebekah
• Robin

Rafaela: *(rah-fah-AY-lah)* (Spanish) Feminine form of Raphael. [RAPHAELLA]

Raina: *(RAY-nah)* (English) Variant form of Regina or Reine (French), meaning "queen." May also be used as a short form of Lorraina and Lorraine. See also Rayna and Reina. [RAINE, RAINEE]

Rainbow: *(RAYN-boh)* (English) The word used as a given name. In the news in the 1990s: comedian/actor Richard Pryor's daughter, Rain. See also Iris. [RAIN]

Raisa: *(RAY-sah, RYE-zah)* (Russian) "Rose." [RAISSA, RAIZA]

Rajani: *(rah-ZHAH-nee)* (Sanskrit) "Night." Hindu mythology: one of the names of the wife of Shiva. [RAJANAE, RAJANEE]

Ramah: *(RAH-mah)* (Hebrew) "High."

Ramona: *(ra-MOH-nah)* (Spanish) "Guards wisely." Feminine form of Ramón, Raymond. [RAMEE, RAMIE]

Rana: *(RAH-nah)* (Arabic) "Gaze upon beauty." Rani is a Hindu title meaning "royal, queen." [RANI]

Ranae: *(ra-NAY)* (American) Variant form of Renée. Also used as a blend with various name endings. See also Renée. [RANAE, RANELLE, RANESSA, RANISHA]

Randi: *(RAN-dee)* (English) Feminine form of Randy, or short form of Miranda. Randa is an Arabic name meaning "beautiful." [RANDA, RANDEE]

Raquel: *(rah-KELL)* (Spanish, Portuguese) Variant of Rachel. [RACQUEL, RACQUELL, RAQUELA, RAQUELLE, ROQUEL]

Rasheeda: *(ra-SHEE-dah)* (Arabic) "Righteous." [RASHEEDAH, RASHIDA]

LESS COMMON CLASSICS; NEW, UNUSUAL NAMES

- Rachelle
- Randi
- Regan
  Raegan
  Reagan
- Regina
- Renée
- Rhiannon
  Rhianna
- Rita

Raven: *(RAY-ven)* (English) A large black bird made famous by Edgar Allen Poe's poem *The Raven*. [RAVINA, RAVYN]

Raya: *(RAY-ah)* (Israeli) "Friend."

Rayann: *(ray-ANN)* (English) A contemporary blend of Ray and Ann. Ray is also a favored prefix with various name endings. See also Rae. [RAYANA, RAYANN, RAYANNA, RAYCINE, RAYE, RAYEANN, RAYLEEN, RAYLENE, RAYLYNN, RAYNELL, RAYNESHA, RAYNISHA]

Rayna: *(RAY-nah)* (Scandinavian) "Counsel." (Israeli) "Song." See also Raina and Reina. [RAYNE, RAYNEE, REYNA]

Reanna: *(ree-ANN-ah)* (Irish) Variant of Rhiannon. [REANNAH, REANNE, REANNON, REEANNE]

Reba: *(REE-bah)* Short form of Rebecca, made familiar by singer Reba McIntyre.

Rebecca: *(ree-BEK-ah)* (Hebrew) "Tied, knotted." Biblical: Rebekah, noted in the Genesis account as a maiden of beauty, modesty, and kindness, became the wife of Abraham's son, Isaac. See also Becky and Riva. [**REBEKAH**, REBECA]

Regan: *(REE-gan, RAY-gun)* (Irish) "Reigning, kingly." [RAEGAN, RAGAN, REAGAN]

Regina: *(re-JEEN-ah)* (Latin) "Queen." [REGEENA, REGENA, REGINE, REJINE]

Reiko: *(RAY-koh)* (Japanese) "Pretty; lovely child." [REI]

Reina: *(RAY-nah)* (Latin) "Queen." Reyna is a short form of Reynalda, meaning "counselor, ruler." See also Raina and Rayna. [**REYNA**, REYNALDA]

Rena: *(REE-nah)* (English) Short form of Irene and Irena. See also Rinah. [REENA, REENE]

Renée: *(ren-NAY)* (French) "Reborn." Phonetic spellings of Renée have resulted in a number of contemporary variants. *Ren-* is also used as a prefix with various endings to create new names. See also Ranae. [RENAE, RENATA, RENAY, RENAYE, RENE, RENEISHA, RENISHA, RENITA, RENNE, RENNIE]

Rexanne: *(reks-AN)* (English) Blend of Rex and Anne. The variants shown here are also used as feminine forms of Rex, following the pattern of Roxanne and its variants. [REXANA, REXANNA, REXINE]

Rhea: *(REE-ah)* (Greek) "Flowing stream." Mythology: Rhea was the mother of Zeus, Poseidon, Hera, and Demeter. Rhea is also a Welsh name referring to a river in Wales. [REYA, RHAE, RHAYA, RHIA]

Rhiannon: *(ree-ANN-an)* (Welsh) "Maiden." Mythology: name of the Welsh horse goddess described in legend as dressed in shining gold and riding a pale horse. Notable in the 1970s: the Fleetwood Mac song "Rhiannon." See also Reanna and Riona. [RHEANNA, RHEANNE, RHIANA, RHIANN, RHIANNA, RHIANNAN, RHIANON, RHYAN, RIANA, RIANE, RIANNA, RIANNE, RIANNON]

Rhoda: *(ROH-da)* (Greek) "Rose." See also Rosa. Biblical: a servant girl who was one of the early Christian disciples.

Rhona: *(ROH-nah)* (Scottish) Variant form of Ronald. [RONA]

Rhonda: *(RON-dah)* (Welsh) "Fierce waters." [RONDA, RHONETTE]

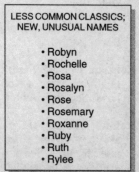

LESS COMMON CLASSICS;
NEW, UNUSUAL NAMES

- Robyn
- Rochelle
- Rosa
- Rosalyn
- Rose
- Rosemary
- Roxanne
- Ruby
- Ruth
- Rylee

Ria: *(REE-ah)* (Latin) Short form of Maria. [RIE]

Richelle: *(ri-SHELL)* (American) Feminine blend of Richard and Rachelle. Also related feminine short forms based on Ricky, Rickie, or Frederica. [RICCA, RICCI, RICKI, RIKKI, RIKKIE]

Riley: *(RY-lee)* (Irish) Variant form of O'Reilly, a personal name of uncertain origin. Lately adopted for girls as well as boys. See also Rylee. [RILEE, RILEIGH]

Rima: *(REE-mah)* (Spanish) "Rhyme, poetry." Literary: in Hudson's *Green Mansions*, Rima was an elusive maiden of the South American rain forest who spoke the language of animals and birds.

Rinah: *(REE-nah)* (Israeli) "Joyful." [RINA]

Riona: *(ree-OH-nah)* (Irish) "Queenly." [RIONNA, RIONNAH]

Risa: *(REE-sah)* (Latin) "Laugh, laughter." Also a short form of names like Marisa. Rise *(rih-ZAY)* is a French form made familiar in the 1950s through the 1970s by opera singer Rise Stevens. [REESA, RISE]

Rita: *(REE-tah)* (Latin) Short form of Margarita, from Margaret. The Italian St. Rita (15th century) has roses for her emblem.

Riva: *(REE-vah)* (Hebrew) Short form of Rebecca. See also Reba. [REVA]

Roberta: *(roh-BER-tah)* (English) "Famed; bright, shining." Feminine form of Robert. Robbie is used occasionally for boys. See also Bobbie and Robin. [ROBBIE, ROBERTHA]

Robin: *(RAH-bin)* (English) Variant of Robert, in popular use as a boy's name since the days of Robin Hood. Now used more for girls. See also Roberta. [**ROBYN**, ROBENA, ROBINA, ROBYNN, ROBYNNE]

Rochelle: *(roh-SHELL)* (French) Feminine variant of Rocco (Italian). St. Rocco (14th century) was a pilgrim and healer. [ROCHELE, ROCHELLA, ROSHELLE]

Roderica: *(rah-der-REE-kah)* (German) "Famous ruler." Feminine form of Roderic.

Rolanda: *(ro-LAHN-dah)* (Latin) "Renowned in the land." Feminine form of Roland. [ROLANDE]

Romina: *(roh-MEEN-ah)* (Latin) "Woman of Rome." Mythology: Roma was the daughter of Evander, who named Rome for her. Romi and Romy are German pet names. [ROMA, ROMALDA, ROMANA, ROMELIA, ROMI, ROMY]

Ronnie: *(RAH-nee)* (English) Short form of Veronica or feminine variant of Ron and Ronald. Roni *(ROH-nee)* is also an Israeli name meaning "song." [RONAE, RONAY, RONELLE, RONI, RONICA, RONIKA, RONISHA, RONNETTE, RONNI]

Rosa: *(ROH-za)* (Latin) "Rose." This most popular flower name for girls has many variants and compounds. Rosa is the Latin form, Rose is English, and both are well-used in English-speaking countries. See also Charo, Raisa, Rhoda, Rosalba, Rosalie, Rosalind, Rosamond, Rose, Roseanne, Rosemary, and Roza. [ROSABELLE, ROSELLA]

Rosalba: *(roh-ZAL-bah)* (Latin) "White rose."

Rosalie: *(ROH-za-lee)* (French) Rosalia *(roh-za-LEE-ah, roh-ZAYL-yah)* is a saint's name. See also Rosa. [ROSALEE, ROSALIA, ROSELIA]

Rosalind: *(RAH-za-lind)* (Latin) A 16th-century poetic creation by Spenser, which has acquired the meaning "beautiful rose." [ROSALEEN, ROSALIN, ROSALINA, ROSALINDA, ROSALINDE, ROSALINE, ROSALYN, ROSALYND, ROSALYNN, ROSELYN, ROSLYN, ROSLYNN]

Rosamond: *(ROH-za-mund)* (French) "Rose of the world; rose of purity." [ROSAMUND, ROZAMOND, ROZAMUND]

Rose: *(rohz)* (English) In the news in the 1990s: Rosie O'Donnell, actress and TV talk show hostess. See also Rosa and Roza. [ROSETTA, ROSETTE, ROSEY, ROSIE, ROSINA, RO-SINE, ROSIO, ROSITA, ROSY]

Roseanne: *(rohz-ANN)* (English) Combination of Rose and Anne. Rossana may be intended as a feminine form of Ross. In the news in the 1990s: actress/comedienne Rose-anne. See also Rosa and Roza. [ROSANA, ROSANNA, RO-SANNE, ROSEANN, ROSEANNA, ROSSANA, ROSSANNA]

Rosemary: *(ROHZ-mare-ee)* (English) Blend of Rose and Mary. Also refers to the fragrant herb, which in folklore is the emblem of remembrance. [ROSEMARIE]

Roshan: *(roh-SHAHN)* (Sanskrit) "Shining light." See also Rachana. [ROSHANA, ROSHANDRA, ROSHAUNDRA, ROS-HAWN, ROSHAWNA]

Rowan: *(ROH-an)* (Gaelic) "Red-berry tree." [ROANNA, ROANNE, ROWEN]

Rowena: *(roh-EEN-ah, roh-ENN-ah)* (Welsh) "Fair one." Rowena was the name of one of the two heroines in Sir Walter Scott's novel *Ivanhoe*. [RHOWENA, ROWENNA]

Roxanne: *(roks-ANN)* (Persian) "Dawn." Roxandra is a contemporary blend of Roxanne and Alexandra, appropriate since Roxanne was the Persian princess Alexander the Great married during his travels of conquest. [ROXANA, ROXANNA, ROXANDRA, ROXANE, ROXANN, ROXEENA, ROX-ENE, ROXI, ROXIE, ROXY]

Roya: *(ROY-ah)* (English) Feminine name based on Roy. [ROYANNA, ROYLEEN, ROYLENE]

Roza: *(ROH-zah)* Variant of Rosa and Rose. The -*z*- spelling reflects the French, Slavic, or Yiddish influence. See also Rosa, Rosalie, Rosalind, and Roseanne. [ROZ, ROZALEE, ROZALYN, ROZANA, ROZANNA, ROZELLA, ROZELLE, ROZETTA, ROZLYN]

Ruby: *(ROO-bee)* (English) "Red." A jewel name. [RUBENA, RUBI, RUBIANNE, RUBIE, RUBINA]

Rudi: *(ROO-dee)* (German) Feminine form of Rudy, from Rudolf. [RUDIE]

Rue: *(roo)* (English) "Regret." The name of an herb used for cooking and in medicine. In Shakespeare's *Hamlet*, Ophelia called rue the "herb-grace o' Sundays." Actress Rue McClanahan has made this name familiar.

Rui: *(ROO-ee)* (Japanese) "Tears; affection."

Ruth: *(rooth)* (Hebrew) "Companion." Biblical: Ruth was the young Moabite widow who said to her Hebrew mother-in-law Naomi, "Where you go, there I shall go also; your people will be my people, your God, my God." [RUTHANN, RUTHANNE, RUTHELLEN, RUTHIE]

Ryan: *(RY-ann)* (Irish) "Royal." Cross-gender use of the surname, probably influenced by Rhiannon. [**RYANN**, RYANA, RYANE, RYANNA, RYANNE]

Rylee: *(RYE-lee)* (Irish) Variant of Riley, an Irish given name of uncertain origin. See also Riley. [RYLEY, RYLIE, RYLINA]

S

Sabelle: *(sa-BELL)* (Latin) Short form of Isabel. [SABELLA]

Sabina: *(sa-BEE-nah)* (Latin) "Of the Sabines." A saint's name in use at least since the second century. See also Sabra.

Sable: *(SAY-bel)* (Slavic) "Black." A highly prized fur, dark brown, almost black. Also used in French and English heraldry as a term for black.

Sabra: *(SAY-brah)* (Israeli, Arabic) "Thorny." A name signifying one who is native born, especially in Israel. Also a variant form of Sabina.

Sabrina: *(sa-BREE-nah)* (English) Meaning uncertain. Mythology: the name of a Celtic maiden in a Welsh tale. See also Breena and Brina. [SABREEN, SABREENA, SABRENA, SABRENE, SABRINNA, SABRYNA]

Sachi: *(SAH-chee)* (Japanese) "Benediction; fortunate." Sachiko *(SAH-chee-koh)* means "blessed child, fortunate child." A trend is developing to drop the *-ko* ending on some names for girls. [SACHIKO]

QUICK REFERENCE
NAMES IN THE TOP 300

- Sabrina
- Sadie
- Samantha
- Sandra
- Sarah
  Sara
- Savannah
  Savanna

Sade: *(shah-DAY, shar-DAY)* Short form of Folasade, a Yoruban/African name meaning "honor confers a crown." The Nigerian singer Sade has greatly influenced popularity of the name and the *shar-*

DAY pronunciation. Sadie is a short form of Sarah. See also Shadiya and Sharde. [SADA, SADEE, SADIA, SADIE, SADINA]

Sadira: *(sa-DEER-ah)* (Persian) "Lotus."

Safiyah: *(sa-FEE-ah)* (Hindi, Swahili) "Pure." (Arabic) "Friend." [SAFIA, SAFIYA]

Sage: *(sayj)* (English) "Wise one." [SAIGE]

Sahara: *(sah-HAH-rah)* (Arabic) "Wilderness." See also Zahara. [SAHARAH, SAHRA]

Saida: *(SAY-dah)* (Arabic) "Huntress; fortunate." Variant form of Zaida. [SAYDA]

Salena: *(sah-LEE-nah)* "The moon." See also Selena. [SALEENA, SALINA]

Sally: *(SAL-ee)* (English) Variant of Sarah. Noted name bearer: actress Sally Field. [SALLEE, SALLIE]

Samantha: *(sa-MAN-thah)* (English) Blend of Sam and Anthea. Samantha became popular in the 1960s due to the TV show *Bewitched* and has kept a strong ranking among name choices ever since.

Sami: *(SAM-ee)* (Arabic) "Exalted." Sammie variants are short feminine forms of Samuel. [SAMIA, SAMMA, SAMMI, SAMMIE, SAMMIJO]

Samira: *(sah-MEER-ah)* (Arabic) "Pleasant." [SAMARA]

Sana: *(sa-NAH)* (Arabic) "Brilliant." (Hindi) "Praise."

Sandra: *(SAN-drah, SAHN-drah)* (English) "Helper of mankind." Short form of Alexandra. [**SANDY**, SANDEE, SANDI, SANDIE, SAUNDRA, SONDRA]

Sapphire: *(SAFF-ire)* (Arabic) "Beautiful." From the Sanskrit "beloved of Saturn." A jewel and color name. Sapphira is very rarely used, probably because the Biblical Sapphira was a woman who was executed by God for lying. Safira *(sa-FEER-ah)* (Spanish) is based on Ceferino, from Zephyr, the name of a third-century pope. [SAFIRA, SAPPHIRA]

Sarah: *(SARE-ah)* (Hebrew) "Princess." Biblical: originally called Sarai, Sarah shared an adventurous nomadic life with her husband Abraham. She is described as being exceptionally beautiful even into her older years. Both Sara and Sarah are used in blended and compound names. See also Sade, Sahara, Sally, Sarina, Shari, Soraya, and Zara. [SARA, SAIRA, SAIRAH, SARABETH, SARAHLEE, SARAHLYNN, SARAI, SARAJANE, SARAJEAN, SARALEE, SARALYN, SARALYNN, SARAMAE, SARI, SARRA, SARRAH]

Sarina: *(sa-REE-nah)* (Latin) Variant of Sara. See also Serena and Sirena. [SAREEN, SAREENA, SARENA, SARENE, SARINNA, SARITA]

Sasa: *(sah-sah)* (Japanese) "Help, aid."

Sasha: *(SAH-shah)* (Russian) Short form of Alexander. [SACHA, SASCHA, SASHEEN]

Satin: *(SAT-en)* (French) The name of the luxury fabric used as a given name. [SATINA]

Savannah: *(sa-VAN-ah)* (Spanish) Literally, a grassland or treeless plain. [SAVANNA, SAVANA, SAVANAH, SAVONNA, SAVONNE]

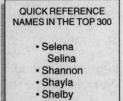

QUICK REFERENCE
NAMES IN THE TOP 300

• Selena
  Selina
• Shannon
• Shayla
• Shelby
• Sierra
• Skylar

Scarlett: *(SCAR-let)* (English) Surname referring to the bright-red color, brought into use as a given name primarily due to Margaret Mitchell's heroine in the novel *Gone With the Wind*. [SCARLET, SCARLETTE]

Seana: *(SHAWN-ah)* (Irish) Feminine form of Sean. See also *Shan-*, Shana, Shawna, and Siana. [SEANNA]

Selena: *(sa-LEEN-ah)* (Greek) "Goddess of the moon." Mythology: Selena was sister to Helios, the sun. In the news: the late Latin pop singer Selena. See also Celina and Salena. [SELENE, SELINA, SELENIA, SELENNA, SELENNE, SELINDA, SELINE]

Selma: *(SEL-mah)* (German) "God's protection." Feminine short form of Anselmo, a saint's name. [SALMA]

Sequoyia: *(seh-KWOY-ah)* (Native American) The giant redwood tree.

Serafina: *(ser-ah-FEE-nah)* (Italian) A Latin saint's name from the Hebrew word *seraphim*, "burning ones," referring to a class of angels. [SERAPHINA]

Serena: *(ser-REE-nah, ser-RAY-nah)* (Latin) "Serene, calm." When spelled Sirena, the name could be a reference to the Sirens, creatures of Greek mythology, who by their irresistible singing lured seamen to their doom. See also Sarina and Sirena. [SEREENA]

Serenity: *(ser-REN-a-tee)* (English, French) Literally, refers to a calm and serene temperament. A virtue name. [SERENE]

Sha-: (American) Blends of *Sha-* plus various name endings, with pronunciation emphasis on the second syllable. Of all the contemporary created names, names beginning with *Sha-* are the most popular. Some may be variants of existing names from African, Arabic, Hindi, Israeli, or other cultures. Others are creative variants of traditional American names. See also *Cha-*, Charlene, Shadiya, Shakeela,

QUICK REFERENCE
NAMES IN THE TOP 300

- Sophia
- Stacy
- Stephanie
- Summer
- Susan
- Sydney
  Sidney

Shalini, Shalisa, *Shan-*, Shanay, Shanell, Shanice, Shantel, Sharise, Sharon, Shawna, *She-*, and Siobhan. [SHADIRA, SHADONNA, SHAKEENA, SHAKIRA, SHALAINA, SHALAINE, SHALANA, SHALANE, SHALAYA, SHALIA, SHALITA, SHALIZA, SHALONDA, SHALYNN, SHAMAINE, SHAMARA, SHAMEKA, SHAMIKA, SHANEDRA, SHANEL, SHANESSA, SHANETTA, SHANIKA, SHANIQUA, SHANIQUE, SHANITA, SHANNAE, SHAQUISE, SHAQUITA, SHARAE, SHARAIA, SHARANA, SHARAY, SHARAYA, SHARAYAH, SHARAYE, SHARINA, SHARITA]

Shadiya: *(sha-DEE-ah)* (Arabic) "Singer." Variant forms may also be phonetic forms of Sade. See also Sharde. [SHADAI, SHADE, SHADI, SHADIA, SHADYA]

Shahnaz: *(SHAH-nahz)* (Farsi) "King's glory."

Shaila: *(SHAY-lah)* (Hindi) "River." See also Shayla. [SHAILI, SHALEE]

Shaina: *(SHAY-nah)* (Israeli) "Beautiful." Shaina and its variants may also be contemporary feminine forms of Shane. See also Shayna. [SHAENA, SHAINAH, SHAINE, SHAYNA, SHAYNE, SHEINA]

Shakeela: *(sha-KEE-lah)* (Hindi) "Beautiful." [SHAKEEL, SHAKILA]

Shalini: *(sha-LEE-nee)* (Hindi) "Modest." [SHALEENA, SHALENA, SHALENE, SHALINA]

Shalisa: *(shah-LEE-sah)* (Hebrew) Variant of Shalishah, a Biblical place name. [SHALISE, SHALISHAH, SHELISA]

Shan- : (American) Blends of *Shan-* and various name endings, with pronunciation emphasis on the second syllable. See also *Sha-*, Shandra, Shanice, Shanti, Shantel, and *She-*. [SHANDEL, SHANDELL, SHANDELLE, SHANDON, SHANTOYA, SHAUNTRICE]

Shana: *(SHAH-nah)* (Irish) "Old; wise." Also a variant of Sean (Irish) and Shayna (Israeli), Shana has been made familiar today by journalist Shana Alexander. See also Seana, Shaina, Shawna, Shayna, and Siana. [SHAN, SHANDA, SHANDI, SHANNA, SHANNAH]

Shanae: *(sha-NAY)* (American) Possibly a phonetic variant inspired by Sinead *(sha-NAYD)*, an Irish form of Jane, following the pattern of Renee and Janae. See also *Sha-*, Shan, and Sinead. [SHANAY, SHANEA, SHANNEA]

Shandra: *(SHAHN-drah)* (Irish) Short form of the Irish name Killashandra, meaning "church of the fortress." May also be a variant of Chandra, "of the moon."

Shanell: *(sha-NEL)* (American) Variant spelling of Chanel. [SHANELLE, SHANNELL]

Shani: *(SHAH-nee)* (Swahili) "A marvel; wondrous."

Shania: *(sha-NYE-ah)* (Native American) "On my way." Contemporary awareness of Shania is due to country-western vocalist Shania Twain.

Shanice: *(sha-NEESE)* (English) A rhyming variant of Janise. [SHANEICE, SHANESE, SHANIECE, SHANISE, SHANNICE]

Shannon: (Irish) "Wise." [SHANNAN, SHANNEN]

Shanti: *(shan-TEE)* (Hindi) "Peaceful." [SHANTA, SHANTAE, SHANTAI, SHANTAY, SHANTE, SHANTEE]

Shantel: *(shan-TEL, shahn-TEL)* (English) "Singer." Variant of Chantel. [SHANTAL, SHANTELL, SHANTELLE]

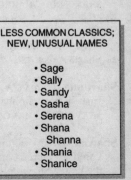

LESS COMMON CLASSICS;
NEW, UNUSUAL NAMES

• Sage
• Sally
• Sandy
• Sasha
• Serena
• Shana
  Shanna
• Shania
• Shanice

Sharde: *(shar-DAY)* (Yoruban) "Honor confers a crown." Phonetic variant of Sade. [SHADAE, SHARDAE, SHARDAI, SHARDAY, SHARDEI]

Shari: *(SHARE-ee)* (English) Variant of Sarah or phonetic form of Sherry. [SHARA, SHARAE, SHAREE, SHARELLE]

Sharik: *(sha-REEK)* (African) "God's child; one on whom the sun shines." [SHARIKA]

Sharise: *(sha-REES)* (English) Variant form of Charise. See also Charis. [SHARICE, SHARISA, SHARISSA]

Sharlene: *(shar-LEEN)* (English) Variant of Charlene and Charla. [SHARLA, SHARLAINE, SHARLAMAINE, SHARLAN, SHARLANA, SHARLANE, SHARLEE, SHARLEEN, SHARLETTA, SHARLINA, SHARLISA, SHARLY, SHARLYN, SHARLYNNE]

Sharmaine: *(shar-MAYN)* (English) Variant spelling of Charmaine. [SHARMAYNE]

Sharmila: *(shar-MEE-lah)* (Sanskrit) "Happy."

Sharon: *(SHARE-en)* (Hebrew) "The plain of Sharon." Biblical place name; the Song of Solomon describes the beloved Shulamite woman as a flower of Sharon. [SHAREEN, SHAREENA, SHARENA, SHARENE, SHARONA, SHARONDA, SHARONNA, SHARRON, SHARYN, SHERRON]

Shasta: *(SHASS-tah)* (Native American) Tribal name, the name of a mountain in California and the name of the Shasta daisy. [SHASTINA]

Shavonne: *(sha-VON)* (American) A phonetic variant of the Irish name Siobhan. [SHAVAUGHN, SHAVON, SHAVONA, SHAVONDA, SHAVONNA, SHEVONNE]

Shawna: (Irish) Feminine variant of Shawn, very much favored as a prefix in blends with various name endings. In the news: Shawntel Smith, the 1995 Miss America. See also

Seana, Shana, and Siana. [SHAUNA, SHAUNDA, SHAUNDEE, SHAUNELLE, SHAUNICE, SHAUNNA, SHAUNTAY, SHAUNTE, SHAWNDA, SHAWNDELLE, SHAWNEE, SHAWNEEN, SHAWNI, SHAWNICE, SHAWNIECE, SHAWNNA, SHAWNTAE, SHAWN-TAY, SHAWNTE, SHAWNTEL]

Shayla: *(SHAY-lah)* (English) A variant form of Shay, possibly of Sheila or Shaila, or a rhyming name based on Kayla. In the news in the 1990s: Shae-lyn Bourre, Olympic ice skating champion. See also Shaila and Shea. [SHAELA, SHAE-LYN, SHAILYN, SHAYLAH, SHAYLEEN, SHAYLENE, SHAYLYN, SHAYLYNN, SHAYLYNNE, SHEALYNN]

Shayna: *(SHAY-na)* (Israeli) "Beautiful." See also Shaina and Shana. [SHAYNAH]

Shayne: (Irish) Variant form of Shane.

She-: (American) Blends of *She-* plus various name endings, with pronunciation emphasis on the second syllable. See also *Sha-*, *Shan-*, and Sherisa. [SHELANNA, SHELONDA, SHE-NELLE, SHEVONDA]

Shea: *(shay)* (Irish) "Courteous." Shai is an Israeli name meaning "gift," and Shaya is an Israeli diminutive of Isaiah. See also Shayla. [SHAY, SHAE, SHAELEE, SHAI, SHAYA, SHAYANA, SHAYDA, SHAYE, SHAYLEE]

Sheba: *(SHEE-bah)* (Hebrew) The name of a kingdom in southern Arabia noted for its great wealth. Biblical: the queen of Sheba journeyed to Jerusalem to see for herself whether accounts about Solomon's great wisdom and wealth were true.

Sheena: *(SHE-nah)* (Scottish) Variant of Jean. Increased interest in this name is probably due to singer Sheena Easton. [SHEENAH]

> **LESS COMMON CLASSICS; NEW, UNUSUAL NAMES**
>
> - Sharon
> - Shawna
> - Shayna
> - Sheila
> - Shelbi
> - Sheridan
> - Shirley
> - Shyanne
> - Shyla

Sheila: *(SHEE-lah)* (Irish) Variant of an Irish form of Celia. Sheela is a Hindi name meaning "gentle." [SHEELA, SHEE-LAGH, SHEILAH, SHELAGH]

Shelby: *(SHEL-bee)* (English) "Willow farm." English surname used as a given name for girls and occasionally for boys. [SHELBI, SHELBIE]

Shelley: *(SHEL-ee)* (English) Surname used as a given name for girls and as a short form of names like Michelle, Rochelle, and Shirley. Noted name bearers: actresses Shelley Long and Shelley Winters. [SHELLEE, SHELLI, SHELLY]

Sheridan: *(SHARE-a-den)* (Irish) "Bright." Surname used as a given name for boys and girls.

Sherilyn: *(SHARE-a-lin)* (American) A blend of Sheryl and Marilyn. In the news in the 1990s: actress Sherilyn Fenn. [SHERELENE, SHERLYNN, SHERYLANN]

Sherisa: *(sher-REE-sah)* Variant based on Cherise or Sherry. See also *She-*. [SHERISE, SHERISSA, SHERITA, SHERRINA, SHERRONDA]

Sherry: *(SHARE-ee)* (English) Short form of Sharon and the many names beginning with *Sher-*. Sherry also may be used in reference to the wine, after the fashion of Brandy. See also Cherie. [SHERAE, SHERAY, SHERAYA, SHEREEN, SHERI, SHERREE, SHERRI, SHERRIE]

Sheryl: *(SHARE-el)* (English) Variant of Cheryl. The Sheryl spelling ensures the soft *sh-* pronunciation. Some of the names listed here also could be considered as variant forms of Shirley. See also Cheryl and *Sha-*. [SHARELL, SHARELLE, SHARRELL, SHERELL, SHERELLE, SHERILL, SHERLENE, SHERRELL, SHERRELLE, SHERRIL, SHERRILL, SHERRYL, SHERYLAYNE]

Shiloh: *(SHY-loh)* (Hebrew) "The one to whom it belongs." See also historical note in boys' index. [SHILO, SHYLOH]

Shirley: *(SURE-lee)* (English) "Bright meadow." Notable name bearers: child actress and U.S. ambassador Shirley Temple-Black and actress Shirley McLaine. See also Sheryl. [SHIRELL, SHIRELLE, SHIRLEE, SHIRLEEN]

Shyanne: *(shy-ANN)* (American) Phonetic form of Cheyenne, a Native American tribal name. [SHIANNA, SHYANNA]

Shyla: *(SHY-lah)* (Hindi) "Daughter of the mountain." Hindu mythology: one of the names of the goddess Parvati. [SHY-LAH]

Siana: *(SHAWN-ah)* (Welsh) Variant of Sian *(shon)*, a Welsh form of Jane. See also Seana, Shana, Shanae, and Shawna. [SIAN, SIANNA]

Sibyl: *(SIB-el)* (Greek) "Prophetess, oracle." See also Cybil and Sybil. [SIBELLA]

Sidney: *(SID-nee)* (English) "From St. Denis." See also Sydney.

Sidonia: *(sih-DOHN-yah)* (Latin) "From Sidon." St. Sidonius (fifth century) lived and wrote about characters and events during the breakup of the Roman Empire in the West. [SI-DONIE]

Sienna: *(see-EN-ah)* (Latin) "From Siena." The city of Siena in Italy; also a brownish-red color.

Sierra: *(see-ERR-ah)* (Latin) "Mountains, mountainous." A name associated with environmental concerns due to the Sierra Club. See also Ciara.

Sigrid: *(SEE-grid)* (Scandinavian) "Beautiful; victorious."

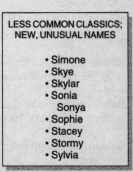

LESS COMMON CLASSICS;
NEW, UNUSUAL NAMES

- Simone
- Skye
- Skylar
- Sonia
  Sonya
- Sophie
- Stacey
- Stormy
- Sylvia

Silvana: *(sil-VAHN-ah)* (Italian) "Woodland, forest." Feminine form of Silvanus. [SILVA, SILVANNA, SILVINA]

Silvia: *(SIL-vee-ah)* (Latin) "Wood, forest." Shakespeare used Silvia for a heroine's name in *Two Gentlemen of Verona*. See also Sylvia.

Simone: *(see-mohn, sih-MOHN)* (French) "Hear, listen." Feminine form of Simon. [SIMONA, SIMONNE, SYMONE]

Sinead: *(sha-NADE)* (Irish) Variant of Jane or Janet. Sinead has been made familiar to Americans by singer Sinead O'Connor.

Siobhan: *(sha-VAHN)* (Irish) Variant of Joan. The unusual spelling of Siobhan is used less frequently than its phonetic variants. See also Shavonne.

Sirena: *(sir-EEN-ah)* (Greek) A variant form of Serena or a reference to the Sirens, creatures of Greek mythology who, by their irresistable singing, lured seamen to their doom. See also Sarina and Serena. [SIRENIA, SIRENNA, SYRENA]

Siri: *(SEER-ee)* (Scandinavian) Variant of Sigrid. [SIRIANA]

Skye: *(sky)* (English) Skye and Sky are used as nicknames for Skyler and Skylar, as nature names, and possibly in reference to the Isle of Skye in Scotland. [SKY, SKYLA]

Skylar: *(SKY-ler)* (Dutch) "Scholar." Phonetic form of the Dutch surname Schuyler. [SKYLER]

Sloane: *(slohn)* (Scottish) "Fighter, warrior." Surname. Sloan is the preferred form for boys.

Sofia: *(so-FEE-ah)* (Latin) Spanish, Italian, and Scandinavian form of Sophia. [SOFIAH, SOFIE]

Solana: *(so-LAH-nah)* (Latin) "Eastern wind." A saint's name.

Solange: *(so-LANZH)* (French) "Solemn, dignified." A saint's name. A fanciful meaning for the name is "angel of the sun."

Sonia: *(SOHN-yah)* (English) Variant of Sophia. [SONYA, SONJA, SONNI]

Sophia: *(so-FEE-ah)* (Greek) "Wisdom." See also Sofia. [SO-PHIE, SOPHY]

Soraya: *(sor-RYE-ah)* (Persian) "Princess." Variant form of Sarah. Notable name bearer: the first wife of the last Shah of Iran. [SOREEYAH]

Stacy: *(STAY-cee)* (English) As a boy's name, a short form of Eustace. Now primarily used for girls, Stacy and Stacey are generally considered to be short forms of Anastacia, after the fashion of Stasia and Stasha. [STACEY, STACEE, STACI, STACIA, STACIE, STASHA, STASIA]

Starla: *(STAR-lah)* (English) Astronomical name based on Star. [STAR, STARLEENA, STARLENA, STARLENE, STAR-LETTE, STARLYN, STARLYNN, STARR]

Stella: *(STEL-ah)* (Latin) "Star." See also Estella.

Stephanie: *(STEFF-a-nee)* (Greek) "Crown, wreath." Feminine form of Stephen. The name of the first Christian martyr was a favored name choice from the earliest centuries of the Christian era. Stephania, a Latin form of the name, was used for girls. The French form Stephanie became popular early in the 20th century. Notable name bearer: actress Stephanie Powers. [STEFANIE, STEPHANY, STEFANA, STE-FANI, STEFANIA, STEFFI, STEPHAINE, STEPHANI, STEPHANIA, STEPHINE, STEVANA, STEVIE]

Stormy: *(STOR-mee)* (English) Name from nature based on the vocabulary word and surname Storm. [STORM, STORMI, STORMIE]

Suellen: *(soo-ELL-en)* (English) A blend of Sue and Ellen. Margaret Mitchell gave the name to one of Scarlett O'Hara's sisters in the novel *Gone With the Wind*. [SUE-LYN]

Sumiko: *(SOO-mee-koh)* (Japanese) "Child of goodness; beautiful child."

Summer: *(SUH-mer)* (English) A nature name; the season used as a girl's name.

Sunita: *(soo-NEE-tah)* (Sanskrit) "Well-behaved."

Sunny: *(SUH-nee)* (English) Literally, sunshine. Sunny implies a happy, cheerful temperament. [SUNNI, SUNNIE]

Susan: *(SOO-zun)* (Hebrew) "Lily." Short form of Susannah. In the apocryphal Book of Tobit, Susannah was a woman of courage who defended herself against wrongful accusation. Susan is the English form, Suzanne is French, and Susana is Spanish. See also Suellen, Xuxa, and Zsa Zsa. [SUSANA, SUZANNE , SUE, SUEANN, SUEANNA, SUEANNE, SUSANNA, SUSANNAH, SUSANNE, SUSETTE, SUSIE, SUSY, SUZAN, SUZANA, SUZANNA, SUZANNAH, SUZETTE, SUZI, SUZIE, SUZY]

Suzu: *(soo-zoo)* (Japanese) "Long-lived." Suzuko: "Spring, autumn child."

Sybil: *(SIH-bul)* (Greek) "Prophetess, oracle." See also Sibyl and Cybil. [SYBILLE]

Sydney: *(SIHD-nee)* (French) "From St. Denis." Sidney is favored as a name for boys, and Sydney is almost entirely used for girls. See also Cydney. [SIDNEY, SYDNEE]

Sylvia: *(SIL-vee-ah)* (English) "Forest." See also Silvia. [SYL-VANA, SYLVIE, SYLVINA, SYLVONNA]

T

Ta-: (American) Blends of *Ta-* plus various name endings, with pronunciation emphasis on the second syllable. See also Tanisha and *Te-*. [TALANI, TALANNA, TALEA, TALEAH, TALEEN, TALENA, TALENE, TALICIA, TALINA, TALISA, TALISHA, TALONA, TALYSSA, TAMEIKA, TAMICA, TAMIKA, TAMIKO, TAMISHA, TANELLE, TANIKA, TARINA, TASHANA, TASHARA, TASHARRA, TASHEENA, TASHINA, TAWANA]

Tabitha: *(TAB-i-thah)* (Aramaic) "Gazelle." Biblical: the Aramaic name of Dorcas, a kindly woman noted for her good works, who was resurrected by Peter. See also Dorcas.

Tacy: *(TAY-cee)* (Latin) "Silence." May also be intended as a short of Anastacia. Initially used as a given name by the Society of Friends, the Quakers. [TACIA]

Taja: *(TAH-zha, TAY-zhah)* (Sanskrit) "Crown." A feminine form of Taj. Taji *(TAH-jee)* is a Japanese surname with the meaning "silver and yellow color." [TAIJA, TAISHA, TAJAH, TAJANAE, TAJANEE, TAJI, TAJIA, TAJIANA]

Talia: *(TAL-yah)* (Hebrew) "Lamb, lambkin." From Taliah. Talia is also a short form of Natalia. Notable name bearer: actress Talia Shire. [TAHLIA, TALIAH, TALYA]

Talitha: *(ta-LEE-tha, TAL-a-thah)* (Hebrew) "Child." Biblical: a reference to the resurrection of Jairus's daughter when Jesus said, "Child, arise."

Tama: *(tah-mah)* (Japanese) "Globe, ball." (Hebrew) "Perfect."

Tamara: *(TAM-a-rah)* (Hebrew) "Palm tree." Russian variant form of Tamar. Biblical: Tamar was a daughter of King David and sister to Absalom. See also Mara, Tammy, and Tara. [TAMAR, TAMARAH, TAMRA, TAMRYN]

Tami: *(TAH-mee)* (Japanese) "Let people see benefit." Tamiko *(TAH-mee-koh)* can mean "Child born in spring." [TAMIKO]

Tammy: *(TAM-mee)* (English) Short form of Thomasina and Tamara. [TAM, TAMI, TAMILYN, TAMLYN, TAMMI, TAMMIE, TAMMIEJO]

Tamsyn: *(TAM-sin)* (English) Short form of Thomasina. See also Tammy. [TAMSEN, TAMSIN]

Tanaya: *(ta-NAY-ah)* (Hindi) "Daughter." [TANAIA, TANEA, TENAYA]

Tani: *(TAH-nee)* (Spanish) Spanish short form of Estanislao, "make famous," from the name borne by several Slavic kings and three saints. [TANIS]

Tanisha: *(ta-NEE-shah)* (African) "Born on Monday." [TANESHA, TANIESHA, TANISHIA]

Tanya: *(TAHN-ya)* (Russian) Short form of Tatiana or Titania. Taina *(TAY-nah)* is a Scandinavian form. See also Tawny and Tonya. [TANIA, TAHNA, TAH-NEE, TAHNI, TAHNIA, TAINA, TANA, TANAMAREE, TANEE, TANJA]

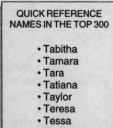

QUICK REFERENCE
NAMES IN THE TOP 300

- Tabitha
- Tamara
- Tara
- Tatiana
- Taylor
- Teresa
- Tessa
- Theresa

Tara: *(TAH-rah)* (Irish) "High hill." Ancient Tara was the site of the "stone of destiny" on which Irish kings were crowned. Hindu mythology: Tara (Sanskrit), "shining," is one of the names of the wife of Shiva. See also Terra. [TARAH, TARALYN, TARALYNN, TARRA, TARRAH]

Taree: *(tah-ree-EH)* (Japanese) "Bending branch."

Taryn: *(TARE-en)* (English) Blend of Tara and Erin. [TARIN, TARRYN, TARYNN]

Tasha: *(TAH-sha)* (Russian) Short form of Natasha, the Russian form of Natalie. See also Latasha. [TASHI, TASHIA, TASSA, TASSIE, TOSHA, TOSHIANA]

Tasia: *(TAH-zha, TAY-zhah)* (American) Short form of Anastasia. See also Taja. [TASHIA, TASYA, TAZIA]

Tate: *(tate)* (Scandinavian) "Cheerful." The surname Tatum is sometimes used as a girl's name, due to actress Tatum O'Neil. [TATUM]

Tatiana: *(tah-sh'-AHN-ah)* (Russian) Feminine form of Tatius, a Roman family clan name. A saint's name. In the news in the 1990s: actress Tatyana Ali. See also Tanya and Tiana. [TATIANNA, TATYANA]

Taura: *(TAW-rah)* (Latin) An astrological name, the feminine form of Taurus. [TAURINA]

Tavia: *(TAY-vee-ah)* (Latin) Short form of Octavia. [TAVA]

Tawny: *(TAW-nee)* (Irish) "A green field." Also an English surname. Tawny and its variants probably are meant to achieve a particular pronunciation of Tanya (*taw-* rather than *tah-*), or they refer to the literal meaning of tawny, the warm sandy color of a lion's coat. [TAWNA, TAWNEE, TAWNEY, TAWNI, TAWNIA, TAWNIE, TAWNYA]

Tayla: *(TAY-lah)* (English) A rhyming variant of Kayla, probably influenced by the popular Taylor. [TAYLIN, TAYLYN]

> QUICK REFERENCE
> NAMES IN THE TOP 300
>
> • Tia
> • Tiana
> • Tiara
> • Tierra
> • Tiffany
> • Tori
> • Tyler
> • Tyra

Taylor: *(TAY-ler)* (English) "Tailor." Surname used as a given name for both boys and girls. Popularity of the name considerably boosted due to characters named Taylor on the soap operas *The Bold and the Beautiful*, *All My Children*, and *Melrose Place*. [TAYLER]

Te-: (American) Blends of *Te-* plus various name endings, with pronunciation emphasis on the second syllable. See also *Ta-*, Tanisha, and Tiana. [TEANA, TEANNA, TELAYNA, TELISA, TELISHA, TENESHA, TENISHA, TEONA, TEONNA]

Tea: *(TAY-ah)* (Latin) Short form of Teresa and Teadora, made familiar in the 1990s by actress Téa Leoni. See also Tia.

Teagan: *(TEE-gan)* (Irish) "Good-looking." Surname. [TEGAN, TEIGE]

Teal: *(teel)* (English) A name from nature; the bird or the blue-green color. [TEELA]

Teddi: *(TED-ee)* (English) Short form of Theodora.

Tempest: *(TEMP-est)* (English) "Turbulent, stormy." Child actress Tempestt Bledsoe has brought attention to the name in recent years.

Teresa: *(ter-REE-sah, ter-RAY-sah)* (Latin) Variant of Theresa. The popularity of two saints, Teresa of Avila and Therese of Lisieux, has resulted in the creation of many variants. See also Terri, Tessa, Theresa, and Tracy. [TERESE, TERESINA, TERESITA, TERESSA, TEREZ, TEREZA, TEREZIA, TRESA, TRESSA]

Terra: *(TARE-ah)* (Latin) "The planet earth." Mythology: the Roman earth goddess, equivalent to the Greek Gaia. See also Tierra. [TERALYN, TERRAH]

Terri: *(TARE-ee)* (English) Short form of Teresa. Also used in contemporary blended names. In the news in the 1990s:

actress Teri Hatcher. [TERI, TERIANA, TERIANN, TERIKA, TERILYNN, TERRIE, TERRIN, TERRY, TERRYN, TERYN]

Tessa: *(TESS-ah)* (English) Short form of Teresa. [TESS, TESSIA, TESSIE]

Thalia: *(THAYL-yah)* (Greek) "Flowering." Mythology: Thalia was the Muse of comedy and one of the Three Graces, goddesses who were the embodiment of beauty and charm.

Thea: *(THEE-ah)* (Greek) "Goddess, godly." Short form of names like Althea and Dorothea. Mythology: the Greek goddess of light; mother of the sun, moon, and dawn.

Thelma: *(THEL-mah)* (Greek) "Will, willful." A literary creation from the 19th century. [TELMA]

Theodora: *(thee-a-DOR-ah)* (Greek) "God-given." Feminine form of Theodore. [TEODORA, THEADORA]

Theresa: *(the-REE-sah, ter-REE-sah)* (Greek) Meaning uncertain; possibly a Greek place name. St. Theresa of Lisieux, France (19th century), who died at age 24, wrote an account of her life published as *The Story of a Soul*, which so affected its readers worldwide that she became the most popular saint of modern times. See also Teresa. [THERESE, THERESSA]

Thomasina: *(TAH-ma-SEE-nah)* (English) "Twin." Feminine form of Thomas. See also Tamsyn and Tammy. [TOMASINA, TOMMI, TOMMIE]

Tia: *(TEE-ah)* (Latin) Short form of Cinthia (Spanish), also a short form of names like Tiana. In the news in the 1990s: twin actresses Tia and Tamera Mowry. See also Tea.

LESS COMMON CLASSICS; NEW, UNUSUAL NAMES

- Talia
- Tanisha
- Tanya
  Tania
- Taryn
- Tasha
- Tatyana
- Tayler
- Tess

Tiana: *(tee-AHN-ah)* (American) Short form of Tatiana. Tiana variants follow the rhyming patterns of Diana variants. See also Tatiana and *Te-*. [TIANNA, TIAHNA, TIANARA, TIANDRA, TIANE, TIANI, TIANNE, TIAUNA, TIONA, TIONNA, TYANA, TYANNA]

Tiara: *(tee-ARH-ah)* (Latin) "Headdress." A tiara is a jeweled headpiece or demicrown. [TIARRA]

Tierra: *(tee-AIR-ah)* (Spanish) "Earth." Used as a variant spelling of Tiara. [TIERA]

Tiffany: *(TIF-a-nee)* (French) Variant of the Greek Theophania, a name referring to the Epiphany, the manifestation of divinity. [TIFFANI, TIFFANIE, TIFFNEY]

Tina: *(TEE-nah)* (Latin) Name ending, particularly of Christina, used as an independent name and in combination with other names. Noted name bearer: rock singer Tina Turner. [TEENA, TINAMARIE]

Tisha: *(TEE-shah)* (American) Short form of Leticia or Latisha. [TIESHA, TYESHA]

Tomiko: *(TOH-mee-koh)* (Japanese) "Happiness child."

Toni: *(TOH-nee)* (English) Short form of Antonia and Antoinette, with contemporary variants based on Toni. See also Tonya. [TONELL, TONETTE, TONIA, TONIESHA, TONISHA]

LESS COMMON CLASSICS; NEW, UNUSUAL NAMES

- Thea
- Tianna
- Tiffani
- Tina
- Toni
- Tracy
- Trisha
- Tristan

Tonya: *(TAHN-yah)* (Russian) "Praiseworthy." Short form of Antonina. See also Tanya and Tawny.

Tori: *(TOR-ee)* (English) Tori short forms and independent names are mostly derived from Victoria, but may also be the feminine use of surnames. Tori (Japanese) means "bird." In the news: actress Tori Spelling and pop singer Tori Amos. See also Tory in boys' index. [TOREY, TORIANA, TORREE, TORREY, TORRI, TORRIE, TORRY, TORY]

Toshi: *(TOH-shee)* (Japanese) "Mirror reflection."

Toya: *(TOY-ah)* (Spanish) Short form of Victoria; also a Japanese surname meaning "house door" or "door into the valley." See also LaToya. [TOYANNA]

Tracy: *(TRAY-see)* (Greek) "From Thracia." Surname dating before the Norman conquest. Also a variant form of Teresa. [**TRACEY**, TRACEE, TRACI, TRACIE]

Trina: *(TREEN-nah)* (Scandinavian) Short form of names with the *-trina* ending. Trena is a Latin term meaning "triple" and sometimes is used in reference to the Trinity. [TREEN, TREENA, TRENA, TRINADETTE, TRINI]

Trisha: *(TRISH-ah)* (English) Short form of Patricia. In the news in the 1990s: singer Trisha Yearwood. See also Teresa for similar-sounding variants. [TRICIA, TRISA, TRISH, TRISH-ANA, TRISSA]

Trista: *(TRISS-tah)* (English) Feminine form of Tristan and/or a rhyming variant of Christa. The spelling of Trysta suggests the English word *tryst*, usually taken to mean a romantic appointment to meet. Tristan is used more for boys than for girls; Tristan variants serve as alternatives to names like Kristen and Christine. [TRISTAN, TRISTANA, TRISTEN, TRISTIN, TRISTINA, TRISTYN, TRYSTA, TRYSTAN, TRYSTIN]

Trixie: *(TRIKS-ee)* (English) "Brings joy." Short form of Beatrix.

Trudy: *(TROO-dee)* (German) "Strength." Short form of names like Gertrude.

Twyla: *(TWYE-lah)* (English) Usage is probably due to dancer/choreographer Twyla Tharp and to a character in a novel by Zenna Henderson. [TWILA, TWYLLA]

Tyler: *(TYE-ler)* (English) Surname used as a given name, probably influenced by the popularity of Taylor. [TYLA, TYLEE, TYLENA]

Tyra: *(TEER-ah, TYE-rah)* (Scandinavian) "Of Tyr, god of battle." In the news in the 1990s: supermodel Tyra Banks and actress Tyra Farrell. [TYREE, TYRENA, TYRENE]

U

Ula: *(OO-lah)* (Spanish) Short form of Eulalie; (Scandinavian) "Wealthy." See also Eulalie.

Ulyssa: *(yoo-LISS-ah)* (Latin) Feminine form of Ulysses, name of the far-traveling hero of Homer's *Odyssey*. [ULISSA]

Ulrika: *(ool-REE-kah)* (Scandinavian) "Wealthy ruler." Feminine form of Ulric, a ninth-century saint's name. [ULRICA]

Uma: *(OO-mah)* (Sanskrit) "Do not." One of the names of the wife of Shiva. Notable in the 1990s due to actress Uma Thurman.

Una: *(OO-nah)* (Latin) "One." Also a phonetic spelling of Oonagh (Irish) "lamb." See also Oonagh.

Unique: *(yoo-NEEK)* (Latin) "Only one." Use of the English word as a given name may be influenced by its similarity to Monique.

Ursula: *(UR-soo-lah)* (Scandinavian) "She-bear." Many legends have risen about St. Ursula (possibly the fourth century) and her maiden companions.

Usha: *(oo-shah)* (Sanskrit) "Dawn." Mythology: daughter of heaven, sister of night.

V

Valencia: *(vah-LEN-cee-ah)* (Latin) "Strong." From Valentinus, a saint's name.

Valentina: *(val-en-TEE-nah)* (Latin) "Strong." Feminine form of Valentine, a saint's name. The custom of sending cards to sweethearts on Valentine's Day arose from an ancient belief that birds begin pairing on February 14, the feast day of St. Valentine (third century). [VALEN, VALENA, VALENE, VALYN]

Valerie: *(VAL-er-ee)* (Latin) "Strong; valiant." Feminine form of Valerius, a Roman family clan name; also the name of a fourth-century Spanish saint. [**VALERIA**, VALAREE, VALARIE]

Van: *(van)* (Dutch) "Of." The Dutch equivalent of *de* in French names. When some early immigrants to America dropped this prefix from their surnames, they converted it to a given name. Van is also used as a short form of Vanessa.

Vanessa: *(va-NESS-ah)* (English) An early-18th-century literary name created by Jonathan Swift. See also Venicia. [VANESA, VANNESSA]

Vania: *(VAHN-yah)* (Latin) "Brings good news." Short form of Evangelina or a variant form of Ivana. See also Vanna. [VANINA, VANYA]

Vanita: *(va-NEE-tah)* (Hindi) "Woman."

Vanity: *(VAN-ih-tee)* (French) Literally means "empty; inflated in pride." [VANITEE]

Vanna: *(VAN-ah)* Short form of Ivana, the Russian feminine form of John, or a variant of Vanessa. Familiarity of Vanna in the 1980s and 1990s is due to Vanna White of the TV game show *Wheel of Fortune*. Vanda is a Czech form of Wanda. [VANA, VANDA, VANETTA]

Velma: *(VEL-ma)* (English) Variant of Wilma or Wilhemina. [VALMA]

Velvet: *(VEL-vet)* (English) The name of the soft-napped fabric used as a given name for girls.

Venetia: *(ve-NEE-shah)* (Latin) A place name: Venice, the "city of canals" in Italy. [VENECIA, VENICIA, VENITA, VENITIA, VENIZIA]

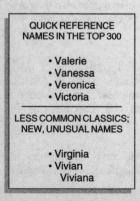

QUICK REFERENCE
NAMES IN THE TOP 300

• Valerie
• Vanessa
• Veronica
• Victoria

LESS COMMON CLASSICS;
NEW, UNUSUAL NAMES

• Virginia
• Vivian
    Viviana

Venus: *(VEE-nus)* (Latin) Roman mythology: the goddess of beauty and love, equivalent to the Greek Aphrodite.

Vera: *(VEER-ah)* (Latin) "Truth." (Russian) "Faith." [VERLA]

Verity: *(VARE-i-tee)* (Latin) "Truthfulness."

Verna: *(VER-nah)* (English) Short form of Laverne or a feminine

form of Vernon. Virna (Italian) became familiar in the
1960s due to actress Virna Lisi. [VERNISHA, VERNITA,
VIRNA]

Veronica: *(ver-RON-ni-kah)* (Latin) "True image." St. Veronica (17th century) was an Italian mystic and saint. See
also Ronnie. [VERONA, VERONIKA, VERONIQUE]

Vianna: *(vee-ANN-ah)* (English) Short form of Viviana, a
saint's name. Vianca is a Spanish variant of Bianca. See
also Vivian. [VIANA, VIANCA, VINA, VIONA]

Victoria: *(vic-TOR-ee-ah)* (Latin) "Conqueror." Feminine
form of Victor. Royal associations from 19th-century England's Queen Victoria and the four-syllable pronunciation
give Victoria connotations of dignity and distinction. Victoria's short forms and nicknames are very informal by con-
trast. Vittoria is an Italian form; Viktoria is Czech. See also
LaToya, Tori, and Toya. [VICKI, VICKIE, VICKY, VIKI, VIKKI,
VIKTORIA, VITTORIA]

Vida: *(VEE-dah, VYE-dah)* (Latin) Short form of Davida. *Vida*
is also the Spanish word for "life." Veda may be used in
reference to the Hindu Veda (Sanskrit), "knowledge."
[VEDA]

Vienna: *(vee-EN-ah)* (Latin) The name of the Austrian city,
used as a given name.

Violet: *(VYE-a-let)* (English) One of the earliest flower names.
Shakespeare used the Latin form Viola for the enterprising
heroine in *Twelfth Night*. [VIOLA, VIOLETA, VIOLETTA, VI-
OLETTE]

Virginia: *(vir-JIN-yah)* (Latin) "Chaste, virginal." See also
Ginger and Ginny. [VIRGENA, VIRGENE, VIRGINA]

Viridiana: *(ver-id-ee-AHN-ah)* (Latin) "Green." An Italian
saint's name.

Viveca: *(VIV-a-kah)* (Latin) "Alive." Viveka (Hindi) means "righteous." Familiar since the 1970s due to Swedish actress Viveca Lindfors. [VIVEKA]

Vivian: *(VIV-ee-en)* (Latin) "Living." An ancient personal name; a saint's name. In Malory's *Morte d'Arthur*, Vivien was the Lady of the Lake and also the enchantress of Merlin. See also Vianna. [VIVIANA, VIVIANE, VIVIANNA, VIVIANNE, VIVIEN, VIVIENNE]

Vondra: *(VAHN-drah)* (Czech) "Womanly; brave." Variant of Andrea. [VONNI, VONNIE]

W

Wanda: *(WAHN-dah)* (German) "Traveler." See also Vanna.

Wava: *(WAY-vah)* (Slavic) "Stranger." Pet name formed from Varvara, the Russian form of Barbara.

Wendy: *(WIN-dee)* (English) Literary: a created name that first appeared in James Barrie's *Peter Pan*. [WENDA, WENDI]

Weslee: *(WEZ-lee)* (English) Feminine form of Wesley. [WESLIA]

QUICK REFERENCE
NAMES IN THE TOP 300

• Wendy
• Whitney

LESS COMMON CLASSICS;
NEW, UNUSUAL NAMES

Whitley

Whitley: *(WHIT-lee)* (English) "White meadow." Occasional use is probably influenced by its similarity to Whitney, and to the character Whitley on the TV show *A Different World*.

Whitney: *(WHIT-nee)* (English) "Fair island." Initial popu-

larity of this surname as a given name is due to singer/
actress Whitney Houston.

Willa: *(WIL-ah)* (German) "Resolute protector." Feminine
form of William.

Willow: *(WIL-oh)* (English) Literally, the willow tree, noted
for its slender, graceful branches and leaves.

Winifred: *(WIN-a-fred)* (Welsh) "Reconciled; blessed." Winifred, a martyred Welsh princess, is traditionally called the
patron saint of virgins. [WINNIE, WYNNE]

Winona: *(wye-NOH-nah)* (Native American) "Firstborn
daughter." Made familiar by actress Winona Ryder. Singer
Wynonna Judd has done the same for her version of the
name. [WINONNA, WYNONNA]

Winter: *(WIN-ter)* (English) Literally, the season. Spring,
Summer, and Autumn complete the roster of season names.

Xandra: *(ZAN-drah)* (Greek) Variant of Alexandra. See also
Zandra. [XANDRIA]

Xanthe: *(ZAN-thah)* (Greek) "Yellow, blonde." [XANTHIA]

Xaviera: *(zay-vee-EHR-ah)* (Arabic) "Bright, splendid."
Feminine form of Xavier. [XAVIA]

Xenia: *(ZAYN-yah)* (Greek) "Welcoming, hospitable." The
New Zealand production of the 1990s TV series *Xena:*

Warrior Princess has brought attention to Xena *(ZEE-nah)* as a girl's name. See also Zaina and Zenia. [XENA, XIA]

Xuxa: *(SHOO-sha)* (Latin) Nickname for Susana used by the hostess of a very popular children's TV show in Brazil.

Xylia: *(ZYE-lee-ah)* (Greek) ''Woodland.'' [XYLA, XYLINA]

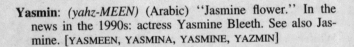

Y

Yasmin: *(yahz-MEEN)* (Arabic) ''Jasmine flower.'' In the news in the 1990s: actress Yasmine Bleeth. See also Jasmine. [YASMEEN, YASMINA, YASMINE, YAZMIN]

Yesenia: *(yeh-SEE-nee-ah)* (Spanish) Phonetic variant of Llesenia, a name made popular by the title character of a 1970s Spanish soap opera. See also Jessenia and Llesenia [YESSENIA]

Ynez: *(ee-NEZ)* (French) ''Chaste.'' Variant of Agnes. See also Inez. [YNES]

Yolanda: *(yoh-LAHN-dah)* (Spanish) Variant of Yolande, a French form of Violet, and the Hungarian Jolanda. [YOLANDE, YOLONDA]

Ysabel: *(EE-sa-bel)* (French) Medieval form of Isabel.

Yumiko: *(yoo-mee-koh)* (Japanese) ''Arrow child.''

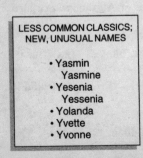

LESS COMMON CLASSICS;
NEW, UNUSUAL NAMES

- Yasmin
  Yasmine
- Yesenia
  Yessenia
- Yolanda
- Yvette
- Yvonne

Yuriko: *(yoo-ree-koh)* (Japanese) "Lily child."

Yvette: *(ee-VET)* (French) Feminine form of Yves. See also Ivette.

Yvonne: *(ee-VAHN)* (French) Feminine variant of Yves, a saint's name. See also Evonne and Ivonne. [YVONNA]

Z

Zahara: *(za-HAH-rah)* (Arabic) "Flowering." (Hebrew) "Shining." See also Sahara, Zara, and Zohra. [ZAHRA]

Zaida: *(ZAY-dah)* (Arabic) "Huntress; fortunate." [ZADA, ZAYDA]

Zaina: *(ZAY-nah)* (Greek) Variant form of Xenia. May also be used as a feminine variant of Zane. See also Zenia. [ZAHNA, ZANA, ZAYNA, ZAYNAH, ZEINA]

Zakiya: *(za-KEE-ah)* (Hebrew) "Pure." [ZAKIA, ZAKIAH, ZAKYLA]

Zalika: *(za-LEE-kah)* (Swahili) "Well-born."

Zandra: *(ZAHN-dra, ZAN-drah)* (Spanish) Variant of Alexandra. See also Xandra.

Zaneta: *(zah-NEE-tah)* (Spanish) A saint's name; variants may also be used as feminine forms of Zane. [ZANETTA, ZANITA]

Zara: *(ZAR-ah)* (Arabic) "Dawning." See also Zahara. [ZAIRA, ZARAH, ZAYRA]

Zarina: *(za-REEN-ah)* (Persian) "Golden." [ZAREEN, ZA-REENA

Zelda: *(ZEL-dah)* (Latin) Short form of Grizelda. The similar-sounding Zelde is a Yiddish name meaning "happiness." [ZELDE]

Zelma: *(ZEL-mah)* (English) Variant form of Selma.

Zenia: *(ZEEN-yah)* (Greek) "Welcoming." Variant of Xenia. Zena is a short form of Zenobia. See also Zaina. [ZENA, ZINA]

Zenobia: *(ze-NOH-bee-ah)* (Latin) Queen Zenobia (third century B.C.) was ruler of the wealthy city of Palmyra in the Arabian desert.

Zhané: *(zha-NAY)* (American) Phonetic variant of Jenae. [ZHANAE, ZHANAYA]

Zia: *(ZEE-ah)* (Arabic) "Light; splendor."

Zita: *(ZEE-tah)* (Greek) A saint's name; also a short form of Rosita.

Zivah: *(zi-VAH)* (Israeli) "Radiant." [ZIVA]

Zoe: *(ZOH-ee)* (Greek) "Life." [ZOEY, ZOIE]

Zohra: *(ZOR-ah)* (Arabic) "Blossom." Biblical: the name of a city in Judah where Samson was born. See also Zahara.

QUICK REFERENCE
NAMES IN THE TOP 300

• Zoe

Zora: *(ZOR-ah)* (Slavic) "Dawn." [ZORAYA, ZOREEN, ZORINA]

Zsa Zsa: *(zhah-zhah)* (Hungarian) Pet name for Susan. Noted name bearer: Hungarian actress Zsa Zsa Gabor.

Zuleika: *(zoo-LAY-kah)* (Arabic) "Fair one." [ZULEICA]

Zulema: *(zoo-LEE-mah)* (Arabic) "Peace." Variant form of Salome or Solomon. [ZULEIMA, ZULEYMA, ZULIMA]

BOYS' NAMES

A

Aaron: *(AIR-an)* (Hebrew) "Lofty; inspired." Biblical: Moses' brother Aaron was the first high priest of Israel. See also Aron. [AAREN, AARYN, ARRON]

Abdullah: *(ab-DUL-ah)* (Arabic) "Servant of God." Abdalla is a Swahili variant. [ABDALLA, ABDUL, ABDULLA]

Abel: *(AY-bel)* (Hebrew) "Exhalation of breath." Biblical: the second son of Adam. The variant form Able is an English surname. [ABELL, ABLE]

Abner: *(AB-ner)* (Hebrew) "Father of light." Biblical: King Saul of Israel's army chief, a valiant warrior and clever strategist.

Abraham: *(AY-bra-ham)* (Hebrew) "Father of multitudes." Biblical: Abraham, celebrated for his great faith, was the ancestor-father of Israel and some of the Arabic peoples. See also Ibrahim. [ABE, ABRAHAN, ABRAHIM]

Abram: *(AY-bram)* (Hebrew) "Exalted father." Biblical: the patriarch Abraham's name before God changed it. Abran *(a-BRAHN)* is the Spanish form. [ABRAN, ABRIAN, ABRIEL]

Absalom: *(AB-sa-lom)* (Hebrew) "Father of peace." Biblical: Absalom, son of King David, was renowned

QUICK REFERENCE
NAMES IN THE TOP 300

• Aaron
• Adam
• Adrian
• Aidan
• Alan
• Albert
• Alex
  Alec
• Alexander
• Alexis

for his handsome appearance and ability to win the loyalty
and allegiance of others.

Ace: *(ayce)* (English) A nickname given to one who excels.
It's also an English surname meaning "noble." [ACEE,
ACIE]

Achilles: *(a-KILL-eez)* (Greek) The mythological hero of the
Trojan War famous for his valor and manly beauty. Also a
saint's name.

Adair: *(a-DARE)* (Scottish) "From the oak tree ford." Used
for boys and girls.

Adam: *(AD-um)* (Hebrew) "Earthling man; from the red
earth." Biblical: in the Genesis account, man was created
from the red earth of Eden. Adan *(a-DAHN)* is the Spanish
form. [ADAMSON, ADAN, ADDAM]

Addison: *(AD-ih-sun)* (English) "Son of Adam."

Adiel: *(AD-ee-el)* (Hebrew) "God is an ornament." [ADEEL,
ADIL]

Adin: *(AY-den)* (Hebrew) "Pleasure given." Biblical: an exile
who returned to Israel from Babylon. [ADEN]

Adlai: *(AD-lay)* (Hebrew) "My ornament." A Biblical name
made noteworthy in the 20th century by the presidential
candidate Adlai Stevenson.

Adolfo: *(a-DOLL-foh)* (German) "Noble wolf." Adolf (13th
century) was a German saint. Religious and family associations keep this name on the somewhat active list in spite
of negative associations with the infamous Adolf Hitler.
[ADOLF, ADOLPH, ADOLPHUS]

Adonis: *(a-DAHN-iss)* (Greek) "Handsome; a lord." Greek
mythology: a youth beloved of Aphrodite. [ADON]

Adrian: *(AY-dree-an)* (Latin) "From Adria (the Adriatic sea region)." A saint's name. [ADRIANO, ADRIEN, ADRION, ADRON]

Adriel: *(AY-dree-el)* (Hebrew) "Of God's flock." A biblical name. [ADRIELL]

Ahmed: *(AH-med)* (Arabic) "Much praised." One of the many names of the prophet Mohammed. [AHMAD, AMAD, AMADI]

Aidan: *(AY-den)* (Irish) "Fiery." St. Aidan (Ireland, seventh century) established the monastery of Lindisfarne, one of the great centers of learning of its time. Notable name bearer: actor Aidan Quinn. [AIDEN]

Akeno: *(ah-kay-noh)* (Japanese) "Bright shining field."

Al: (English) A short form of names beginning with *Al-*.

Alain: *(al-LAYN)* (French) Variant form of Alan. See also Alan and Allen. [ALLAIN]

Alan: *(AL-an)* (Gaelic) "Fair, handsome." Alun is a Welsh form. See also Alain and Allen. [ALUN]

Alaric: *(AL-a-ric)* (German) "Rules all." Historical: the Gothic king who plundered Rome in A.D. 410. St. Alaricus (10th century) was the son of a duke who turned to the religious life. [ALARICK, ALRIC, ALRICK]

Alasdair: *(AL-as-dare)* (Scottish) Variant of Alexander. [ALASTAIR, ALDAIR, ALISTAIR, ALISTAIRE, ALISTER, ALLISTER]

Albert: *(AL-bert)* (German) "Noble; bright." One of the most famous

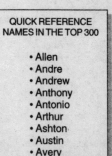

QUICK REFERENCE
NAMES IN THE TOP 300

- Allen
- Andre
- Andrew
- Anthony
- Antonio
- Arthur
- Ashton
- Austin
- Avery

Alberts was Prince Albert, consort of Queen Victoria, who was noted for his enthusiastic support of the application of science to the modern industrial age. Albert Einstein devised the theory of relativity when still a young man. [ALBERTO]

Albin: *(AL-bin)* (English) "White." Alban and Albin are English surnames probably based on Alba, a Spanish and Italian place name. St. Alban (fourth century), according to legend, was the first martyr of Britain. [ALBAN, ALBEN, ALBYN]

Albion: *(AL-bee-on)* (Latin) "White cliffs." Albion is an ancient poetic name for Britain.

Alden: *(ALL-den)* (English) "Wise/old; friendly." [ALDAN, ALDIN]

Aldo: *(ALL-doh)* (Italian) "Old one, elder." [ALDIS, ALDON]

Aldric: *(ALL-drik)* (French) "Old/wise ruler." St. Aldric (ninth century) was a bishop of Le Mans, France. [ALDRICH, ALDRIN]

Alejandro: *(al-ay-HAHN-droh)* (Spanish) Variant form of Alexander. [ALEJANDRINO, ALEXANDRO]

Alex: *(AL-ex)* (English) Short form of Alexander. Alek is a Russian form; Aleko is Greek. [ALEC, ALECK, ALEK, ALEKO]

Alexander: *(al-ek-ZAN-der)* (Greek) "Defender of mankind." Alexander the Great (356–323 B.C.) conquered and ruled the greater part of the known world before his death at the age of 33. History describes him as a man of high physical courage, impulsive en-

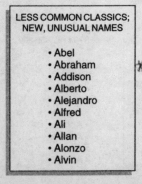

LESS COMMON CLASSICS;
NEW, UNUSUAL NAMES

- Abel
- Abraham
- Addison
- Alberto
- Alejandro
- Alfred
- Ali
- Allan
- Alonzo
- Alvin

ergy, and fervid imagination. Alessandro is an Italian form; Alexandre and Alixandre are French. See also Alasdair, Alejandro, Alex, Alexis, Lex, Sandy, and Zander. [ALESSANDRO, ALEXAN, ALEXANDRE, ALIXANDRE]

Alexis: *(a-LEX-iss)* (Greek) Short form of Alexander. St. Alexis (fifth century) was widely popular in the Middle Ages. [ALEXEI, ALEXI, ALEXIO]

Alfonso: *(al-FON-so)* (Spanish) "Ready, eager." Alfonso has been favored by Spanish royalty. Alphonse is a French form. [ALFONSE, ALFONZO, ALPHONSE, ALPHONSO]

Alford: *(AL-ford)* (English) "The old ford."

Alfred: *(AL-fred)* (English) "Elf-wise counselor." Alfredo *(al-FRAY-doh)* is the Latin form. [**ALFREDO**, ALF, ALFIE]

Ali: *(al-LEE)* (Arabic) "The greatest." Variant of Allah, title of the Supreme Being in the Muslim faith. The homonym Allie is most often a short form of names beginning with *Al-*. [ALLIE, ALY]

Allard: *(AL-erd)* (English) "Noble; brave."

Allen: *(AL-en)* (Gaelic) Variant of Alan. Allen is an English and American preference; Allan is Scottish. See also Alain. [ALLAN, ALLYN]

Allon: *(AL-en)* (Hebrew) "Great tree." [ALON]

Alonzo: *(a-LON-zoh)* (Spanish, Italian) Variant form of Alphonse; see Alfonso. [ALANZO, ALONSO]

Alton: *(ALL-tun)* (English) "From the old town." See also Elton. [ALSTON]

Alva: *(AL-vah)* (Hebrew) "Sublime." Biblical: Alvah was a place and tribal name. [ALVAH, ALVAN]

Alvaro: *(AL-vah-roh)* (Spanish) "Truth-speaker; guardian." [ALVAR]

Alvern: *(AL-vern)* (Latin) "Spring, greening." See also Elvin.

Alvin: *(AL-vin)* (English) "Wise friend." [ALVYN, ALWIN, ALWYN]

Alvis: *(AL-viss)* (English) "All-knowing."

Amadeus: *(ah-ma-DAY-us)* (Latin) "Loves God." A saint's name that became widely familiar as Wolfgang Mozart's middle name due to the 1987 movie *Amadeus*, which dramatized the famed composer's life. [AMADEO]

Ambrose: *(AM-brohz)* (Greek) "Immortal." St. Ambrose (eighth century) was a tutor and friend of Charlemagne.

Amery: *(AY-mer-ee)* (Irish) "Ridge, long hill." See also Amory. [AMRY]

Ames: *(aymz)* (French) "Friend." Rare.

Amil: *(AH-meel)* (Hindu) "Invaluable."

Amir: *(a-MEER)* (Arabic) "Prince." (Israeli) "Powerful." [AMEER]

Amon: *(AY-mon)* (Hebrew) "Trustworthy, faithful." Biblical. Also the name of one of the gods of Thebes in Egypt.

Amory: *(AM-er-ee)* (German) "Brave; powerful." See also Amery and Emory.

Amos: *(AYM-ess)* (Hebrew) "Bearer of burdens." Biblical: the prophet who wrote the book of Amos.

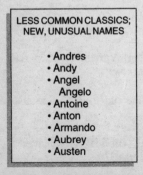

LESS COMMON CLASSICS;
NEW, UNUSUAL NAMES

- Andres
- Andy
- Angel
  Angelo
- Antoine
- Anton
- Armando
- Aubrey
- Austen

Anders: *(AN-ders)* (Scandinavian) Variant form of Andrew. [ANDERSON]

Andino: *(an-DEE-noh)* (Latin) Italian short form of Andrew.

André: *(AHN-dray)* (French) Variant form of Andrew. Andrei is a Slavic form. Aundre *(AWN-dray)* is an American phonetic variant. See also Andres and Andrew. [ANDREE, ANDREI, AUNDRE]

Andres: *(AHN-drays)* (Spanish) Variant form of Andrew. Andreas and Andreus are Greek forms. [ANDREAS, ANDREUS, ANDRIUS]

Andrew: *(AN-droo)* (Greek) "Manly; brave." Biblical: the first chosen of the 12 apostles. St. Andrew is the patron saint of Scotland and Russia. Andras is a Welsh form. See also Anders, Andino, Andre, Andres, Andrian, Jedrek, and Kendrew. [**ANDY**, ANDRAS, ANDRIEL]

Andrian: *(AN-dree-en)* (American) A blend of Andrew and Adrian.

Andrik: *(AN-drik)* (Slavic) Variant form of Andrew. [ANDRIC, ANDRICK]

Angel: *(AHN-hail, AIN-jel)* (Greek) "Messenger." Biblical: name for the spirit creatures sent by God to men as His messengers. Hispanic male usage is dominant for this cross-gender name. [**ANGELO**, ANGELINO]

Angus: *(ANG-guss)* (Scottish) "Singular; choice."

Ansell: *(AN-sul)* (German) "God's protection." Variant form of Anselmo. [ANSEL]

Anselmo: *(an-SEL-moh)* (Latin) "God's protection." St. Anselm (11th century) was archbishop of Canterbury during William the Conqueror's reign. [ANSELM]

Anson: *(AN-sun)* (English) "Anne's son." A surname.

Antares: *(an-TARE-ees, an-TAHR-ees)* (Greek) The name of a giant red star, the brightest in the constellation Scorpio.

Anthony: *(AN-tha-nee)* (Latin) "Highly praiseworthy." Mark Antony (82–30 B.C.), Roman triumvir and general, shared a throne and a tempestuous political career with Queen Cleopatra of Egypt. St. Anthony (third century) founded the first Christian monastic order and is traditionally renowned for his resistance to the devil. See also Antoine, Anton, Antonio, and Tony.

Antoine: *(AN-twahn)* (French) Variant form of Anthony. In the news in the 1990s: actor Antwon Tanner. [ANTWAN, ANTWON]

Anton: *(an-tohn)* (Slavic) Variant form of Anthony. Antone *(AN-tohn)* is a contemporary variant. [ANTONE]

Antonio: (Latin) Spanish and Italian variant of Anthony. [ANTINO, ANTONIUS]

Apollo: (Greek) "Destroyer." Mythology: the Greek and Roman god of light, music, and poetry. The name comes from Appollyon, Greek translation of the Hebrew word *abaddon*, meaning "destroyer." Biblical: Apollo was one of the early Christian disciples.

Aram: *(AIR-am)* (Assyrian, Hebrew) "High, exalted."

Aramis: *(AIR-a-miss)* In fiction, the famous swordsman from Alexander Dumas's *The Three Musketeers*, notable for his ambition and religious aspirations.

Archer: *(AR-cher)* (English) "A bowman." An English surname from medieval times when bows and arrows were essential hunting and fighting equipment.

Archie: *(AR-chee)* (English) "Valuable; bold." A short form of Archibald. [ARCHIBALD]

Ardell: *(ar-DELL)* (Latin) "Eager, industrious." [ARDEL]

Ardon: *(ARD-en)* (Hebrew) "Bronze." A biblical name. Arden (Celtic) means "lofty; eager." [ARDEN]

Ari: *(AIR-ee)* (Hebrew) "Lion." (Scandinavian) "Eagle." Also a short form of Aristides (Greek) meaning "the best." [ARIE, ARISTIDE, ARIUS]

Aric: *(AIR-ik)* (Scandinavian) "Rule with mercy." See also Eric. [AARIC, ARICK, ARIK, ARRICK]

Ariel: *(AR-ee-el)* (Hebrew) "Lion of God." Biblical: a name for Jerusalem. Shakespeare gave this name to a prankish spirit in *The Tempest*. More frequently used for girls in the 1990s.

Arion: *(AR-ee-en)* The name of a Greek poet and musician. Mythology: the name of the magic horse born to Poseidon and Demeter. Arian is a Welsh form. [ARIAN, ARIEN]

Arjay: *(ar-jay)* (American) Phonetic spelling of the initials *R.* and *J.*

Arlen: *(AR-len)* (Hebrew) "Pledge." [ARLAN, ARLAND, ARLANDO, ARLIN]

Arley: *(AR-lee)* (English) Variant of Harley or Arlen. [ARLEIGH, ARLIE]

Arlo: *(AR-loh)* (Latin) "Strong; manly." Italian variant of Charles. Noted name bearer: folksinger Arlo Guthrie.

Arman: *(ar-MAHN)* (Spanish, Russian) Short form of Armando; Armani is a related Italian surname made familiar by the men's clothing designer. [ARMANI, ARMANTE]

Armando: *(ar-MAHN-doh)* (Spanish) "Army man." Armand is a French form; Armond is Italian. Variant of Herman. [ARMAND, ARMOND, ARMONDO]

Armon: *(AR-men)* (Hebrew) "High place." [ARMEN, ARMIN]

Arnan: *(AR-nen)* (Hebrew) "Quick; joyful." Biblical: a descendant of King David. Arnon means "torrent valley." [ARNON]

Arne: *(arn)* (Scandinavian) "Eagle."

Arni: *(AR-nee)* (Hebrew) "High." Biblical: an ancestor of Jesus.

Arnold: *(AR-nold)* (English, German) "The eagle rules." Famous name bearer: actor Arnold Schwarzenegger. [ARNALDO, ARNEL, ARNELL, ARNIE, ARNO, ARNOLDO]

Aron: *(AIR-en)* (Hebrew) Spanish, Slavic, and Scandinavian form of Aaron. Aron is the spelling used for Elvis Presley's middle name.

Arsenio: *(ar-SEE-nee-oh)* (Greek) "Virile, masculine." According to tradition, St. Arsenius the Great (fourth century) tutored the sons of the Roman emperor Theodosius. The actor/television personality Arsenio Hall has brought the name into prominence. [ARCENIO, ARSENE]

Arthur: *(AR-ther)* (Celtic) "Noble; courageous." King Arthur of Britain (sixth century) and his Round Table of knights have become legendary figures. Arturo is the Spanish form. [**ARTURO**, ART, ARTIE, ARTUR]

Arvin: *(AR-vin)* (English) "The people's friend." [ARVIE, ARVIS, ARVON, ARVYN, ARWIN, ARWYN]

Asa: *(AY-sah)* (Hebrew) "Healer, physician." Biblical: name of the third king of Judah. [ASE]

Asher: *(ASH-er)* (Hebrew) "Happy; happiness." Biblical: Asher, the eighth son of Jacob, was promised a life blessed with abundance.

Ashley: *(ASH-lee)* (English) "Meadow of ash trees." A surname. As a given name, Ashley is now used mostly for girls. Literary: Ashley Wilkes is the man long loved by Scarlett O'Hara in Margaret Mitchell's novel *Gone With the Wind*. Ashley is also an English saint's name (17th century). [ASHLEN, ASHLIN]

Ashton: *(ASH-ton)* (English) "Ash tree town." A surname used as a given name. [ASH, ASHFORD, ASHTIN, ASTON]

Ashwin: *(ASH-win)* (Hindu) A calendar month. [ASHWYN]

Atticus: *(AT-a-kuss)* (Latin) "From Athens." Literary: the name of Scout's father in the novel *To Kill a Mockingbird*. An Armenian saint's name (fifth century).

Aubrey: *(AW-bree)* (French) "Rules with elf-wisdom." Variant form of Alberic. St. Aubrey (12th century) was one of the founders of the Cistercian order. [AUBRY]

Auden: *(AW-den)* (English) "Old friend." Audie is a short form. Noted name bearer: Audie Murphy, a 1950s actor who was also the most decorated American soldier in World War II. [AUDELL, AUDIE]

Audric: *(AW-drik)* (English) "Old/wise ruler." Variant form of Aldericus, the name of an eighth-century French saint.

August: *(AW-gust)* (Latin) "Majestic dignity; grandeur." St. Augustine (sixth century) was the first archbishop of Canterbury. [AGUSTIN, AGUSTINE, AGUSTUS, AUGUSTINE, AUGUSTUS]

Aurelio: *(aw-REE-lee-oh)* (Latin) "Golden." Spanish form of Aurelius. Aurelian (third century) was one of the great Roman Emperors. [AURELIAN, AURELIANO, AURELIUS]

Austin: *(AW-sten)* (French) Variant of Augustine. St. Augustine (seventh century) was sometimes called Austin. In America, the name carries Western associations due to Stephen Austin, a frontiersman and one of the founders of the Republic of Texas. The state capital is named in his honor. [AUSTEN, AUSTYN]

Avery: *(AY-vree)* (English) "Rules with elf-wisdom." [AVRY]

Axel: *(AX-el)* (Scandinavian) Variant of Absalom.

Ayers: *(airz)* (English) "Heir to a fortune."

B

Bailey: *(BAY-lee)* (French) Comes from the word meaning "steward" or "public official"; a man in charge. Used for girls as well as boys. [BAYLEY]

Banner: *(BAN-ner)* (English) "Flag; ensign bearer."

Barak: *(ba-RAHK, BARE-ek)* (Hebrew) "Flash of lightning." Biblical: a valiant fighting man who cooperated with the prophetess Deborah to win victory in a battle against overwhelming odds. See also Barric. [BARRAK]

Baran: *(BARE-en)* (Russian) "The ram; forceful, virile." See also Baron.

Barclay: *(BAR-klay)* (Scottish) "The birch tree meadow." See also Berkley. [BARTLEY]

Bard: *(bard)* (English) "Minstrel, singer-poet." St. Bardo

(11th century) was a German saint. [BAIRD, BARDEN, BAR-DON]

Barnabas: *(BAR-na-bus)* (Hebrew) "Son of comfort." Biblical: a first-century missionary companion of Paul. Bernabe is a Spanish form. See also Barney. [BARNABY, BERNABE]

Barnett: *(bar-NET)* (English) "Of honorable birth." [BARNET]

Barney: *(BAR-nee)* (English) Short form of Barnabas and Barnaby.

Baron: *(BARE-an)* (French) A title of nobility used as a given name. Also the Hebrew phrase *Bar Aaron*, "son of Aaron." [BARR, BARRON]

Barrett: *(BARE-et)* (English) Variant of Barnett. [BARRET]

Barric: *(BARE-ik)* (English) "Grain farm." A place name. See also Barak. [BARRICK, BERIC]

Barry: *(BARE-ee)* (Irish) "Fair-haired." Variant form of Bairre, from *fionnbharr*, "white hair." St. Bairre (seventh century) founded a monastery that became the city of Cork in Ireland. [BARRIE, BARRINGTON]

Bartholomew: *(bar-THAWL-oh-myoo)* (Hebrew) "The son of Tolmai (the farmer)." Biblical: one of the twelve apostles, known as the patron saint of tanners and vintners. Variants listed here are related English surnames. [BART, BARTEL, BARTH, BARTON, BATES]

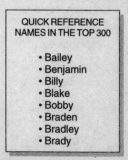

QUICK REFERENCE
NAMES IN THE TOP 300

- Bailey
- Benjamin
- Billy
- Blake
- Bobby
- Braden
- Bradley
- Brady

Bartram: *(BAR-tram)* (Scandinavian) "Glorious raven." The raven was consecrated to Odin, the Norse god of war, and was the emblem of the Danish royal standard. See also Bertram.

Baruch: *(BAR-ook)* (Hebrew) "Blessed." Biblical: one Baruch was Jeremiah's scribe-secretary.

Basil: *(BAZ-el)* (Greek) "Royal, kingly." St. Basil (fourth century) of Caesarea was called "the Great." [BASILIO]

Baxter: *(BAK-ster)* (English) "Baker." An occupational name.

Bayard: *(BAY-erd)* (French) "Auburn-haired." The name of a 16th-century French knight and national hero renowned for his valor and purity of heart. [BAY, BAYLEN]

Beale: *(beel)* (English) "Handsome." [BEAL, BEALL]

Beau: *(boh)* (French) "Handsome." See also Bo. [BEAUDAN, BEAUDINE]

Ben: *(ben)* (English) Short form of names like Benjamin and Benedict. Benn is an English surname. [BENJI, BENJY, BENN, BENNIE, BENNY]

Benedict *(BEN-a-dikt)* (Latin) "Blessed." A name used by 15 popes and a monastical order, the Benedictines. Shakespeare's Benedick in *Much Ado About Nothing* is a self-assured, witty bachelor. [BENEDETTO, BENEDICK, BENITO]

Benjamin: *(BEN-ja-men)* (Hebrew) "Son of the right hand." Biblical: the 12th and most beloved son of the patriarch Jacob.

Benjiro *(ben-jee-roh)* (Japanese) "Enjoy peace."

Bennett: *(BEN-et)* (English) Variant of Benedict. Noted name bearer: publisher Bennett Cerf. [BENNET, BENSON]

Bentley: *(BENT-lee)* (English) "Grassy meadow."

QUICK REFERENCE
NAMES IN THE TOP 300

- Brandon
  Branden
- Brendan
  Brenden
  Brendon
- Brennan
- Brent
- Brett
- Brian

Benton: *(BEN-ten)* (English) "Settlement in a grassy place."

Berkley: (English) "The birch tree meadow." Noted name bearer: cartoonist Berkeley Breathed. Also see Barclay and Burke. [BERK, BERKE, BERKELEY]

Berlyn: *(BER-lin)* (German) "Son of Berl." See also Burl. [BERL, BERLE, BURLIN]

Bern: (Scandinavian) "Bear." [BERNE, BERNELLE, BURNELL]

Bernard: *(ber-NARD)* (German) "Strong as a bear." A saint's name. See also Bjorn. [BARNARD, BERNARDO, BERNIE, BURNARD]

Bert: *(bert)* (English) "Illustrious." Short form of names like Albert and Bertram. [BERTIE, BERTIN, BERTON]

Bertram: *(BER-trum)* (English, German) "Glorious raven." See also Bartram and Bertrand.

Bertrand: *(BER-trand, ber-TRAND)* (French) Variant form of Bertram. A saint's name. Famous name bearer: philosopher Bertrand Russell.

Bevan: *(BEV-en)* (Welsh) "Son of Evan."

Billy: *(BIL-ee)* (English) Nickname for William, now often used as an independent name. Billie is frequently used for girls. In the news in the 1990s: country-western singer Billy Ray Cyrus. [BILL, BILLIE]

Birch: *(berch)* (English) "Bright, shining; the birch tree." A nature name and surname.

Bjorn: *(bee-YORN)* (Scandinavian) "Bear." Famous name bearer: Swedish tennis champion Bjorn Borg. See also Bernard.

Blade: *(blayd)* (English) "Knife, sword." This surname has been in use since medieval times.

Blaine: *(blayn)* (Scottish) Surname, meaning uncertain. St. Blaine (seventh century) was a Scottish saint. [BLANE, BLANEY, BLAYNE]

Blair: *(blare)* (Scottish) "Field, plain." Used somewhat more for girls than for boys.

Blaise: *(blayz)* (French) "Lisp, stutter." The homonym Blaze means "fire." Blaise Pascal was a brilliant 17th-century child prodigy, mathematician, scientist, and philosopher; he invented the calculating machine and hydraulic press before he died at age 39. A fourth-century saint's name. [BLAIS, BLAISDELL, BLAIZE, BLASE, BLAYZE, BLAZE]

Blake: *(blayk)* (English) "Dark, dark-haired." Can also mean the reverse: "fair, pale." Made familiar in the 1980s due to the fictitious character Blake Carrington on the TV series *Dynasty*. [BLAKELY, BLAKEMAN]

Bo: *(boh)* (Scandinavian) Nickname and short form occasionally used for boys and, due to actress Bo Derek, for girls. See also Beau.

Bobby: *(BAH-bee)* (English) Short form of Robert. Bobbie is more frequently used for girls. [BOB, BOBBIE]

Boden: *(BOH-den)* (Scandinavian) "Shelter." St. Bodey (16th century) was an English saint. [BEAUDEAN, BODIE, BODIN, BODINE]

Boone: *(boon)* (English) "Good; a blessing." Daniel Boone, the American frontier hero, has influenced the use of the surname as a given name.

Borak: *(bor-AHK)* (Arabic) "The lightning." According to legend, Al Borak was the name of the magical horse that bore Mohammed from earth to the seventh heaven.

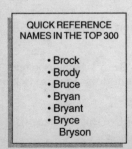

QUICK REFERENCE
NAMES IN THE TOP 300

- Brock
- Brody
- Bruce
- Bryan
- Bryant
- Bryce
  Bryson

Borg: *(borg)* (Scandinavian) "Castle." Familiar to sci-fi fans as the name of an invincible hive-species on the 1990s TV series *Star Trek: The Next Generation.*

Boris: *(BOR-iss)* (Russian) "Fighter." St. Boris is known as the patron saint of Moscow.

Bowen: *(BOH-en)* (Welsh) "Son of Owen." [BOWIE]

Boyce: *(boyce)* (French) "Lives near the wood."

Boyd: *(boyd)* (Scottish) "Blonde, fair-haired."

Brad: *(brad)* (English) "Broad, wide." Also used as a short form of names like Bradford and Bradley. [BRADD]

Braddock: *(BRAD-uk)* (English) "Broad-spreading oak."

Braden: *(BRAY-den)* (English, Irish) "Broad hillside." [BRADDON, BRADON, BRAEDEN, BRAEDON, BRAYDEN, BRAYDON]

Bradley: *(BRAD-lee)* (English) "Broad clearing in the wood." Also related English surnames. [BRADFORD, BRAD-LEE, BRADSHAW]

Brady: *(BRAY-dee)* (Irish) "Broad."

Bram: *(bram)* (Scottish) "Bramble; a thicket of wild gorse." (Hebrew) Short form of Abraham and Abram. Noted name bearer: Bram Stoker, author of *Dracula.*

Brand: *(brand)* (English) "Fiery torch, beacon; sword." May also derive from Brandon. Brandt is a German form; Brando is Italian. [BRANDELL, BRANDO, BRANDT]

LESS COMMON CLASSICS;
NEW, UNUSUAL NAMES

- Barry
- Beau
- Blaine
- Brad
- Braxton
- Brayden
- Brennen
- Brice
- Byron

Brandon: *(BRAN-den)* (English) "Beacon on the hill; gorse-covered hill." [**BRANDEN**, BRANDAN, BRANDIN, BRANDYN]

Brannon: *(BRAN-en)* (Irish) Variant of Brandon. [BRANNA, BRANNEN]

Branson: *(BRAN-sun)* (English) "Son of Brand." [BRANSEN]

Brant: *(brant)* (English) Variant of Brand. Joseph Brant, a Mohawk, was a renowned strategist who fought on the British side during the American Revolution. He was also a devout scholar who translated Christian religious works into his native tongue. [BRANSTON, BRANTLEY, BRANTON]

Breck: *(brek)* (Gaelic) "Freckled." [BREXTON]

Brendan: *(BREN-den)* (Irish) "Prince." St. Brendan of Ireland (sixth century) is famed for his scholarship and adventurous traveling, including a seven-year voyage to a land that some think may have been North America. Noted name bearer: Irish playwright and wit Brendan Behan. [**BRENDEN, BRENDON**]

Brennan: *(BREN-an)* (Irish) Variant form of Brendan. [BRENN, BRENNEN, BRENNON]

Brent: *(brent)* (English) "Hilltop." [BRENDT, BRETEN, BRENTLEY, BRENTLY, BRENTON]

Brett: *(bret)* (English) "Brit." A native of Brittany (France), or Britain (England). [**BRET**, BRETTON, BRITT, BRITTAIN, BRITTAN, BRITTON]

Brewster: *(BREW-ster)* (English) "One who brews ale." See also Webster.

Brian: *(BRY-en)* (Celtic) "He ascends." Historical: Brian Boru (10th century) was a high king of Ireland and one of its greatest national heroes. See also Bryan and Bryant. [BRIEN, BRION]

Brice: *(bryce)* (English, French) "Of Britain." St. Brice (fifth century) was a French saint. See also Bryce.

Brick: *(brik)* (English) "Bridge." [BRICKMAN, BRIGHAM, BRIK]

Brock: *(brahk)* (English) Variant form of Brook. The related surnames are English and German/Jewish variants of names like Baruch. [BROC, BROCKMAN, BROCKTON, BROXTON]

Broderick: *(BRAH-der-ik)* (Welsh) "Son of Roderick." [BRODERIC, BRODERICK, BRODRIC]

Brodie: *(BROH-dee)* (Scottish) Place name. There is a Castle Brodie in Scotland. [BRODEN, BRODY]

Bronson: *(BRAHN-sun)* (English) "Brown's son." [BRON]

Brooks: *(brux)* (English) "Water, stream." [BROOK, BROOKE]

Bruce: *(brooce)* (Scottish) Surname used since medieval times, now a common given name, especially in Scotland. The tale of "the Bruce" (Robert, King of Scotland in the 14th century), who watched and learned the value of perseverance from a spider spinning a web, has become a part of the world's folklore. Notable in modern times: rock musician Bruce Springsteen and actor Bruce Willis.

Bruno: *(BROO-noh)* (German) "Brown." A saint's name.

Bryan: *(BRY-an)* (English) Very popular variant form of Brian. [BRYON]

Bryant: *(BRY-ant)* (English) Variant form of Brian. Briant (16th century) was an English saint. Notable name bearer: talk show host Bryant Gumbel. [BRIANT]

Bryce: *(bryce)* (Scottish) "Of Britain." Surname form of Brice. [**BRYSON**, BRYCEN, BRYCETON, BRYSTON]

Buck: *(buk)* (English) The word for a male goat or deer, used as a given name or nickname. Also an English slang word used to describe a sportsman, a dandy. [BUCKLEY]

Bud: *(bud)* (English) "Brother." Nickname used since medieval times. [BUDDY]

Buell: *(BYOO-ell)* (German) "Hill dweller." Use of surnames like Buell, Buford, and Beauregard as given names stems from the custom of naming sons after commanding officers during and after the Civil War. In the North, names like Grant and Scott became popular choices.

Burdett: *(ber-DETT)* (French) Surname used as a given name. [BURDETTE]

Burke: *(berk)* (English) "Fortified hill." See also Berkley. [BOURKE]

Burl: *(berl)* (English) "Fortified." Made familiar in the 1950s by folksinger/actor Burl Ives. See also Berlyn. [BURLE, BURLEIGH, BURRELL]

Burne: *(bern)* (English) "Bear; brown." [BURNELL, BURNETTE, BURNEY, BYRNE]

Burt: *(bert)* (English) "Fortified." [BURTON]

Byron: *(BYE-ron)* (English) Surname often used as a given name. The variant form Biron was the name of a character in Shakespeare's *Love's Labours Lost*. [BIRON]

C

Cable: *(KAY-bel)* (English) "Ropemaker." An English surname. [CABE]

Cadell: *(kay-DELL)* (Welsh) "Spirit of battle." Variants may be in reference to Cadoc, a sixth-century Welsh saint. See also Kade. [CADE, CADEN, CADOC, CAYDEN]

Caelan: *(KAY-lan)* (Gaelic) Meaning uncertain; possibly a contemporary variant of Cailean (Scottish). [CAILEAN, CAILIN, CALAN, CALEY]

Caesar: *(SEE-zer)* (Latin) Caesar was the title of the Roman emperors after Augustus Caesar. Czar (Russian) and Kaiser (German) are variant forms. St. Caesarius (fourth century) was physician to two emperors. See also Cesar.

Cain: *(kayn)* (Hebrew) "Something produced." Biblical: Cain, the firstborn son of Adam, killed his brother in jealous anger and spent the rest of his life as a wanderer in exile. See also Kain.

Caine: *(kayn)* (English) Medieval place name and surname. No connection to the biblical Cain. See also Kane.

Cal: *(kal)* (English) Short form of names beginning with *Cal-*.

Calder: *(KAHL-der)* (English, Scottish) "Rough waters."

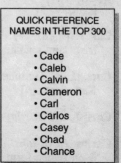

QUICK REFERENCE
NAMES IN THE TOP 300

- Cade
- Caleb
- Calvin
- Cameron
- Carl
- Carlos
- Casey
- Chad
- Chance

Cale: *(kayl)* (English) Surname derived from Charles.

Caleb: *(KAY-leb)* (Hebrew) "Dog; tenacious and aggressive." Biblical: Caleb, a companion of Moses and Joshua, was noted for his astute powers of observation and fearlessness in the face of overwhelming odds.

Callum: *(KAL-um)* (Gaelic) "Dove." See also Colm. [CALUM]

Calvert: *(KAL-vert)* (English) "Cowherd, cowboy." [CAL-BERT]

Calvin: *(KAL-vin)* (Latin) "Bald." A Roman family clan name. Noted name bearer: U.S. President Calvin Coolidge. More familiar in the 1990s due to Bill Watterson's cartoon feature *Calvin and Hobbes.*

Camden: *(KAM-den)* (Scottish) "Winding valley."

Cameron: *(KAM-er-en)* (Scottish) "Bent nose." This nickname of an especially valorous ancestor became the surname of one of the oldest clans in Scotland. [CAM, CAMREN, CAMRON]

Camilo: *(ka-MEE-loh)* (Latin) "Free-born child; noble." Masculine form of Camille. [CAMILLO]

Cardell: *(kar-DEL)* (French) Surname, meaning uncertain. [CARDELLE]

Carey: *(KARE-ee)* (Welsh, Irish) "Of the dark ones." An Irish saint's name (16th century). See also Cary.

Carl: *(karl)* (German) Variant of Charles. See also Carlos and Karl. [CARLIN]

Carlisle: *(KAR-lyle)* (English) "Carl's island." [CARLYLE]

Carlos: *(KAR-lohs)* (Spanish) Variant form of Charles. Carlo is an Italian form. See also Carl. [CARLITO, CARLO]

Carlton: *(KARL-ten)* (English) "Free men's town." See also Charlton. [CARLETON, CARLSON, CARSTON]

Carmelo: *(kar-MAY-loh)* (Hebrew) "Fruitful orchard." Refers to Mount Carmel in Palestine. [CARMELLO]

Carnell: *(kar-NEL)* (English) "Defender of the castle." Carne *(karn)* is a Welsh variant of the English surname Cairn, meaning a landmark or memorial made of piled-up stones. [CARNE, CARNELLE]

Carrick: *(KARE-ik)* (Irish) "Rock."

Carrington: *(KARE-ing-ton)* (English) Place name and surname.

Carson: *(KAR-sen)* (Scottish) Surname, meaning uncertain. [CARSEN]

Carter: *(KAR-ter)* (English) "One who transports goods." An occupational surname. [CARTRELL]

Cary: *(KAR-ee)* (Welsh) "Loving." Noted name bearer: actor Cary Grant. See also Carey.

Casey: *(KAY-see)* (Irish) "Alert; vigorous." See also Kasey. [CACE, CACEY, CASE, CAYCE]

Casimir: *(KAH-zee-meer)* (Slavic) "Enforces peace." A saint's name (15th century). See also Kasimir. [CASIMIRO, CAZ]

Caspar: *(KAS-per)* (Persian) "Keeper of the treasure." In medieval tradition, Caspar was one of the three Magi who traveled from afar to find the baby Jesus. [CASPER]

Cassian: *(KASH-en)* (French) Variant form of Cassius. A fourth-century saint's name.

> **QUICK REFERENCE NAMES IN THE TOP 300**
>
> - Chandler
> - Charles
> - Chase
> - Christian
> - Christopher
> - Clayton
> - Cody
> - Colby
> - Cole

Cassidy: *(KAS-ih-dee)* (Irish, Welsh) "Curly-headed." [CASS]

Cassius: *(KASH-us)* (Latin) Roman family clan name. Shakespeare's Julius Caesar depicts Caius Cassius as politically ambitious. In modern times, Cassius Clay was the birth name of the heavyweight boxing champion Muhammad Ali.

Cecil: *(SESS-ul, SEE-sul)* (Latin) "Blind." Also a Welsh surname. St. Cecilius was a priest of Carthage (third century). [CECILIO]

Cedric: *(SED-rik)* (Welsh) "Gift of splendor." See also Kedrick. [CEDRICK, CEDRIK]

Cedro: *(SED-droh)* (Spanish) Cedro and Cidro *(SEE-droh)* are Spanish short forms of Isadoro.

Cesar: *(sez-ZAR)* Spanish variant form of Caesar. Cezar is a Slavic form. Cesare *(CHEZ-a-ray)* is Italian. Noted name bearer: labor leader Cesar Chavez. See also Caesar. [CESARE, CESARIO, CEZAR, CHEZARE]

Chad: *(chad)* (English) A medieval given name of uncertain meaning. Also a short form of various surnames. St. Chad was a seventh-century English saint. [CHADD, CHADRIC, CHADRICK, CHADWICK]

Chan: *(chahn)* (Spanish) Nickname for John. Chano and Chayo are similar Spanish short forms for names ending in *-ano* and *-rio*. Chan is also a Chinese family name. The Sanskrit name Chan means "shining." [CHANO, CHAYO]

Chance: *(chans)* (English) Variant form of Chauncey *(CHAWN-see)* from the French chancellor. Chance probably is also used in the sense

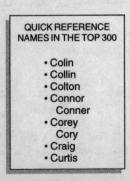

QUICK REFERENCE
NAMES IN THE TOP 300

- Colin
- Collin
- Colton
- Connor
  Conner
- Corey
  Cory
- Craig
- Curtis

of "fortune; a gamble." [CHAUNCE, CHAUNCEY, CHAUNCY, CHONCEY]

Chancellor: *(CHAN-sa-ler)* (French) "Doorkeeper." A surname and title of high office, as in the Lord Chancellor of England or the chancellor of a university. [CHANCELOR]

Chandler: *(CHAND-ler)* (English) "Candlemaker." A surname popular for use as a given name, probably due to the character of Chandler Bing on the TV series *Friends*.

Channing: *(CHAN-een)* (English) "Young wolf." [CHANN, CHANNE, CHANNON]

Charles: *(charlz)* (English, French) "A man." French variant form of Carl, adopted by the English especially since the 17th-century reigns of kings Charles I and II. Charles and its variant forms have been favored by the royalty of several countries, including the present Prince of Wales. Charlie and Charly are occasionally used for girls. See also Arlo, Carl, Carlos, Charlie, Charlton, and Karl. [CHARLESON, CHAS, CHAZ, CHICK, CHUCK]

Charlie: *(CHAR-lee)* (English) Nickname for Charles, popular as an independent name. [CHARLEY, CHARLY]

Charlton: *(CHARL-ten)* (English) "Charles's town." Noted name bearer: actor Charlton Heston. See also Carlton. [CHARLESTON, CHARLETON]

Charro: *(CHAR-oh)* (Spanish) Nickname for a cowboy, especially in Argentina.

Chase: *(chayce)* (English) "Huntsman." [CHACE, CHASEN, CHAYCE]

Che: *(chay)* (Spanish) Short form of Jose, made familiar as a given name by the Latin-American revolutionary Che Guevara.

Cherokee: *(CHARE-oh-kee)* (Native American) "People of a different speech." The name of one of the largest tribes, used as a given name.

Chester: *(CHES-ter)* (English) "Camp of soldiers." [CHESS, CHESTON, CHET]

Chevy: *(CHEV-ee)* (French) "Horseman; knight." A short form of Chevalier. Actor-comedian Chevy Chase has brought the name into modern notice. [CHEVAL, CHEVALIER, CHEVALL]

Cheyne: *(chayn)* (French) "Oak-hearted." [CHANE, CHANEY, CHAYNE, CHENEY]

Chico: *(CHEE-koh)* (Spanish) "Boy, lad." Also a Spanish short form of Ezekiel.

Chiko: *(chee-koh)* (Japanese) "Arrow; pledge."

Chris: *(kris)* (English) Short form of Christopher and Christian. Cris is a Spanish form. [CRIS]

Christian: *(KRIS-chen)* (Greek) "Follower of Christ, the Anointed." The *Cr-* spellings are Spanish forms. Occasionally used for girls. Noted name bearer: actor Christian Slater. [**CRISTIAN**, CHRISTAN, CHRISTOS, CRISTIEN, CRISTON, CRISTOS]

LESS COMMON CLASSICS;
NEW, UNUSUAL NAMES

- Caden
- Camden
- Carlton
- Carson
- Carter
- Cedric
- Cesar
- Chaz
- Clarence
- Clay

Christopher: *(KRIS-toh-fer)* (Latin) "With Christ inside." The legend of St. Christopher as the patron saint of travelers grew from the story of a giant who made his living carrying people across a river. According to the legend, one day he carried across a child whom he discovered was actually Christ. Christofer and Christoffer are German forms. Christophe *(kris-TAWF)* is French. See also Cristofer. [CHRISTOFER, CHRISTOFFER, CHRISTOPHE]

Cisco: *(SIS-koh)* (Spanish) Diminutive of Francisco.

Clancy: *(KLAN-see)* (Irish) "Red-headed fighter."

Clarence: *(KLARE-ence)* (Latin) "Bright, shining; gentle." Noted name bearer: author Clarence Day.

Clark: *(klark)* (English) "Cleric, secretary." Noted name bearer: the fictional Clark Kent of *Superman* fame. [CLARKE]

Claude: *(klawd)* (Latin) "Lame." Claudius was the Roman emperor who succeeded Caligula. St. Claudius (third century) was a Roman tribune who converted to Christianity. [CLAUD, CLAUDIO, CLAUDIUS]

Clayton: *(KLAYT-'en)* (English) Place name and surname derived from Clay. [CLAIBORNE, CLAY, CLAYBORNE, CLAYBURN]

Clement: *(KLEM-ent)* (Latin) "Clemency, mercy." A name borne by 14 popes. Clemens is a Danish form. [CLEM, CLEMENS, CLEMENTE]

Cletus: *(KLEE-tus, KLAY-tus)* (Greek) "Illustrious." A short form of Anacletus. St. Cletus (first century) was elected Pope in A.D. 76. [CLEO, CLEON, CLETE, CLETIS, CLEYTUS]

Cleveland: *(KLEEV-land)* (English) "Land of cliffs." [CLEVE]

Clifford: *(KLIF-erd)* (English) "Cliff-side ford." [CLIFF, CLYFORD]

Clifton: *(KLIF-ten)* (English) "Town by the cliff."

Clinton: *(KLIN-ten)* (English) "Hillside town." Famous name bearer: actor Clint Eastwood. [CLINT]

Clive: *(kleeve, klyve)* (English) "Cliff." [CLEAVON, CLEVE]

Clovis: *(KLOH-viss)* (German) "Renowned fighter." Variant form of Louis.

Clyde: *(klyd)* (Scottish) Refers to the Clyde River in Scotland.

Coburn: *(KOH-bern)* (Scottish, English) Surname and place name. [COBY]

Cochise: *(ko-CHEECE)* (Native American) The name of a renowned warrior, chief of the Chiricahua Apache.

Cody: *(KOH-dee)* (Irish, English) "Helpful." See also Kody. [CODELL, CODEY, CODIE]

Colby: *(KOHL-bee)* (English) "Dark, dark-haired." See also Kolby. [COLBERT, COLBEY]

Cole: *(kohl)* (English) A short form of Nicholas. The related surname Colman is also a saint's name. [COLEMAN, COLEY, COLMAN, COLSON]

Colin: *(KOH-lin, KAH-lin)* (English, Irish, Scottish) Short form of Nicholas. See also Collin. [COLAN, COLYN]

Collier: *(KAWL-yer)* (English) "Coal miner."

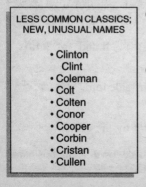

LESS COMMON CLASSICS;
NEW, UNUSUAL NAMES

- Clinton
  Clint
- Coleman
- Colt
- Colten
- Conor
- Cooper
- Corbin
- Cristan
- Cullen

Collin: *(KAH-lin)* (Scottish) Variant form of Colin. [COLLEN, COLLINS]

Colm: *(kolm)* (Irish) "Of St. Columba." A name used in reference to St. Columba (sixth century) of Ireland, who founded the monastery of Iona. Modern name bearer: actor Colm Meaney of *Star Trek: Deep Space Nine* fame. See also Callum. [COLUM]

Colt: *(kolt)* (English) "Young horse; frisky." Variants are English surnames used as given names. [COLTER, COLTRANE, COULTER]

Colton: *(KOHL-ton)* (English) "Coal town." See also Kolton. [COLTEN]

Conan: *(KOH-nan)* (Irish, Scottish) "Hound." St. Conan (seventh century) was an Irish missionary on the Isle of Man. A name made familiar in the 1980s through the novels and movies about *Conan the Barbarian*. Noted name bearers: talk show host Conan O'Brien and Sir Arthur Conan Doyle, author of the Sherlock Holmes mysteries.

Connal: *(KAHN-al)* (Irish) "High; mighty." [CONAL, CONALL, CONN, CONNELL]

Connor: *(KAH-ner)* (Irish) "Hound-lover." See also Konnor. [CONNER, CONOR]

Conrad: *(KAHN-rad)* (German, Slavic) "Brave; wise." The name of nine saints. See also Konrad.

Conroy: *(KAHN-roy)* (Irish) "Wise advisor."

Constantine: *(KAHN-stan-teen)* (Latin) "Constant, steadfast." Notable name bearer: Constantine the Great, the fourth-century emperor who made Christianity the official state religion of the Roman Empire. [CONSTANTINO]

Conway: *(KAHN-way)* (Welsh) Place name and surname.

Cooper: *(KOO-per)* (English) "Barrelmaker." May also be the English form of a German surname meaning "coppersmith."

Corbett: *(KOR-bet)* (French) "Raven." [CORBET, CORBY]

Corbin: *(KOR-bin)* (French) "Raven-haired." St. Corbinian was a seventh-century French saint. Variants are English

surnames used as given names. Modern name bearer: actor
Corbin Bernsen. See also Korbin. [CORBEN, CORBYN, COR-
VIN]

Cordell: *(kor-DEL)* (English) "Cordmaker." See also Kor-
dell. [CORD, CORDALE, CORDAY]

Cordero: *(kor-DARE-oh)* (Spanish) "Lamb." [CORD]

Corey: *(KOR-ee)* (English, Irish) "Hill hollow." See also
Cory and Kory. [CORLEY, CORREY, CORRICK, CORRY]

Cormac: *(KOR-mac)* (Irish) "Raven's son." Historical: the
third-century Irish king who founded schools of military
science, law, and literature at Tara. St. Cormac (10th century) was king of Munster, Ireland. [CORMACK, CORMICK]

Cornelius: *(kor-NEEL-yus)* (Latin) "Horn; hornblower." Biblical: Cornelius was a Roman centurion who was baptized
by Peter. [CORNEL, CORNELIO, CORNELL]

Corrin: *(KOR-in)* (Irish) "Spear-bearer." [CORIN, CORLAN,
CORRAN, CORREN]

Cort: *(kort)* (English) "Courtier, court attendant." Variant
form of Courtney. Courtney now is used primarily for girls.
See also Curt, Kort, and Kurt. [CORTLAND, COURT, COURT-
LAND, COURTENAY, COURTNEY]

Cortez: *(kor-TEZ)* (Spanish) "Courteous." Variant of Curtis.
Historical: surname of the Spanish explorer and adventurer
who with a small expeditionary force conquered the Aztec
civilization of Mexico. [CORTES]

Corwin: *(KOR-wen)* (Gaelic) "From beyond the hill." [COR-
WYN]

Cory: *(KOR-ee)* (English) Surname. See also Corey and Kory.

Coyan: *(KOY-an)* (French) "Modest." [COYNE]

Coyle: *(koyl)* (Irish) "Leader in battle."

Craig: *(krayg)* (Scottish) "Rock, rocky."

Creed: *(kreed)* (English) "Belief; guiding principle." Creedon is an Irish surname. [CREEDON]

Creighton: *(KRAYT-en)* (Scottish) "Border dweller." [CRAYTON]

Crispin: *(KRIS-pin)* (Latin) "Curly-haired." St. Crispin was a third-century martyr who came to be known as the patron of shoemakers, especially in England. Modern name bearer: actor Crispin Glover. [CRESPIN]

Cristian: (Latin) "Follower of Christ." See Christian. [CRYSTIAN]

Cristofer: *(kris-TOH-fer)* (Latin) Spanish form of Christopher. [**CRISTOPHER**, CRISTOFOR, CRISTOVAL]

Croydon: *(KROYD-en)* (English) Surname and place name. [CROY]

Cruz: *(krooz)* (Spanish, Portuguese) "Cross." [CRUZITO]

Cullen: *(KULL-en)* (Irish) "Good-looking lad." [CULLAN, CULLIN]

Curran: *(KER-an)* (Gaelic) "Dagger." [CURRIE, CURRY]

Curt: *(kert)* (English) Short form of Curtis. See also Cort and Kurt.

Curtis: *(KERT-iss)* (English) "Courteous." See also Curt, Kort, and Kurtis. [CURTISS]

Cyd: *(sid)* (English) Variant short form of Sydney.

Cydney: *(SID-nee)* (English) Variant form of Sydney. Cyd is the short form.

Cyrano: *(SEER-a-noh)* (French) Cyrano de Bergerac was a 17th-century soldier and science fiction writer. His talents and his extraordinary nose provided the inspiration for Rostand's *Cyrano de Bergerac*. Cyran was a seventh-century French saint. [CYRAN]

Cyril: *(SEER-el)* (Greek) "Master, lord." The name of at least eight saints. [CY, CYRILL]

Cyrus: *(SY-russ)* (Persian) "Enthroned." Historical: Cyrus the Great conquered Babylon at the height of its powers and founded the Persian Empire. Biblical: Cyrus is prophetically named in the book of Isaiah as the one who would overthrow Babylon and liberate the captive Israelites. Also the name of a fourth-century saint, a doctor in Alexandria.

Czar: *(zar)* (Russian) "Caesar, emperor." See also Cesar.

D

Da- and D'-: (American) Blends of *Da-* plus various endings, with pronunciation emphasis on the second syllable. Names beginning with *D'-* (meaning "of") follow an Italian style of surnames. See also Damario, *De-*, and Deshawn. [D'AMANTE, D'AMICO, D'ANDRE, D'ANGELO, DAJOHN, DAJON, DAJUAN, DAMAR, DAMARCO, DAMARKO, DAMONE, DAMONT, DAMONTE, DAQUAN, DASEAN, DASHAE, DASHAUN, DASHAWN, DASHONN, DAVAR, DAVAUGHN, DAVON, DAWAYNE]

Dace: *(dayce)* (French) "Of the nobility." May also be used as a form of Dasius or Datius, saints' names from the fourth and sixth centuries. Dacio is a Spanish name meaning "from Dacia." [DACEY, DACIAN, DACIO]

Dadrian: *(DAY-dree-en)* (American) A contemporary rhyming variant of Adrian. [DADE]

Daegan: *(DAY-gan)* (Irish) "Black-haired." Variant form of Deegan. [DAGEN, DEEGAN]

Dag: *(dag)* (Scandinavian) "Day." Mythology: the son of Night who brought the daylight as he rode his horse around the earth. Famous name bearer: U.N. Secretary-General and Nobel Peace Prize winner Dag Hammarskjöld. [DAEG]

Dai: *(dah-ee)* (Japanese) "Large." Also a Welsh short form of David.

Dakota: *(da-KOH-tah)* (Native American) "Friend, ally." Tribal name. [DAKOTAH]

Dale: *(dayl)* (English) "Valley." [DAEL, DALEN]

Dallan: *(DAL-en)* (Irish) "Blind." St. Dallan of Ireland (sixth century) was a poet known for his great learning. [DAL, DALAN, DALLEN, DALLIN, DALLON, DALON]

Dallas: *(DAL-iss)* (Scottish) "From the dales, the valley meadows." Name of the Texas city and surname used as a given name.

Dalton: *(DOLL-ton)* (English) "From the valley town." See also Delton. [DAULTON]

Damario: *(da-MAH-ree-oh)* (Spanish) Masculine form of Damaris. (Greek) "Gentle." [DEMARIO]

Damian: *(DAY-mee-en)* (Greek) Variant of Damon. The Belgian priest Father Damien is honored as the man who gave his life helping the lepers of Molokai in Hawaii. St.

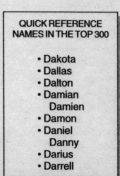

QUICK REFERENCE
NAMES IN THE TOP 300

- Dakota
- Dallas
- Dalton
- Damian
  Damien
- Damon
- Daniel
  Danny
- Darius
- Darrell

Damian (third century) is known as the patron saint of physicians. [**DAMIEN**, DAMIANO, DAMION]

Damon: *(DAY-mon)* (Greek) "One who tames, subdues." [DAMAN, DAYMON]

Dan: *(dan)* (Hebrew) "Judge." Biblical: Dan was the fifth son of Jacob and founder of one of the 12 tribes of Israel. While Dan is an independent name, it's also used as a short form of Daniel. [DANN]

Dana: *(DAY-nah)* Variant of Daniel or Dane.

Dane: *(dayn)* (English) "From Denmark." Variants Daine and Dayne are English/French surnames occasionally used as given names. [DAIN, DAINE, DANON, DAYNE, DAYNER]

Daniel: *(DAN-yel)* (Hebrew) "God is my judge." Biblical: the prophet and writer of the book of Daniel was a teenager when he was taken to Babylon after the destruction of Jerusalem in 607 B.C. He survived a politically motivated death sentence in a lions' den. Many prominent men have had the name since, among them statesman Daniel Webster and frontiersman Daniel Boone. Danilo is a Spanish form; Dantrell is a contemporary blended variant. [DANNY, DANELL, DANILO, DANTRELL]

QUICK REFERENCE
NAMES IN THE TOP 300

• Darren
• David
• Dennis
• Derek
  Derrick
• Destin
• Devin
• Devon
  Devan
• Dillon

Danno: *(dah-noh)* (Japanese) "Field gathering." Surname.

Dante: *(DAHN-tay)* (Spanish, Italian) "Enduring." Historical: Dante Alighieri, considered one of the great poets of all time, wrote *The Divine Comedy*, notable for the graphic description of the medieval version of Hell known as Dante's Inferno. See also Donte. [DANTAE, DANTEL, DAUNTE]

Danton: *(dan-TONE, dan-TAHN, DAN-tun)* (French) Variant of Anthony. [D'ANTON]

Darby: *(DAR-bee)* (Irish) "Without envy."

Darcel: *(dar-SELL)* (French) "Dark." Variant of the surnames Darcy or D'Arcy. [DARCELL, DARCIO, DARCY, D'ARCY]

Darence: *(DARE-ence)* (American) Blend of Darrell and Clarence. [DARRANCE, DARRENCE, DERRANCE]

Darin: *(DARE-en)* (English) Meaning uncertain; possibly a form of Darren (Irish). Darin and the variants listed here are surnames. Usage may be to preserve a family surname or may be phonetic variations of the basic sound of Darin. [DARAN, DAREN, DARON, DARRIN, DARRON, DARRYN, DARYN, DERREN, DERRIAN, DERRIN]

Dario: *(DAR-ee-oh)* (Latin) Variant of Darius.

Darion: *(DARE-ee-un)* (Greek) "Gift" or possibly a variant of Darius. Of unknown origin, Darien has poetic significance; John Keats described the moment of discovery when explorers stood "silent, upon a peak in Darien." [DARIAN, DARIEN, DARRIAN, DARRIEN, DARRION]

Darius: *(da-RYE-us, DARE-ee-us)* (Medo-Persian) "He possesses." Possibly a royal title, like Caesar. Historical: Darius the Mede assumed the kingship of Babylon after its conquest by Cyrus. See also Dario. [DARRIUS]

Darnell: *(dar-NEL)* (English) "Hidden." Place name and surname. [DARNEIL, DARNEL]

Darold: *(DARE-old)* (American) Blend of Daryl and Harold or Gerald. [DARROLD, DERALD, DERROLD]

Darrell: *(DARE-el)* (English) "Open." A surname and given name that dates from at least the 11th century. Darrell is much favored for spelling variants in every possible combination. See also Darryl. [DAREL, DARIEL, DARIELL, DAR-ROLL, DERELL, DERRALL, DERRELL, DERRILL]

Darren: *(DARE-en)* (Irish) Origin uncertain. Possible meaning: "little great one." See also Darin.

Darrick: *(DARE-ik)* (American) Variant spelling of Derrick, from Derek, or a phonetic spelling of Darroch. See also Darroch and Derek. [DARIC, DARICK]

Darroch: *(DARE-ahk)* (Irish) "Strong; oak-hearted." See also Derek. [DARROCK]

Darryl: *(DARE-ul)* (English) Variant of Darrell. Daryl is occasionally used for girls. Noted name bearer: baseball player Darryl Strawberry. See also Darrell. [DARYL, DARREL, DARRYLL, DARYLE, DARYLL, DERRYL]

Dartagnan: *(dar-TAN-yan)* (French) Dumas's swashbuckling tale *The Three Musketeers* was based on the real D'artagnan's memoirs.

Darvell: *(dar-VEL)* (French) "Town of eagles."

Darvin: *(DAR-vin)* (English) Blend of Daryl and Marvin, or a variant form of Darwin. [DERVIN]

Darwin: *(DAR-win)* (English) "Dear friend." Historical: Charles Darwin, 19th-century naturalist, was the first major exponent of human evolution. [DARWYN]

David: *(DAY-vid)* (Hebrew) "Beloved." Biblical: one of the most remarkable personalities in the Scriptures. David was a shepherd, musician, poet, soldier, statesman, prophet, and king. He wrote about half of the Psalms and very likely

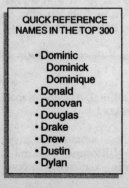

QUICK REFERENCE
NAMES IN THE TOP 300

- Dominic
  Dominick
  Dominique
- Donald
- Donovan
- Douglas
- Drake
- Drew
- Dustin
- Dylan

composed music for them as well. He is the only David mentioned in the Bible; his name occurs there more than a thousand times. Today there are variants of the name in almost every language group. St. David (sixth century) is the patron saint of Wales. See also Dai, Davion, Davis, Davyn, and Dawson. [DAVE, DAVEY, DAVIE, DAVIEL, DAVY]

Davion: *(DAY-vee-an)* (American) Blend of David and Darrion. [DAVEON]

Davis: *(DAY-viss)* (English) Surname. Variant of David. [DAVIDSON, DAVIES, DAVISON, DAYSON, DAYTON]

Davon: *(DAY-ven, da-VAHN)* (American) Contemporary variant of Davyn or a use of *Da-* plus Von. See also *Da-* and Davyn. [DAVONN]

Davyn: *(DAY-ven, DAV-en)* (Welsh) Variant form of David. Davin is a French form. [DAVIN]

Dawson: *(DAW-sun)* (English) "David's son." Surname occasionally used as a given name.

Dax: *(daks)* (French) Place name; a town in southwestern France that dates from before the days of the Roman occupation. Familiar today as the name of a character on the TV show *Star Trek: Deep Space Nine*. [DACK, DAXTON]

Daylon: *(DAY-len)* (American) Daylon and its variants probably are rhyming variants of the name Waylon, or are uses of various surnames as given names. [DAELAN, DALEN, DALYN, DAYLAN, DAYLEN, DAYLIN, DEYLIN]

De-: (American) Blend of *De-* plus various endings, with pronunciation emphasis on the second syllable. These given names follow the French style of aristocratic surnames using the prefix *de-*. Capitalizing the second syllable is optional; names of this type appear both ways in contemporary usage. See also *Da-*, Deandre, and DeShawn.

[DEANGELO, DEANTE, DEANTHONY, DEJOHN, DEJON, DE-
JUAN, DELEON, DELON, DELORAN, DELOREAN, DEMAR, DE-
MARCO, DEMARCOS, DEMARCUS, DEMARIO, DEMARR,
DEMAURI, DEMOND, DEMONTE, DEONDRE, DEONTAE,
DEONTE, DERELLE, DEROYCE, DESEAN, DESHAY, DEVAL, DE-
VANE, DEVANTE, DEVAUGHN, DEVAUN, DEVELL, DEVONN,
DEVONTE, DEWAYNE]

Deacon: *(DEE-ken)* (Greek) "Dusty one; servant." Title of a
ministerial assistant in a Christian congregation. [DEAKIN,
DEKE, DEKEL, DEKLE]

Dean: *(deen)* (English) "From the valley." Dean is a surname
and a title name, signifying a church official or the head of
a school. In the news in the 1990s: actor Dean Cain. [DE-
ANE, DENE]

Deandre: *(dee-AHN-dray, dee-ahn-DRAY)* (American) An especially popular *De-* name. See also Andre. [D'ANDRE,
DEANDRAE, DEANDRE]

Declan: *(DECK-lan)* (Irish) The name of an Irish saint (sixth
century).

Dedrick: *(DEE-drik)* (Dutch) "Gifted ruler." Variant form of
Diedrick. Dieter is a German form. [DEDRIC, DIEDRICK, DI-
ETER, DIETRICH]

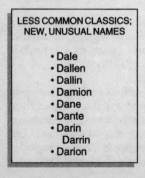

LESS COMMON CLASSICS;
NEW, UNUSUAL NAMES

• Dale
• Dallen
• Dallin
• Damion
• Dane
• Dante
• Darin
   Darrin
• Darion

Deion: *(DEE-ahn)* (American) Variant form of Dion, from Dionysus. Noted name bearer: football
player Deion Sanders. [DEON]

Deker: *(DEH-ker)* (Hebrew)
"Piercing." Biblical: Deker was
the father of one of Solomon's 12
deputies. [DECKER, DEKKER]

Del: *(del)* (French) Surname prefix
meaning "of the." Used today as

an independent name and as a short form of names beginning with *Del-*.

Delaney: *(de-LANE-ee)* (Irish) "Dark challenger." (French) "From the elder tree grove." [DELANE, DELANIE, DELANO]

Delbert: *(DEL-bert)* (English) "Noble; bright." [DALBERT]

Delmar: *(DEL-mar)* (French) "Of the sea." [DELMER, DELMORE]

Delmon: *(DEL-mun)* (English) "Of the mountain." The English surname Delman means "man from the valley." [DELMAN, DELMONT]

Delroy: *(DEL-roy)* (French) "From the king." [DELRAY, DELRICK, DELRICO, DELRON]

Delton: *(DEL-tun)* (English) "From the town in the valley." See also Dalton.

Delvin: *(DEL-vin)* (English, Irish) "Godly friend." [DELVON, DELWIN, DELWYN]

Demetrius: *(de-MEE-tree-us)* (Greek) "Of Demeter." Mythology: Demeter is the Greek goddess of corn and harvest. Her withdrawal for the part of the year that her daughter Persephone must spend with the god of the underworld is the reason for winter. St. Demetrius (fourth century), together with St. George, was patron saint of the Crusaders. See also Dimitri. [DEMETRI, DEMETRIO, DEMITRI, DEMITRIUS]

Denis: *(de-NEES)* (French) Variant form of Dionysius. St. Denis (third century) was the first bishop of Paris and is the patron saint of France. [DENYS]

> LESS COMMON CLASSICS;
> NEW, UNUSUAL NAMES
>
> • Darnell
> • Darryl
> • Davis
> • Dean
> • Deandre
> • Deion
>   Deon
> • DeMarcus
> • Demetrius

Dennis: *(DEN-iss)* (English) Variant of Dionysius. Mythology: Dionysius is the Greek god of wine, responsible for the growth of the vines in spring and the originator of wine-making; he is equivalent to the Roman god Bacchus. Biblical: a judge of Athens who was converted to Christianity by the apostle Paul. In the news in the 1990s: basketball player Dennis Rodman. [DENNIE, DENNISON, DENNY]

Denver: *(DEN-ver)* (English, French) Possibly a variant of the French surname Danvers, meaning "from Anvers." Contemporary use may refer to the name of the capital city of Colorado. Notable name bearer: actor Denver Pyle.

Denzel: *(DEN-zul)* (English) A place-name in Cornwall. Noted name bearer: actor Denzel Washington. [DENZELL, DENZIL]

Derek: *(DARE-ik)* (English) "Gifted ruler." From Theodoric. Many phonetic variants have come into popular usage. See also Darrick, Darroch, and Dirk. [DAREK, DERECK, DERICK, DERIK, DERREK, DERRICK, DERRIK, DERYCK, DERYK]

Derry: *(DARE-ee)* (Irish) "Oak grove." Surname; also the original name of the Irish city of Londonderry.

Derwin: *(DER-win)* (English) "Gifted friend." Derwent is a similar-sounding English surname referring to the Derwent River in England. [DERVIN, DERVON, DERWENT, DERWYN, DURWIN]

Des: *(dez)* (English) Short form of names beginning with *Des-*, occasionally used as an independent name.

Deshawn: *(de-SHAWN)* (American) DeShawn is an especially popular prefix name. See also *De-* and *Da-*. [DESEAN, DE-SHANE, DESHAUN, DESHON]

Desi: *(DEZ-ee)* (Latin) "Yearning; sorrow." Short form of Desiderus. [DEZI]

Desmond: *(DEZ-mund)* (Gaelic) "From South Munster." An Irish surname referring to Munster, one of the five regions of ancient Ireland. [DESMUND, DEZMOND]

Destin: *(DESS-tin, des-TEEN)* (French) "Destiny." The French surname Destan means "by the still waters." [DESTAN, DESTON]

Destry: *(DESS-tree)* (English) Variant of a French surname. Destry has the flavor of the American west due to the classic Western film *Destry Rides Again*. [DESTREY, DESTRIE]

Dev: *(dev)* (English) Short form of names beginning with *Dev-*. Also a Sanskrit title meaning "divine, god."

Deverel: *(DEV-er-al)* (French) Surname; a variant form of Deveraux, referring to a location in France. [DEVERAL, DEVEREAU, DEVEREAUX, DEVERELL]

Devin: *(DEV-in)* (French) "Divine, perfect." Devin is a favored name for boys. There are numerous spelling variants. See also Devon.

Devlin: *(DEV-lin)* (Irish) "Misfortune." [DEVLAND, DEVLON, DEVLYN]

Devon: *(DEV-en)* (English) Name of the county in England, noted for its beautiful farmland. See also Devin. [DEAVON, DEVAN, DEVEN, DEVEON, DEVION, DEVONN, DEVRON, DEVYN]

Dewey: *(DOO-ee)* (English) Place name and surname; possibly a Welsh form of David.

Dexter: *(DEKS-ter)* (Latin) "Right-handed." [DEX, DEXTON]

Dick: *(dik)* (English) One of the rhyming nicknames from medie-

LESS COMMON CLASSICS;
NEW, UNUSUAL NAMES

- Denzel
- Desmond
- Devante
- Devonte
- Dexter
- Diego
- Dorian
- Duncan
- Dwayne

val times. Richard was shortened to Rick, then rhymed to Dick, and variants like Dickson and Dix (which is also the French word meaning "ten") followed. Today Dick is rarely used as an independent name. See also Richard. [DICKSON, DIX, DIXON]

Diego: *(dee-AY-go)* (Spanish) Variant of James.

Dillon: *(DIL-un)* (Irish) "Like a lion." See also Dylan. [DILAN, DILLEN]

Dimitri: *(de-MEE-tree)* (Slavic) Variant of Demetrius. In Catholic tradition, Dimas *(DEE-mas)* was the name of the compassionate thief who died with Jesus at Calgary. See also Demetrius. [DIMAS, DIMITRIOS, DIMETRIUS]

Dino: *(DEE-no)* (Italian, Spanish) Short form ending of names like Bernardino.

Dion: *(DYE-on, DEE-on)* (Greek) Short form of Dionysius. Diandre and Diondre are blends of Dion and Andre. See also Deion. [DEON, DIANDRE, DIONDRE, DIONTE, DONDRE]

Dirk: *(derk)* (Dutch) "Ruler." Variant of Derek and Dietrich. See also Dedrick.

Dolan: *(DOH-lan)* (Irish) "Dark; bold."

Dolphus: *(DOLL-fuss)* (German) Short form of Adolphus.

Dominic: *(DAH-ma-nik)* (Latin) "Of the lord." The French spelling of Dominique is also used for girls. A saint's name. [**DOMINICK, DOMINIQUE**, DOMENICO, DOMINGO, DOMINICO, DOMINIK]

Don: *(dahn)* (English) Short form of names beginning with *Don-*. Mythology: the Irish Donn was known as king of the underworld. Use of the Welsh Gaelic surname Donne as a given name may be in honor of John Donne, the 17th-century poet. Donnan was a seventh-century Irish saint. [DONN, DONNAN, DONNE, DONNIE, DONNY]

Donald: *(DAHN-ald)* (Scottish) "Great chief." Donald is one of the clan names of Scotland. See also Donnell.

Donato: *(doh-NAH-toh)* (Spanish, Italian) "Gift from God." A short form of Donatello. [DONATELLO, DONZEL]

Donnell: *(DAHN-el, don-NEL)* (Scottish, Irish) "World mighty." Also used as a variant of Donald. [DONAL, DO-NELL, DONNEL]

Donovan: *(DAH-na-vun)* (Irish) "Brown-haired chieftain." [DONAVAN, DONAVON]

Donte: *(DAHN-tee, dahn-TAY)* (American) Contemporary phonetic variant of Dante. See also Dante. [DONTAE, DON-TAY, DONTAYE, DONTELL, DONTRELL]

Dorian: *(DOR-ee-en)* (Greek) "Descendant of Dorus." Literary: in Oscar Wilde's novel *The Picture of Dorian Gray*, Dorian was granted the wish that he would retain perpetual youth and beauty. A portrait of him changed to show the ravages of time and eventually caused his death. [DORIEN, DORION]

Doron: *(DOR-en)* (Israeli) "Dweller."

Dorran: *(DOR-en)* (Irish) "Dark-browed." Contemporary usage of Dorran and other related surnames listed here as variants is probably influenced by the rhyming patterns of favored names like Darren, Darryl, and Torrance. [DORAN, DORRANCE, DORREL, DORRELL, DORREN, DORRIN]

Douglas: *(DUG-less)* (Scottish) "From the dark river." Historical: there were two branches of this powerful Scottish clan and family—the Black Douglases and the Red Douglases. The lords of these clans are key figures in Sir Walter Scott's novels. [DOUG, DOUGLASS]

Dov: *(dahv)* (Hebrew) "Bear."

Dover: *(DOH-ver)* (Welsh) "Water." Name of the British seaport on the English Channel.

Doyle: *(doyl)* (Irish) "Dark stranger."

Drake: *(drayk)* (English) "Dragon." From Drakon (Greek). Drago is an Italian form; Draco is Latin. [DRACO, DRACON, DRAGO, DRAKON]

Drew: *(droo)* (English) Short form of Andrew. Dru is a French form. [DRU, DRUE]

Duane: *(d'wayn)* (Irish) "Dark." Historical note: many Irish and Scottish names have the meaning "dark" or "black." Most Gaels had brown hair and dark skin coloring that contrasted with the fair hair and pale skin of Norwegian and Swedish invaders. Duante *(d'wan-TAY)* is a contemporary creation. See also Dwayne. [DUANTE, DUAYNE, DUWAYNE]

Duarte: *(d'-WAR-tay)* (Spanish) "Prosperous guardian." Variant of Edward. [DUARDO]

Dugan: *(DOO-gen)* (Gaelic) "Dark."

Duke: *(dook)* (English) Title used as a nickname or given name. Duke is also a short form of Marmaduke. Duke has Western associations because it was the nickname of actor John Wayne, best known for his roles in films of the American West.

Dumont: *(doo-MONT)* (French) "Of the mountain."

Duncan: *(DUN-kin)* (Scottish) "Dark warrior." Literary: in Shakespeare's *Macbeth*, Duncan is king of Scotland.

Dunstan: *(DUN-sten)* (English) "Brown stone." St. Dunstan (10th century) restored the monastery system in England after the devastating Viking raids of previous decades.

Durand: *(der-RAND)* (French) "Firm, enduring." [DURAN, DURANT, DURANTE, DURRANT]

Durbin: *(DER-bin)* (Latin) "City-dweller."

Dureau: *(dur-ROW)* (French) "Strong." [DURELL, DURRELL]

Dustin: *(DUS-tin)* (English) "A fighter." The exposure given to this name by actor Dustin Hoffman has been a major influence on contemporary usage. Popularity is also influenced by the rhyming similarity to another favored name, Justin. [DUSTAN, DUSTON, DUSTY, DUSTYN]

Duval: *(doo-VAL)* (French) "Of the valley."

Dwade: *(dwayd)* (American) This blend of Dwayne and Wade could be given the combined meaning "dark traveler."

Dwayne: *(d'wayn)* (Irish) "Dark." See also Duane. [DA-WAYNE, DEWAYNE, DWAIN, DWAINE, DWANE]

Dwight: *(Rhymes with light)* (English) Surname, meaning uncertain. Noted name bearer: U.S. President Dwight David Eisenhower.

Dylan: *(DIL-an)* (Welsh) "From the sea." Mythology: a legendary Welsh hero. See also Dillon. [DYLLAN, DYLLON]

E

Eagan: *(EE-gan)* (Irish) "Fiery; forceful." [EGAN, EGON]

Eamon: *(EE-mon, AY-mon)* (Irish) "Prosperous protector." Variant of Edmund. [EAMES]

Earl: *(erl)* (English) "Nobleman." Name based on the English title. [EARLE, ERLE]

Easton: *(EES-tun)* (English) "From East town." [EATON]

Eben: *(EBB-an, EE-ben)* (Hebrew) "Stone." Biblical: a memorial stone erected by the prophet Samuel to mark a critical defeat and a victory in Jewish history. [EBAN]

Eddie: *(ED-ee)* (English) Short form of names beginning with *Ed-*. [ED, EDDY]

Eden: *(EED'n)* (Hebrew) "Pleasure." Biblical: the name of the gardenlike first home of Adam and Eve. Also used for girls.

Eder: *(EE-der)* (Hebrew) "Flock." Biblical: the tower of Eder near Hebron was built as a watchtower from which shepherds could watch their flocks. The name became a symbol of God's watchfulness over his people.

Edgar: *(ED-gar)* (English) "Fortunate and powerful." Edgardo is the Spanish form. [EDGARDO]

Edison: *(ED-ih-sun)* (English) "Son of the fortunate warrior." [EDSON]

Edmund: *(ED-mund)* (English) "Prosperous protector." See also Eamon. [EDMON, EDMOND, EDMUNDO]

QUICK REFERENCE
NAMES IN THE TOP 300

- Eddie
- Edward
- Edwin
- Eli
- Elijah
- Eric
  Erik
- Ethan
- Evan

Edric: *(ED-rik)* (English) "Power and good fortune." [EDDRICK, EDRICK, EDRIK]

Edsel: *(ED-sul)* (German) "Noble; bright."

Edward: *(ED-werd)* (English) "Prosperous guardian." A favorite name of British royalty. Eduard is a

French form; Eduardo is Spanish and Portuguese. See also Eddie and Ned. [EDUARD, EDUARDO, EDWARDO]

Edwin: *(ED-win)* (English) "Rich in friendship." St. Edwin (sixth century) was an Anglo-Saxon king. [EDWYN]

Efrain: *(eh-fra-EEN)* (Spanish) Variant form of Ephraim. See also Efron and Ephraim. [EFREN, EFRAN]

Efron: *(EFF-ron)* (Hebrew) "Young stag." [EPHRON]

Einar: *(EYE-nar)* (Scandinavian) "One warrior." [EINER]

Ekon: *(EE-kun)* (Nigerian) "Strong."

Elam: *(EE-lam)* (Hebrew) Biblical: one of the five sons of Noah's son Shem.

Elbert: *(EL-bert)* (German) "Bright; famous." [ELBER]

Eldred: *(EL-dred)* (English) "Old/wise ruler." St. Eldred (ninth century) was a Benedictine slain by Vikings. Eldridge Cleaver was a noted African-American writer. [ELDRIAN, ELDRICK, ELDRIDGE, ELDWIN]

Eleazar: *(el-ee-AY-zar)* (Hebrew) "God has helped." Biblical: the son of Aaron and later his successor as high priest of Israel. [ELIEZER, ELIAZAR]

Elgin: *(EL-jin)* (English) "Noble, white." [ELGINE, ELJIN]

Eli: *(EE-lye)* (Hebrew) "Ascended; my God." Biblical: Eli was a high priest who judged Israel for 40 years and instructed the boy Samuel. [ELY]

Elias: *(ee-LYE-us)* (Greek) Variant short form of Elijah. [ELIA]

LESS COMMON CLASSICS;
NEW, UNUSUAL NAMES

- Earl
- Eduardo
- Elias
- Elliot
  Elliott
- Emmanuel
- Enrique
- Erick
- Everett

Elihu: *(ee-LYE-hew)* "My God is He." Biblical: a young man whose fiery defense of God's righteousness is recounted in the Book of Job.

Elijah: *(ee-LYE-jah)* (Hebrew) "My God is Jehovah." Biblical: Elijah, one of the foremost prophets of Israel. The Book of Kings recounts many miracles performed for and by him. Notable in the 1990s: actor Elijah Wood. See also Elias, Elliot, Ellis, and Ilya. [ELIJA]

Elisha: *(ee-LYE-shah)* (Hebrew) "God is salvation." Biblical: faithful attendant and successor to the prophet Elijah. Sometimes used for girls as a variant of Elise.

Ellery: *(EL-er-ee)* (Latin) "Joyful, happy." Familiar since the 1930s due to the fictional sleuth Ellery Queen, the pen name of writers Frederic Dannay and Manfred Lee.

Elliot: *(EL-ee-ut)* (English) Variant of Elijah. [ELLIOTT, ELIOT, ELLIOTT]

Ellis: *(EL-iss)* (English) Variant of Elias, from Elijah. [ELLISON, ELLISTON, ELSON]

Elmer: *(EL-mer)* (English) "Famed; noble." Elmo is a short form of Erasmus, the name of a noted Dutch scholar. The electrical phenomenon sometimes seen in the rigging of ships at sea is called St. Elmo's fire. [ELMO, ELMORE]

Eloy: *(EE-loy)* (Latin) "Chosen one." Short form of Eligius, the name of a French saint (sixth century).

Elrod: *(ELL-rod)* (Hebrew) "God is king." [ELRAD]

Elroy: *(EL-roy)* (Latin) "The king." (Irish) "Red-haired youth." [ELRIC, ELRICK]

Elton: *(EL-ten)* (English) "From the old town." Famous name bearer: singer Elton John. [ELDEN, ELDON, ELSON, ELSTON]

Elvin: *(EL-vin)* (English) "Elf-wise friend." Variant of Alvin.
[ELVERN, ELVYN, ELWIN, ELWYN]

Elvis: *(EL-viss)* (English) Variant of Elvin. Brought into prominence by the late singer/actor Elvis Presley, the name continues to be quietly but steadily used. Other noted name bearers: world champion figure skater Elvis Stojko and football player Elvis Grbac.

Elwood: *(EL-wud)* (English) "Forest dweller."

Emerson: *(EM-er-sun)* (English) "Son of Emery." See also Emory. [EMERSEN]

Emilio: *(eh-MEEL-ee-oh)* (Latin) Spanish form of Emil, from a Roman clan name with the possible meaning "industrious." The German/English form Emil *(AY-mul)* is in rare use today. Emile *(ay-MEEL, EH-meel)* is a French form. See also Emlyn. [EMELIO, EMIL, EMILE, EMILIANO]

Emlyn: *(EM-lin)* (Welsh) Variant of Emil or Emma. [EMLEN]

Emmanuel: *(ee-MAN-yoo-el)* (Latin) "With us is God." Variant of the Hebrew name Immanuel. Biblical: a name-title applied to the Messiah. Emanuele is an Italian form. See also Manuel. [EMANUEL, EMANUELE]

Emmett: *(EM-it)* (English) Male variant of Emma, a girl's given name from medieval times. Today, actor M. Emmet Walsh features his unusual middle name rather than his first name, Michael. [EMMET]

Emory: *(EM-er-ee)* (English) "Brave; powerful." Variant of Amory. St. Emerus (eighth century) was a French saint. See also Amory and Emerson. [EMERY]

Enoch: *(EE-nuk)* (Hebrew) "Trained and dedicated." Biblical: Enoch was the father of Methuselah, the oldest living man named in the Bible.

Enrique: *(ahn-REE-kay)* (Spanish) "Rules his household." Variant of Henry. Enrico is an Italian form. [ENRICO]

Ephraim: *(EF-ram)* (Hebrew) "Doubly fruitful." Biblical: one of Joseph's two sons by his Egyptian wife Asenath. Noted name bearer: stage and screen actor Efrem Zimbalist, Jr. See also Efrain and Efron. [EFRAIM, EFREM, EPHREM]

Eran: *(AIR-en)* (Hebrew) "Roused, awakened."

Eric: *(AIR-ik)* (Scandinavian) "Ever kingly." Scandinavian legend relates that the Viking sea rover Ericson (son of Eric the Red) landed on the shores of America 500 years before Christopher Columbus. Today actor Eriq La Salle has generated interest in the French spelling. Erich is a German form. See also Aric and Ericson. [ERIK, ERICH, ERICK, ERIQ, ERIX, ERYK]

Ericson: *(AIR-ik-sun)* (Scandinavian) "Eric's son." [ERICKSEN, ERIKSON]

Erin: *(AIR-en)* (Gaelic) Poetic name for Ireland. Eron is a Spanish variant of Aaron. Today, Erin is more commonly used for girls. [ERI, ERON]

Ernest: *(ERN-ist)* (English) "Serious; determined." Variant form of Ernst (German). Literary: Oscar Wilde's comedy *The Importance of Being Earnest* makes the name Earnest a key feature of the plot. Famous name bearer: novelist Ernest Hemingway. Ernesto is a Spanish form. [ERNESTO, EARNEST, ERNIE, ERNST]

Errol: *(AIR-ul)* (Scottish) "Earl, nobleman." Made familiar in the 1930s due to Errol Flynn, famous for his swashbuckling roles. [ERROLL]

Erskine: *(ERS-kin)* (Scottish) "Ascending." Noted name bearer: Erskine Caldwell.

Erwin: *(ER-win)* (English) "Friend." Erwin and the Ervin variants derive from Irving. Famous name bearer: basketball player Earvin "Magic" Johnson. See also Irving. [EAR-VIN, ERVIN, ERVINE, ERVING]

Esau: *(EE-sah)* (Hebrew) "Hairy." Biblical: Esau, the older twin brother of Jacob, was a skilled and adventurous hunter.

Esmond: *(EZ-mund)* (English) "Protector." [ESMUND]

Esteban: *(ess-TAY-ban)* (Spanish) Variant of Stephen. [ES-TEVAN, ESTEVON]

Ethan: *(EE-than)* (Hebrew) "Enduring; overflowing." Biblical: a man of Israel noted for his wisdom. Famous name bearer: American patriot Ethan Allen.

Etienne: *(eh-t'-YIN)* (French) Variant of Stephen.

Eugene: *(yoo-JEEN)* (Greek) "Well-born." St. Eugenius (seventh century), bishop of Toledo, Spain, was also a musician and poet. See also Gene. [EUGENIO]

Eustace: *(YOO-stiss)* (Greek) "Productive." According to legend, St. Eustace (second century) was a Roman general who was converted and martyred. [ESTES, EUSTIS]

Evan: *(EV-an)* (Welsh) Variant of a Gaelic name anglicized as John. See also Evian. [EVANN, EVIN, EVON, EVYN]

Everard: *(EV-er-ard)* (English) "Hardy; brave." [EVARADO, EVERADO]

Everett: *(EV-er-et)* (English) "Hardy; brave." Variant form of Everard. [EVERT, EVERTON]

Evian: *(EV-ee-an)* (American) Usage may be as a variant of Evan, influenced by the town in France famous for Evian springwater. If considered a blended name (Evan and Ian), Evian could take on the meaning of "John-John." [EVION]

Ewen: *(YOO-en)* (Irish) A variant form of Evan. See also Keon. [EUAN, EWAN]

Ezekiel: *(ee-ZEE-k'-yul)* (Hebrew) "God strengthens." Biblical: Ezekiel was a prophet who was among the captives taken to Babylon at the first fall of Jerusalem; he wrote the Book of Ezekiel while in captivity. Esequiel is a Spanish form. See also Zeke. [EZEQUIEL, ESEQUIEL]

Ezra: (Hebrew) "Help." Biblical: a fifth-century-B.C. Jewish priest, scholar, copyist, and historian who wrote the two Chronicles and the Book of Ezra and began the compiling and cataloging of the Old Testament. [ESRA, EZRAH]

F

Fabian: *(FAY-bee-en)* (Latin) From Fabius, a Roman clan name; the name of several Roman emperors and 16 saints. Fabien is a French form; Fabiano is Italian. See also Fabio. [FABIANO, FABIEN, FABION, FAVIAN]

Fabio: *(FAH-bee-oh)* (Italian) Short form of Fabiano. Strongman artist's model Fabio has brought modern recognition to the name. [FAVIO]

Faine: *(fayn)* (English) "Good-natured." Fane is a Welsh form. [FANE]

Falco: *(FAL-koh)* (Latin) Surname having to do with falconry. Falke is a German form. [FALCON, FALK, FALKE, FALKEN]

Faraji: *(fah-RAH-jee)* (Swahili) "Consolation."

Farid: *(fah-REED)* (Arabic) "Exceptional, unequaled." (Hindi) "Wide."

Farley: *(FAR-lee)* (English) "Fair meadow." Surname. [FAR-LEIGH, FARLOW]

Faron: *(fah-ROHN)* (Spanish) "Pharaoh." St. Faro (seventh century) was a French bishop. [FARO]

Farran: *(FARE-en)* (Irish) "The land." Similar-sounding variants: Farren (English), "adventurous"; Ferron, "iron-worker." Farran, Farren, and Farrin are also used for girls. [FARREN, FARRIN, FARRON, FERRIN, FERRON]

Farrell: *(FARE-el)* (Irish) "Brave." [FARREL, FERRELL]

Farris: *(FARE-iss)* (English) "Iron-strong." [FARIS, FERRIS]

Federico: *(fed-er-EE-koh)* (Spanish, Italian) "Peaceful ruler." Variant of Frederick. [FREDERICO]

Felipe: *(feh-LEE-pay)* (Spanish) Variant of Philip. [FELIPPE]

Felix: *(FEEL-iks)* (Latin) "Happy." Biblical: Roman procurator of Judea during Paul's time, a wily politician. The name of three popes and numerous saints. Feliciano is a Spanish and Italian form. [FELICIANO]

Fergus: *(FER-gus)* (Scottish) "Man of strength." St. Fergus the Pict (eighth century) was an Irish missionary in Scotland. [FERGUSON]

Fernando: *(fer-NAHN-doh)* (Spanish) "Adventurer." Fernand is a French form. St. Ferdinand of Castile (13th century) was king of Castile and Leon. See also Hernando. [FERDINAND, FERNAND]

Fidel: *(fee-DEL)* (Latin) "Faithful." Noted name bearer: Fidel Castro, the revolutionary who became president-for-life of Cuba. [FIDAL, FIDELLO]

Finn: *(fin)* (Irish) "Fair." Mythology: Finn MacCumhail was a legendary Irish hero (third century) somewhat like the English Robin Hood. His warrior-followers were called Fini-

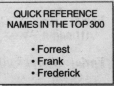

QUICK REFERENCE
NAMES IN THE TOP 300

• Forrest
• Frank
• Frederick

ans. St. Finnian of Clonard (fifth and sixth century) was called "The Teacher of Irish Saints" because a number of students at his school became very prominent ecclesiastics. [FINIAN, FINNEGAN, FINNIAN]

Fitz-: *(fits)* (English) Surname prefix meaning "son of." [FITZGERALD, FITZHUGH, FITZPATRICK]

Fletcher: *(FLECH-er)* (English) "Arrowmaker." [FLETCH]

Flint: *(flint)* (English) Place name and surname. Also a name from nature, referring to the hard quartz that produces a spark of fire when struck by steel.

Florian: *(FLOR-ee-an)* (Slavic, Latin) "Flower." Masculine form of Flora, from a Roman clan name. St. Florian (fourth century) was a Roman officer under Diocletian who came to be called the patron of Poland and Austria.

Floyd: *(floyd)* (English) Variant of Lloyd.

Flynn: *(flin)* (Irish) "Son of a red-haired man." [FLINN, FLYN]

Fonso: *(FAHN-soh)* (Latin) Short form of Alfonso. [FONSIE, FONZELL, FONZIE, FONZO]

Fontaine: *(fahn-TAYN)* (French) "Fountain, water source." Fontana is an Italian form. [FONTANA, FONTANE, FON-TAYNE, FONTEYNE]

Ford: *(ford)* (English) Literally, a shallow place used to cross a river or stream. Surname. [FORDE]

Forrest: *(FOR-est)* (English) "Woodland." St. John Forest (16th century) was one of the numerous English priests who were martyred during the conflicts between King Henry VIII and the Pope. [FOREST, FORESTER, FORRESTER]

Fortino: *(for-TEEN-oh)* (Latin) "Strong; fortunate." [FOR-TUNATO]

Foster: *(FAW-ster)* (English) "Forest ranger."

Francis: *(FRAN-sis)* (Latin) "From France." Traditionally, Frances is the feminine form. Noted name bearer: Francis Sinatra, also known as Frank. St. Francis of Assisi (12th century) is remembered as the gentle saint who delighted in God's works as revealed by nature. See also Frank.

Francisco: *(frahn-CEES-koh)* (Spanish) Variant of Francis. Francesco is an Italian form. [FRANCESCO, FRISCO]

Frank: *(frank)* (English) "Free; a free man." Frankie is occasionally used for girls. Franz *(frahnz)* is a German form; François *(frah-SWAH)* is French. See also Francis and Francisco. [FRANKIE, FRANCO, FRANÇOIS, FRANKY, FRANTZ, FRANZ]

Franklin: *(FRANK-lin)* (English) "Free man, landholder." [FRANKLYN]

Fraser: *(FRAY-zer)* (Scottish) "Of the forest men." One of the major clans of Scotland. Frasier *(FRAY-zher)* is notable today due to the popular TV comedy series. [FRASIER, FRAZER, FRAZIER]

Frederick: *(FRED-er-ik)* (German) "Peaceful ruler." Frederik is a Scandinavian form; Frederic is French. Fritz is a nickname. An interesting contemporary variant is used by actor Fredro Starr. See also Federico. [FREDDY, FRED, FREDDIE, FREDERIC, FREDERIK, FREDRIC, FREDRICK, FREDRIK, FRITZ]

Freeman: *(FREE-man)* (English) Surname used as a given name. Literally, a free man, one freed from bound servitude to an overlord. Name of an English saint (16th century). [FREMAN]

Fremont: *(FREE-mont)* (French) "Noble protector."

LESS COMMON CLASSICS; NEW, UNUSUAL NAMES

- Fabian
- Felix
- Fernando
- Francis
- Francisco
- Franklin
- Fredrick

G

Gabriel: *(GAY-bree-el)* (Hebrew) "God's able-bodied one." Biblical: the archangel Gabriel is the only angel besides Michael named in the canonical Scriptures. Gavriel is a Jewish variant. [GABE, GABRIAN, GAVRIEL]

Gage: *(gage)* (French) "Pledge."

Galen: *(GAY-len)* (Greek) "Tranquil." The name of a second-century physician whose research provided a basis for accepted medical practices for 1,500 years. [GAELAN, GALAN, GALYN]

Galvin: *(GAL-vin)* (Irish) "Sparrow."

Gannon: *(GAN-on)* (Irish) "Fair."

Gardner: *(GARD-ner)* (English) "Keeper of the garden." [GARD, GARDINER]

Gareth: *(GARE-eth)* (Welsh) "Gentle." Sir Gareth, noted for his modesty and bravery, was a knight of King Arthur's Round Table. [GARRETH]

QUICK REFERENCE
NAMES IN THE TOP 300

- Gabriel
- Gage
- Garrett
- Gary
- Gavin
- George
- Gerald
- Grant
- Gregory

Garland: *(GAR-land)* (French) "Wreath; prize." Surname. [GARLAN, GARLEN, GARLYN]

Garnet: *(GAR-net, gar-NET)* (French) "Keeper of grain." Surname. May also be used in reference to the gemstone. [GARNELL, GARNER, GARNETT]

Garrad: *(GARE-ad)* (English) Variant of Garret, from Gerald. [GARED, GARRED, GERRED]

Garrett: *(GARE-et)* (English) "Spear ruler." Variant of Gerald. See also Gerritt. [GARETT, GARRET, GARRITT]

Garrick: *(GARE-ik)* (English) "Rules by the spear." [GARRIK]

Garrison: *(GARE-a-son)* (English) "Spear-fortified town." Noted name bearer: humorist, writer, and radio personality Garrison Keillor. [GARSON]

Garron: *(GARE-on)* (French) "Guardian." Use of Garron and variants listed here are probably the use of family surnames or as rhyming variants following the pattern of Darin variants. [GARAN, GAREN, GARIN, GARION, GARON, GARRAN, GARREN, GARRIN, GERON]

Garth: *(garth)* (Scandinavian) "Garden." Noted name bearer: country-western singer Garth Brooks.

Garve: *(GAR-vee)* (Irish) "Rough, rugged." [GARVEY]

Garvyn: *(GAR-ven)* (English) "Spear friend; ally." [GARVIN]

Gary: *(GARE-ee)* (English) "Spear." Famous since the 1930s due to actor Gary Cooper. [GAREY, GARREY, GARRY]

Gavin: *(GAV-en)* (Scottish, Welsh) "White hawk." A form of the medieval name Gawain. Gavino is an Italian form. Gavan is the name of an English saint (17th century). Noted name bearer: actor Gavin MacLeod. See also Gwayne. [GAVAN, GAVINO, GAVYN]

Gene: *(jeen)* (English) Short form of Eugene. Geno is an Italian short form. [GENO]

Geoffrey: *(JEF-ree)* (English) "Peaceful." Geoff *(jef)* is an English short form. See also Jeffrey. [GEFFREY, GEOFF]

George: *(jorj)* (English) "Farmer." St. George, a knight who became the patron saint of England, achieved legendary status through the medieval depiction of his struggle with a fire-breathing dragon, symbolic of the devil. Giorgio *(jee-OR-jee-oh)* is an Italian form. Use of the Geordi variants may be influenced by the character Geordi LaForge on the TV series *Star Trek: The Next Generation*. See also Joren, Jorge, Keoki, and Yuri. [GEORDI, GEORDIE, GEORGIO, GIORGIO]

Gerald: *(JARE-ald)* (German) "Rules by the spear." Geraldo (her-AL-doh) is a Spanish form. Notable in the 1990s: talk show host Geraldo Rivera. See also Garrad, Garrett, Jarrett, Jarrod, and Jerald. [GERALDO, GERE, GEROLD, GERRALD, GERRELL]

Gerard: *(je-RARD)* (French) "Spear-strong." The name of numerous saints. Gerardo is a Spanish form; Gerhard is German. Noted name bearer: French actor Gérard Depardieu. See also Jerard. [GERARDO, GERHARD, GERRARD]

Germain: *(jer-MAYN)* (French) "Brotherly." From Germanus (Latin), the name of seven saints. See also Jermaine. [GERMAYNE]

Geronimo: *(hare-ROH-nee-moh, jer-RAH-nah-moh)* (Spanish) "Sacred name." Variant of Jerome, a saint's name. The Native American Geronimo (19th century) was one of the last of the renowned Apache warrior chiefs.

LESS COMMON CLASSICS; NEW, UNUSUAL NAMES

- Garret
- Geoffrey
- Gerardo
- Giovanni
- Glenn
  Glen
- Graham
- Grayson
- Griffin

Gerritt: *(GARE-it)* (Dutch) Variant form of Gerald. See also Garrett. [GERRIT]

Gerry: *(JARE-ee)* (English) Short form of names beginning with *Ger-*. See also Jerry.

Giacomo: *(JOCK-a-moh)* (Italian) Variant of James and Jacob.

Gian: *(jon)* (Italian) Short form of John, often used in combination with other names. Gianni is equivalent to Johnny. [GIANCARLO, GIANFRANCO, GIANLUCA, GIANNI]

Gideon: *(GIH-dee-en)* (Hebrew) "One who cuts down." Biblical: a judge of Israel who won battles through skillful planning and faith rather than strength of arms alone.

Gilbert: *(GIL-bert)* (English) "Bright lad." Gilberto is a Spanish form. [GILBERTO]

Giles: *(jiles)* (Greek) "Young shield." Gil *(gil)* is mostly used as a short form of Gilbert; it is also an Israeli name meaning "joy." [GIL]

Gilmore: *(GIL-mor)* (Scottish) "Sword bearer." [GILMAR, GILMER]

Gilroy: *(GIL-roy)* (Scottish) "Serves the king."

Gino: *(JEE-no)* (Italian) Short form of names like Gian and Giovanni. [GENO]

Giovanni: *(joh-VAHN-ee)* (Italian) Variant of John. See also Jovan. [GEOVANI, GEOVANNI, GEOVANNY, GEOVANY, GIOVANI, GIOVANNY, GIOVONNI]

Giuliano: *(joo-lee-AH-noh)* (Italian) Variant of Julian, Julio. [GIULIO]

Giuseppe: *(jeh-SEP-ee)* (Italian) Variant of Joseph.

Glenn: *(glen)* (Gaelic) "Valley." [GLEN, GLENDALE, GLENDON, GLENDYN, GLYNN]

Godfrey: *(GAHD-free)* (German) "God's peace." A saint's name.

Gordon: *(GORD-en)* (English, Scottish) "From the marshes." Name of one of the great Scottish clans.

Grady: *(GRAY-dee)* (Irish) "Man of rank." [GRADEN, GRADON]

Graham: *(GRAY-em)* (Scottish) "Farm home." [GRAEME]

Grant: *(grant)* (English, Scottish) "Bestow; great, tall." Noted name bearer: writer Grantland Rice. [GRANTLAND]

Grayson: *(GRAY-sun)* (English) "Gray-haired; son of the Gray family; son of Gregory." [GRAY, GRAYSEN, GREY, GREYSON]

Greg: *(greg)* (English) Short form of Gregory. The double consonant ending on a short form usually indicates an English surname, as in Gregg. [GREGG, GREGSON]

Gregorio: *(greh-GORE-ee-oh)* (Italian, Spanish, Portuguese) Variant form of Gregory.

Gregory: *(GREG-er-ee)* (Greek) "On the watch." The first of the 16 popes to bear the name was called Gregory the Great. He founded monasteries, reorganized papal administation and fostered the development of the Gregorian chants. Gregor is a Scottish and German variant; Gregori is Russian; Grigor is Welsh and Russian. See also Greg and Gregorio. [GREGOR, GREGORI, GRIGOR]

Griffin: *(GRIF-en)* (Welsh) "Fighting chief; fierce." Mythology: in Greek mythology and medieval legend, the Gryphon was a fierce creature with the foreparts of an eagle and the hindquarters of a lion. [GRIFF, GRIFFEN, GRIFFITH, GRYPHON]

Grover: *(GROVE-er)* (English) "Grove dweller."

Guillermo: *(gui-YARE-mo)* (Latin) Variant of William. Guillaume *(gee-OHM)* is a French form. [GILLERMO, GUILLAUME]

Gunther: *(GUN-ther)* (German) "Battler, warrior." Gunnar is a Scandinavian variant. [GUNNAR, GUNNER]

Gustav: *(GOO-stahv)* (German) "Royal staff." Gustavo is a Spanish form. [GUSTAVO, GUS, GUSTAF, GUSTAVE]

Guy: *(gye)* (Welsh) "Lively." Guido is an Italian form.

Gwayne: *(gwayn)* (Welsh) "White hawk." Variant of the medieval name Gawain.

Gyan: *(GYE-en)* (Sanskrit) "Knowledge."

H

Hadrien: *(HAY-dree-en)* (Latin) "Dark." Variant form of Adrian. The Roman emperor Hadrian (second century A.D.) was a gifted writer and architect; he caused Hadrian's Wall to be built in Britain. [HADRIAN]

Hakim: *(hah-KEEM)* (Arabic) "Wise." Noted name bearer: basketball player Hakeem Olajuwon. [HAKEEM]

Hakon: *(HAH-ken)* (Scandinavian) "High-born." [HAAKON, HAKAN]

Hal: *(hal)* (English) A nickname for Henry.

Halden: *(HAL-den)* (English) "From Denmark." [HALDANE]

Halen: *(HAY-len)* (Swedish) "Hall." [HALE, HALLEN, HAYLAN]

> **QUICK REFERENCE**
> **NAMES IN THE TOP 300**
>
> • Harley
> • Harold
> • Harrison
> • Hayden
> • Henry
> • Hunter

Halim: *(ha-LEEM)* (Arabic) "Gentle."

Hamid: *(ha-MEED)* (Arabic) "Thankful to God." (Hindu) "Friend." A variant of Mohammed.

Hamilton: *(HAM-ul-tun)* (Scottish) Place name and surname of one of the great noble families in Scotland.

Hampton: *(HAMP-tun)* (English) Place name and surname.

Hank: *(hank)* (English) Nickname for Henry.

Hans: *(hahns)* (Scandinavian, German, Dutch) Variant of John. [HAN, HANSEN, HANSON]

Hari: *(HAH-ree)* (Sanskrit) "Lion." Mythology: one of the names of Vishnu.

Harley: *(HAR-lee)* (English) "Meadow of the hares." Variants listed here are related surnames. [HARLAN, HARLAND, HARLEN, HARLON, HARLOW]

Harman: *(HAR-man)* (French) Variant of Herman. Harmon (Hebrew), "palace," is a biblical place name. [HARMEN, HARMON]

Harold: *(HARE-uld)* (Scandinavian) "Army commander." Herald is also literally "one who proclaims." [HARALD, HARRELL, HERALDO, HERLAD]

Harper: *(HAR-per)* (English) "Harpist, minstrel."

Harry: *(HARE-ee)* (English) The English version of the French pronunciation of Henri *(aw-REE)*. It's used as a nickname of Henry as well as of variants like Harrison, "Harry's son," and Harris. Noted name bearer: actor Harrison Ford. [**HARRISON**, HARRIMAN, HARRIS]

Hart: *(hart)* (English) "Strong; brave." Hart and Hartley are surnames of two English saints (16th century). [HARTE, HARTFORD, HARTLEY, HARTMAN]

Harvey: *(HAR-vee)* (English) "Eager for battle." Variant form of Herve (French). [HERVE]

Hassan: *(hah-SAHN)* (Arabic) "Good-looking." Hasani *(ha-SAHN-ee)* is a Swahili variant. [HASAN, HASANI, HASSAIN]

Haven: *(HAY-ven)* (English) "A place of safety; shelter."

Hayden: *(HAY-den)* (English) "The hill meadow." [HAYDAN, HAYDON, HAYES]

Heath: *(heeth)* (English) Surname and place name. *Heath* is a word for untended land where certain flowering shrubs grow. Literary: Heathcliff was the dark hero of Emily Brontë's *Wuthering Heights*. [HEATHCLIFF]

Heber: *(HEE-ber)* (Hebrew) "Partner." Biblical: an ancestor of Abraham. Also an Irish name of uncertain meaning.

Hector: *(HEK-tor)* (Greek) "Steadfast." In Homer's *Iliad*, Hector was a prince of Troy.

Hendrik: *(HEN-drik)* (Scandinavian, Dutch) Variant of Henry. [HENRICK, HENRIK]

Henry: *(HEN-ree)* (German) "Rules his household." A favored royal name of England and France. The second son of the current Prince of Wales is named Henry. Henri is a French form; Heinrich is German; Henryk is Polish. See also Enrique, Hal, Hank, Harry, and Hendrik. [HEINRICH, HENRI, HENRIQUE, HENRYK]

Herbert: *(HER-bert)* (German) "Illustrious warrior." An island in Lake Derwentshire, England, is named in honor of St. Herbert (seventh century). [HERB]

Hercules: *(HERK-yoo-lees)* (Greek) "In Hera's service." Mythology:

LESS COMMON CLASSICS;
NEW, UNUSUAL NAMES

- Harry
- Heath
- Hector
- Holden
- Houston
- Howard

the Greek Hercules was a son of Zeus who possessed extraordinary strength. The name was borne by at least two saints, but may be better known through Agatha Christie's fictional Belgian detective Hercule Poirot.

Herman: *(HER-man)* (German) "Soldier." St. Herman (11th century) wrote the famous hymn "Salve Regina." See also Harmon.

Hermes: *(HER-mees)* (Greek) "Messenger." Mythology: Hermes was a messenger for the gods on Olympus and was himself the god of eloquence. He was called Mercury by the Romans.

Hernando: *(air-NAHN-doh)* (Spanish) "Adventurous." Variant of Ferdinand. [HERNAN, HERNANDEZ]

Herschel: *(HER-shul)* (Yiddish) "Deer." Noted name bearer: football player Herschel Walker. [HERSHEL, HIRSCH]

Hilario: *(ee-LAH-ree-oh)* (Latin) "Joyful, glad." Variant of Hilary (Greek), the name of more than 30 saints.

Hiram: *(HYE-rum)* (Hebrew) "My brother is exalted." Biblical: the king of Tyre, friendly to King David and King Solomon. [HYRAM]

Holden: *(HOHL-den)* (English) "Sheltered valley." Holman is a related surname meaning "man from the valley." [HOLMAN]

Hollis: *(HAH-liss)* (English) "The holly tree."

Holmes: *(holms)* (English) "Home by the river."

Holt: *(holt)* (English) "By the forest."

Homer: *(HOH-mer)* (Greek) "Given as hostage; promised." Two of the greatest works of Greek epic poetry, the *Iliad* and the *Odyssey*, are attributed to Homer. [HOMAR]

Horace: *(HOR-ess)* (Latin) From Horatius, a Roman family clan name. [HORACIO, HORATIO, HORATIUS]

Houston: *(HEW-ston)* (Scottish) Place name and surname. The name's association with the American West is due to the Texan general Sam Houston and the city in Texas that bears his name.

Howard: *(HOW-erd)* (English) "Noble watchman." Surname of one of the great houses of English nobility. [HOWIE]

Hubert: *(HEW-bert)* (German) "Bright, intelligent." A saint's name.

Hugh: *(hew)* (German) "A thinker." The name of numerous saints. Huw is a Welsh form. Notable in the 1990s: actors Hugh Grant and Hugh Beaumont. See also Hugo. [HUEY, HUGHIE, HUW]

Hugo: *(HEW-goh)* (Latin) Variant form of Hugh. See also Keegan. [UGO]

Humberto: *(oom-BARE-toh)* (Spanish) "Big; bright." A saint's name.

Humphrey: *(HUM-free)* (German) "Peace; strength." A saint's name. Notable name bearer: actor Humphrey Bogart.

Hunter: *(HUN-ter)* (English) "Pursuer." [HUNT, HUNTINGTON, HUNTLEY]

Hussain: *(hoo-SAYN)* (Arabic) "Good." Hussein was the name of the founder of Shiite Islam. [HUSAIN, HUSAYN, HUSSEIN]

Hyatt: *(HYE-et)* (English) Surname used as a given name.

I

Ian: *(EE-an, EYE-an)* Scottish form of John. [IAIN]

Ibrahim: *(ee-bra-HEEM)* (Arabic) Variant of Abraham. [IBRAHEEM]

Ignacio: *(eeg-NAH-see-oh)* (Latin) "Fiery." St. Ignacius of Loyola was the founder of the Catholic Jesuit order. [INIGO]

Igor: *(EE-gor, EYE-gor)* (Russian) "Warrior of peace."

Ilya: *(ILL-yah)* (Russian) Short form of Elijah.

Immanuel: *(ih-MAN-yoo-el)* (Hebrew) "With us is God." [IMAN, IMANI]

Ingram: *(ING-grum)* (Scandinavian) "Raven of peace."

Ira: *(EYE-rah)* (Hebrew) "Full-grown." Biblical: the name of a priest or chief minister to King David.

Irving: *(ER-ving)* (English) "Friend." See also Ervin. [IRVIN, IRVEN, IRVINE, IRVYN, IRWIN]

Isaac: *(EYE-zik)* (Hebrew) "Laughter." Biblical: the only son of Abraham by his wife Sarah. Famous name bearer: violinist Itzhak *(ITS-hahk)* Perlman. [IKE, ISA, ISSAC, ITZHAK, IZAAC, IZAAK]

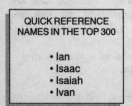

QUICK REFERENCE
NAMES IN THE TOP 300

- Ian
- Isaac
- Isaiah
- Ivan

Isaiah: *(eye-ZAY-ah)* (Hebrew) "Salvation of Jehovah." Biblical: one of the major prophets and writer of the Book of Isaiah. Isais is a Latin form. Noted name bearer: basketball player Isiah Thomas. [ISAIS, ISIAH, IZAIAH]

Ismael: *(EES-mah-el)* (Hebrew) "God listens." Spanish form of Ishmael. Biblical: the son of Abraham by Sarah's Egyptian slave woman Hagar. Among his descendants were Bedouin tribes and Mohammed (seventh century), founder of Islam. Literary: because Ishmael was cast out to wander in the desert, the name is often used symbolically, as in Herman Melville's novel *Moby Dick*. [ISHMAEL]

Israel: *(IS-rah-el)* (Hebrew) "God perseveres, contends." Biblical: when Jacob, son of Isaac, was in his nineties, God changed his name to Israel as a token of blessing. His 12 sons became the ancestors of the Israelite nation.

Ivan: *(ee-VAHN, EYE-van)* (Russian, Slavic) Variant of John. Ivanhoe is a medieval variant Sir Walter Scott used for the Saxon hero of his novel *Ivanhoe*. [IVANHOE, IVANO]

Ives: *(eve)* (Scandinavian) "Archer's bow." Variant of Yves, from Ivar. Ivo is a saint's name. See also Yves. [IVAR, IVO, IVON, IVOR]

J

Ja-: (American) Blends of *Ja-* plus various endings, with pronunciation emphasis on the second syllable. See also *Je-*. [JALEN, JALENN, JAMAINE, JAMAR, JAMARI, JAMARR, JAMELLE, JAMON, JAMOND, JAQUAN, JAQUILLE, JARAY, JARONN, JAVAUGHN, JAVON, JAVONTE, JAYVON]

Jabari: *(ja-BAR-ee)* (Swahili) "Valiant."

Jabin: *(JAY-bin)* (Hebrew) "God has built." A biblical name.

Jacan: *(JAY-kin)* (Hebrew) "Trouble." A biblical name. [JACHIN]

Jace: *(jayce)* (English) Variant short form of Jason. [JACEN, JACY, JAYCE]

Jacinto: *(ha-CEEN-toh)* (Spanish) Masculine form of the Greek name Hyacinth, meaning "alas."

Jack: *(jak)* (English) Name based on John or Jacques, the French form of Jacob. Jackie is used more for girls than for boys. See also Jackson and Jacques. [JACKIE, JACKY]

Jackson: *(JAK-son)* (English) "Son of Jack." [JACSON, JAX, JAXON, JAXSON]

Jacob: (JAY-kub) (Hebrew) "Supplanter." Biblical: the son of Isaac and Rebekah and twin brother of Esau. Jacob fathered 12 sons and a daughter, who became the ancestors of the nation of Israel. Jacobo is a Spanish form; Yakov *(YAH-kav)* is Russian. See also Giacomo, Jack, Jacques, Jake, and James. [JACOBO, JACOBUS, JAKOB, YAKOV]

Jacques: *(zhahk)* (French) Variant form of Jacob. The Scottish Jock is a phonetic form of Jacques. [JOCK]

Jadon: *(JAY-don)* (Hebrew) "Jehovah has heard." A biblical name. [JADE, JADEN, JADER, JAEDON, JAYDEN, JAYDON]

Jadrian: *(JAY-dree-en)* (American) Blend of Jay or Jade and Adrian.

Jaeger: *(JAY-ger)* (German) "Hunter." The similar sounding Jagur, a biblical place name, is an Aramaic name meaning "heap of stones; marker." [JAGGER, JAGUR]

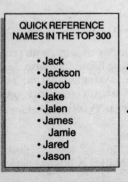

QUICK REFERENCE
NAMES IN THE TOP 300

- Jack
- Jackson
- Jacob
- Jake
- Jalen
- James
   Jamie
- Jared
- Jason

Jago: *(JAY-goh)* (English) Variant of James used in Cornwall.

Jairo: *(HYE-roh)* (Spanish) Variant of Jairus *(JARE-us)*, a Hebrew name meaning "Jehovah enlightens." Jarius is a contemporary blend of *Jar-* and Darius. Biblical: Jairus was the father of a young girl resurrected by Jesus. [JAIRUS, JARIUS]

Jake: *(jayk)* (English) Short form of Jacob, well-used as an independent name.

Jakeem: *(ya-KEEM)* (Hebrew, Arabic) "Raised up." [JAKIM]

Jamal: *(ja-MAL)* (Arabic) "Handsome." Notable in the 1990s: actor Malcolm-Jamal Warner. [JAHMAL, JAMAAL, JAMAEL, JAMAHL, JAMALL, JAMEEL, JAMEL, JAMIEL, JAMIL, JAMILE]

James: *(jayms)* (English) Variant of Jacob. Biblical: one of the 12 apostles of Jesus, who possibly was also a cousin of Jesus. The King James Bible is named in reference to James I of England (16th–17th century). Spanish pronunciation of Jaime: *HYE-may*, Scottish: *JAY-mee*. See also Diego, Jacob, Jago, Jamison, Kimo, and Santiago. [JAIME, JAMIE, JIMMY, JAYME, JAYMES, JEM, JIM, JIMMIE]

Jamin: *(JAY-min)* (Hebrew) "Right hand of favor." A biblical name; one Jamin was a grandson of Jacob. [JAMIAN, JAMIEL, JAMON, JAYMIN]

Jamison: *(JAY-ma-sun)* (English) "Son of James." [JAMESON, JAMIESON]

Jan: *(yahn, jan)* (Dutch, Slavic) Variant of John. See also Jansen. [JANO]

Janak: *(JAN-ik)* (Hindu) Mythology: the father of Sita. Janek (Czech, Polish) is a form of John. [JANEK]

Jansen: *(JAN-sen)* (Scandinavian) "Son of John." [JANSE, JENSEN, JENSON, JANTZEN]

Japheth: *(JAY-feth)* (Hebrew) "May He grant ample room." Biblical: the oldest of Noah's three sons.

Jarah: *(JAY-rah)* (Hebrew) "He gives sweetness; honey." Biblical: a descendant of Jonathan, son of King Saul. Jarrah (Arabic) means "vessel." See also Jeriah. [JARRAH]

Jared: *(JARE-ed)* (Hebrew) "Descending." Biblical: Jared was a pre-Flood ancestor of Jesus. Jered was a descendant of Judah. The modern popularity of Jared initially was due to the character Jared on the 1960s TV Western *Big Valley*. Many variants with the same sound have come into use. See also Jarrod and Jerrod. [JARAD, JAROD, JARYD, JERAD]

Jarek: *(YAH-rik, JARE-ik)* (Polish) "January child." See also Jerrick.

Jarell: *(JARE-el, ja-RELL)* (English) Possibly a form of Jarl, but the numerous spelling variants suggest that it is frequently used as a blend of *Jar-* and Darell. See also Jerrell. [JAREL, JARREL, JARRELL, JARRYL, JARYL]

Jareth: *(JARE-eth)* (American) Blend of *Jar-* or *Jer-* and Gareth, or a variant of Jarah. [JARRETH, JERETH]

Jarl: *(jarl)* (Scandinavian) Roughly equivalent to the English title of Earl. See also Jarell.

Jaron: *(JARE-on, ja-RAHN)* (Israeli) "Cry of rejoicing." Some of the many contemporary names similar to Jaron may be based on a blend of the sound of Jared or Jerry and Darren, or are the use of surnames. [JARAN, JAREN, JARIN, JARRAN, JARREN, JARRON, JARYN, JERAN, JEREN, JERREN, JERRIN, JERRON]

Jarrett: *(JARE-et)* (English) Variant and surname form of Garrett. [JARETT, JARRET, JERETT, JERRETT]

QUICK REFERENCE
NAMES IN THE TOP 300

- Jay
- Jeffrey
  Jeffery
- Jeremiah
- Jeremy
- Jerry
- Jesse
  Jessie
- Jimmy

Jarrod: *(JARE-ed)* (English) Variant and surname form of Garrett, from Gerald. See also Jared and Jerrod. [JARRED, JARRAD, JARRYD]

Jarvis: *(JAR-viss)* (English) Variant of the French name Gervaise, meaning "spearman." [JARVEE, JARVELL, JERVIS]

Jason: *(JAY-sun)* (Greek) "A healing." Biblical: an early Christian associate of Paul. Greek mythology: Jason was leader of a group of warrior heroes called the Argonauts. In the news: singer J'son. See also Jace and Jayson. [JACE, JAISON, JASE, JASEN, JAYCE, J'SON]

Jasper: *(JAS-per)* (Greek) Variant form of Caspar or Gaspar. Jasper is also a semiprecious gemstone, harder than glass, and red or reddish brown. Biblical: the jasper mentioned in the Book of Revelation actually may refer to a diamond. [JASPAR]

Javan: *(JAY-van)* (Hebrew) "Ionian." Biblical: the grandson of Noah who settled in the islands and coast lands of the Mediterranean. He's identified as the ancestor of the ancient Greeks. [JAYVEN, JAYVON]

Javier: *(HAH-vee-air)* (Spanish, Portuguese) "Bright." Variant of Xavier.

Jay: (English) Short form of names like Jason and Jacob. Jay and Jai are also Sanskrit names meaning "victorious." Mythology: Jay is the name of various deities in Hindu classical writings. [JAE, JAI, JAYE, JAYRON, JAYRONN]

Jaycee: (American) Phonetic name based on initials. [JAYAR, JAYDEE, JAYVEE]

Jaylen: *(JAY-len)* (American) Contemporary blend of Jay and Len,

QUICK REFERENCE
NAMES IN THE TOP 300

- Joel
- John
  Johnny
- Jon
- Jonah
- Jonathan
  Johnathan
  Johnathon
  Jonathon

possibly a rhyming variant of Gaylen. Biblical: Jalon (Hebrew) was a descendant of Judah. [JALON, JAYLAN, JAYLIN, JAYLON]

Jayson: *(JAY-sun)* (American) A contemporary form of Jason. [JAYCEN, JAYSEN]

Je-: (American) Blend of *Je-* plus various endings, with pronunciation emphasis on the second syllable. See also *Ja-*. [JEMAR, JEMARIO, JERAE, JERELL, JERELLE, JERON, JERONE, JEVAN, JEVON]

Jean: *(jeen)* (French) Variant of John. Jean is sometimes hyphenated with a second name, and the French pronunciation *(zhahn)* may be used. [JEAN-CARLO, JEAN-LUC, JEAN-PAUL, JEANPIERRE]

Jediah: *(je-DYE-ah)* (Hebrew) "Jehovah knows." Jada is a short form of the name; both are biblical names. [JADA, JEDAIAH]

Jedidiah: *(jed-ah-DYE-ah)* (Hebrew) "Beloved of Jehovah." Biblical: a "blessing" name given in infancy to King Solomon, David's second son by Bathsheba. [JED, JEDADIAH, JEDD, JEDEDIAH]

Jedrek: *(JED-rik)* (Polish) "A strong man." Variant of Andrew. [JEDRICK]

Jefford: *(JEF-erd)* (English) Surname and place name.

Jeffrey: *(JEF-ree)* (English) "Peaceful." Variant of Geoffrey. The three-syllable alternate spelling Jeffery *(JEF-er-ree)* has been used since medieval times. See also Geoffrey. [JEFFERY, JEFF, JEFFERSON, JEFFRY]

Jehu: *(JAY-hew)* (Hebrew) "Jehovah is He." Biblical: Jehu was a military commander of Israel, later king, who was noted for his pell-mell style of chariot driving.

Jemal: *(je-MAHL)* (Arabic) "Handsome." Variant of Jamal.

Jerald: *(JARE-uld)* (English) Variant and surname form of Gerald. [JERALDO, JEROLD, JERRALD, JERROLD]

Jerard: *(je-RARD)* (French) Variant of Gerard. Jerrard is also an English surname. [JERARDO, JERRARD]

Jeremiah: *(jare-ah-MYE-ah)* (Hebrew) "Jehovah exalts." Biblical: one of the major prophets, a scholar. Besides writing the Book of Jeremiah and Lamentations, Jeremiah compiled and wrote the histories of I and II Kings. Jeremias is a Spanish form. See also Jeremy. [JEREMIAS]

Jeremy: *(JARE-a-mee)* (English) Variant of Jeremiah, in use since the Middle Ages. [JERAMIE, JERAMY, JEREMIE]

Jeriah: *(jer-RYE-ah)* (Hebrew) "Jehovah has seen." A biblical name. Jerah is the name of a Hebrew lunar month; also a given name. See also Jarah. [JERAH, JERRAH]

Jericho: *(JARE-a-koh)* (Arabic) "City of the moon." Biblical: a city in Canaan destroyed when its walls fell down. [JERICO]

Jeriel: *(JARE-ee-el)* (Hebrew) "God has seen." Biblical: a descendant of Jacob through his son Issachar. See also Jerrell. [JERRIEL]

Jermaine: *(jer-MAIN)* (Latin) "Brotherly." Variant of Germaine. Familiar in modern times due to singer Jermaine Jackson. [JERMAIN, JERMANE, JERMAYNE]

Jerome: *(jer-OME)* (Greek) "Sacred name." St. Jerome (fourth century) was a scholar who prepared the Latin Vulgate, the standard accepted text of the Bible in the common language of the time. See also Geronimo. [JERONIMO]

QUICK REFERENCE
NAMES IN THE TOP 300

- Jordan
- Joseph
  José
- Joshua
- Josiah
- Juan
- Julian
- Justin

Jerrell: *(JARE-el)* (English) Probably a further extension of the Jarell variants, or a variant of Jeriel. See also Jarell and Jeriel. [JEREL, JERRALL, JERREL, JERRYL, JERYL]

Jerrick: *(JARE-ik)* (American) Meaning could be "strong, gifted ruler" if Jerrick is used as a blend of Jerold and Derrick. The variants shown here may be spelling variants, or forms of Polish and Dutch surnames. See also Jarek. [JERIC, JERICK, JERRIC]

Jerrod: *(JARE-ed)* (English) Variant of Garrett. See also Jared and Jarrod. [JERAD, JEROD, JERRAD, JERRED, JERRYD]

Jerry: *(JARE-ee)* (English) Used as an independent name, Jerry is also a short form of names beginning with *Jer-*. Noted name bearers: actors/comedians Jerry Lewis and Jerry Seinfeld. See also Gerry.

Jesse: *(JESS-ee)* (Hebrew) "Jehovah exists." Biblical: the shepherd father of King David. Jessie is also used for girls. The similar-sounding Jesiah is a variant form of Joshua. [JESSIE, JESS, JESSEY, JESIAH, JESSY]

Jestin: *(JESS-tin)* (Welsh) Variant of Justin. [JESSTIN, JESTON]

Jesus: *(JEE-zus)* (Hebrew) Short form of Joshua, from the Hebrew name Jehoshua, meaning "Jehovah is salvation." The name of the biblical Christ is very frequently used as a given name in Hispanic cultures. Spanish pronunciation is *hay-SOOS*.

Jethro: *(JETH-roh)* (Hebrew) "Overflowing, abundance." Biblical: Moses' father-in-law, a priest of Midian. [JETT]

Jiro: *(jee-roh)* (Japanese) "Second son."

Joaquin: *(wah-KEEN)* (Spanish) Short form of the Hebrew name Jehoichin, meaning "Jehovah has established." Joaquin Miller was a noted and colorful 19th-century poet-adventurer of the American West. According to medieval

Catholic tradition, Joachim was the name of the Virgin Mary's father. [JOACHIM]

Job: *(johb)* (Hebrew) "Persecuted." Biblical: a man called by God "blameless and upright." Job is proverbial as an example of patience under trial. [JOBE, JOBY]

Joben: *(JOH-ben)* (Japanese) "Enjoy cleanness."

Jody: *(JOH-dee)* (English) Nickname for Joseph and Jude.

Joe: (English) Short form of Joseph. Joemar is occasionally used as a blend of Joseph and Mary. [JOEMAR, JOEY, JO-MAR]

Joed: *(JOH-ed)* (Hebrew) "Jehovah is witness." A biblical name.

Joel: *(JOH-ul)* (Hebrew) "Jehovah is God." Biblical: a prophet and writer of the Book of Joel. [JOELL]

John: *(jahn)* (Hebrew) "Jehovah has been gracious; has shown favor." Biblical: the name of the longest-lived of the 12 apostles, who was especially loved by Christ. Also the name of John the Baptist, who baptized Christ in the Jordan river. Dozens of variant forms, given names and surnames, male and female, have been created in almost every language. For a few examples, Jan is a Dutch and Slavic form; Janos is Czech; Joao is Portuguese; and the Johan variants are German and Swiss. Possibly the most popular name in history; kings, popes, saints, heroes, villains, and men of every degree between have borne the name. A contemporary trend seems to be building to hyphenate John, Jean, Jon, Sean, and Shawn with various other names. See also Evan, Evian, Ewen, Gian,

> **LESS COMMON CLASSICS;
> NEW, UNUSUAL NAMES**
>
> • Jace
> • Jaden
> • Jaime
> • Jakob
> • Jamal
> • Jaron
> • Jarrod
>   Jarred
> • Javier
> • Jaxon

Giovanni, Hans, Ian, Ivan, Jack, Jan, Jansen, Jean, Jon, Jonathan, Jonte, Juan, Keon, Keoni, Sean, Shane, and Shawn. [**JOHNNY**, JAN, JANOS, JOAO, JOHAN, JOHANN, JOHANNES, JOHN-CARLO, JOHN-MICHAEL, JOHNN, JOHNNIE, JOHN-PATRICK, JOHN-PAUL, JOHNSON]

Jomei: *(joh-may)* (Japanese) "Spread light."

Jon: *(jahn)* (English) Variant of John or short form of Jonathan, Jon is also used in the French fashion, hyphenated with a second name. See also Jean. [JON-CARLO, JON-COREY, JON-DAVID, JON-LUKE, JONN, JONNIE, JONNY, JON-TAE, JONTE, JON-PAUL]

Jonah: *(JOE-nah)* (Hebrew) "Dove." Biblical: because Jonah was on board a ship when God caused it to sink, sailors have traditionally used the name to personify someone who brings bad luck. [JONAS]

Jonathan: *(JAHN-a-thun)* (Hebrew) "Jehovah has given." Biblical: the son of King Saul, Jonathan was noted for his manliness, generosity, and unselfishness. He saved David's life when Saul would have killed him. [**JOHNATHAN, JOHNATHON, JONATHON**]

Jonte: *(jahn-TAY)* (American) Variant of Jon combined with the favored end sound of Dante. [JOHNTAY, JOHNTE, JONTAE, JONTELL, JONTEZ]

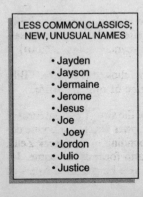

LESS COMMON CLASSICS; NEW, UNUSUAL NAMES

• Jayden
• Jayson
• Jermaine
• Jerome
• Jesus
• Joe
  Joey
• Jordon
• Julio
• Justice

Jorah: *(JOR-ah)* (Hebrew) "He has reproached." Biblical.

Joram: *(JOR-am)* (Hebrew) "Jehovah is exalted." Jorim was an ancestor of Mary. [JORIM]

Jordan: *(JOR-dan)* (Hebrew) "Down-flowing." Name of the major river in Palestine, used as a given name since the Crusades. The short form Jordi is also a Catalan variant form of George. Jourdaine and Jourdan are French forms. [JORDAIN, JORDELL, JORDEN, JORDI, JORDON, JORDY, JORDYN, JOURDAINE, JOURDAN]

Jorell: *(jor-ELL)* (American) Usage probably inspired by the fictional character Jor-El, father of Superman. See also Jarell and Jerrell. [JORAN, JOREL, JORREL, JORRELL]

Joren: *(JOR-en)* (Scandinavian) Variant of George. [JORAN, JOREY, JORIAN, JORN, JORON, JORRY, JORY]

Jorge: *(HOR-hay)* (Spanish, Portuguese) "Farmer." Variant of George. [JORJE]

Joseph: *(JOH-sef)* (Hebrew) "May Jah give increase." Biblical: the son of Jacob who, sold by his brothers into slavery, rose to become a supreme power in Egypt. Also Jesus' earthly father, a carpenter. Jose *(hoh-ZAY)* is a Spanish form. See also Guiseppe, Jody, and Joe. [JOSE, JOSEF, JOSELITO, JOSEPHUS]

Joshua: *(JOSH-yoo-ah)* (Hebrew) "Jehovah is salvation." Short form of Jehoshua. Biblical: Joshua was an attendant and helper to Moses during the Israelites' 40-year trek through the Sinai wilderness. He was appointed by God to lead the Israelites after the death of Moses. Josue is a Spanish form. [JOSH, JOSS, JOSUE]

Josiah: *(jo-SYE-ah)* (Hebrew) "Jehovah has healed." Biblical: king of Judah at age eight after his father was assassinated, Josiah ruled well for 31 years. [JOSIAS, JOZIAH]

Jotham: *(JO-tham)* (Hebrew) "May Jehovah complete." Biblical: a king of Judah during a time of military strife.

Jovan: *(jo-VAHN)* (Latin) "Father of the sky." Variant form of Jove, from Jupiter. Mythology: Jupiter was the supreme deity of Roman mythology, corresponding to the Greek Zeus. Some 20 saints have used the Latin form of the name, Jovanus. The Jovani variants may also be phonetic forms of

Giovanni. [JEOVANI, JEOVANNI, JEOVANY, JOVANI, JOVANN, JOVANNI, JOVANNY, JOVANY, JOVI, JOVIN, JOVITO, JOVON]

Juan: *(wahn)* (Spanish) Variant form of John, often used in combination with other names. [JUANCARLOS, JUANITO, JUANLUIS, JUANPABLO]

Jubal: *(JOO-bal)* (Hebrew) "The ram." Biblical: Jubal was the inventor of the harp and the pipes, and the founder of music making.

Judah: *(JOO-dah)* (Hebrew) "The praised one." Biblical: Judah was the fourth of Jacob's 12 sons. Judas, the Greek form of Judah, is very rarely used, due to the infamy of Judas Iscariot. Jude, a brother of James, wrote one of the shortest pieces in the Bible, the Book of Jude. See also Jody. [JUDD, JUDE, JUDSON]

Julian: *(JOO-lee-en)* (Latin) "Jove's child." Variant of Julius, the family clan name of several of the most powerful Roman emperors. Biblical: Julius, a Roman centurion, saved Paul's life during a hazardous voyage. See also Giuliano. [JULIO, JULIUS, JULES, JULIANO, JULIEN]

Junior: *(JOON-yer)* (Latin) "The younger one." Occasionally used as a given name, though more usually the abbreviation *Jr.* is attached to a full name when it is identical to a father's or grandfather's name.

Justice: *(JUSS-tiss)* (English) "To deliver what is just." A virtue name. See also Justus. [JUSTYCE]

Justin: *(JUS-tin)* (English) "Just, upright, righteous." Variant of Justus. St. Justin (second century) was a Greek philosopher who wrote of the moral values of Christianity. See also Jestin. [JUSTAIN, JUSTAN, JUSTEN, JUSTINO, JUSTYN]

Justus: (Latin) "Upright, just." Biblical: an early disciple of Christ, a man considered as a replacement for Judas Iscariot as one of the 12 apostles. [JUSTIS]

K

Kacey: *(KAY-see)* Variant of Casey or a creation based on the initials K.C. See also Casey and Kasey. [KACY, K.C.]

Kade: *(kayd)* (Scottish) "From the wetlands." See also Cadell. [KADEN, KADON, KADRICK]

Kadir: *(kah-DEER)* (Arabic) "Spring greening."

Kaelan: *(KAY-lan)* (Gaelic) Meaning uncertain. See also Caelan and Kellen. [KAEL, KAELIN, KALAN, KALEN, KALEY, KALIN]

Kaemon: *(kah-ay-mon)* (Japanese) "Joyful; right-handed." Old samurai name.

Kahlil: *(kah-LEEL)* (Arabic) "Friend." Famous name bearer: poet Kahlil Gibran. See also Khalil. [KAHLEIL, KALIL]

Kai: *(kye)* (Welsh, Scandinavian) "Keeper of the keys." Variant of Kay. Kai is also a Hawaiian name meaning "the sea." Kaimi *(kye-EE-mee)* is a Hawaiian name meaning "the seeker." [KAIMI]

Kain: *(kayn)* (Hebrew) "Acquire." Variant of Kenan. Biblical: refers to the tribe of Kenites or to a city in Judah. See also Cain and Kenan.

Kalani: *(kah-LAH-nee)* (Hawaiian) "The sky; chieftain."

QUICK REFERENCE
NAMES IN THE TOP 300

- Kade
  Kaden
- Karl
- Kasey
- Keaton
- Keegan
- Kennan
- Kelly
- Kelvin

Kaleb: *(KAY-leb)* (Hebrew) "Dog; tenacious and aggressive." See also Caleb.

Kalvin: *(KAL-vin)* See also Calvin and Kelvin. [KALVYN]

Kamden: *(KAM-den)* "Winding valley." See also Camden. [KAMDON]

Kameron: *(KÆM-er-en)* See also Cameron. [KAM, KAMRON, KAMRYN]

Kana: *(KAH-nah)* (Hawaiian) Mythology: a Maui demigod who could take the form of a rope and stretch from Molokai to Hawaii. Kano (Japanese) means "one's masculine power, capability." [KANO]

Kane: *(kayn)* (Irish) "Fighter." Kane *(kah-NAY)* is also a Japanese surname meaning "putting together; money." See also Caine. [KAIN, KAINE, KAYNE]

Kannon: *(KAN-en)* (Japanese) Variant of Kuan-yin, the Buddhist deity of mercy. Kannan (Sanskrit) is a variant of Krishna. [KANNAN, KANNEN]

Kanoa: *(ka-NOH-ah)* (Hawaiian) "The free one."

Karim: *(kah-REEM)* (Arabic) "Generous; a friend." The Koran lists generosity as one of the 99 qualities of God. Noted name bearer: basketball great Kareem Abdul-Jabbar. [KAREEM, KHARIM]

Karl: *(karl)* (German) "Man, manly." See also Carl. [KAREL, KARLE, KARLIN, KARLO, KARLOS, KARLTON, KARSON]

Kasey: *(KAY-see)* (Irish) "Alert; vigorous." Variant of Casey. See also Kacey.

Kasimir: *(KAZ-e-meer)* (Slavic) "Enforces peace." The name of the patron saint of Poland; also a favored name of Polish royalty. See also Casimir. [KAZ, KAZIMIR]

Kaspar: *(KAS-per)* (Polish) "Keeper of the treasure." Variant of Caspar.

Kassidy: *(KAS-a-dee)* See also Cassidy. [KASS]

Kassim: *(kah-SEEM)* (Arabic) "Divided." [KASEEM, KASIM]

Keane: *(keen)* (Irish) "Fighter." [KEENE, KEYNE]

Keandre: *(kee-AHN-dray)* (American) A contemporary blend of *Ke-* and Andre. [KEONDRE]

Keanu: *(kee-AH-noo)* (Hawaiian) "The breeze." Noted name bearer: actor Keanu Reeves.

Kearn: *(kern)* (Irish) "Dark." [KEARNE, KEARNEY]

Keaton: *(KEE-ton)* (English) "Place of hawks." [KEETON]

Kedrick: *(KEH-drik)* (English) "Gift of splendor." Variant of Cedric. [KEDDRICK, KEDRIC]

Keefe: *(keef)* (Irish) "Noble, gentle."

Keegan: *(KEE-gen)* (Irish) "A thinker; fiery." Variant of Hugh. [KAGAN, KAGEN, KEAGAN, KEGAN]

Keenan: *(KEE-nen)* (Irish) "Fighter." Notable name bearers: actors Keenan Wynn and Keenan Ivory Wayans. See also Keane and Kenan. [KEENEN, KEENON, KEN-NAN, KENNON]

Keiji: *(KAY-jee)* (Japanese) "Govern with discretion."

Keir: *(KEE-er)* (Irish) "Dusky; dark-haired." A name initially made familiar in the 1970s by the actor Keir Dullea. [KEER]

> **QUICK REFERENCE NAMES IN THE TOP 300**
>
> - Kendall
> - Kendrick
> - Khalil
> - Kolton
> - Korey
> - Kristian
> - Kurt
> - Kurtis

Keitaro: *(kay-tah-ROH)* (Japanese) "Blessed."

Keith: *(keeth)* (Scottish) "Woodland." The family name of hereditary earls marshals of Scotland from the 11th century.

Kelby: *(KEL-bee)* (Scandinavian) "Place by the fountain; spring."

Kellen: *(KEL-en)* (Gaelic) Possibly from an ancient given name meaning "slender." See also Kaelan. [KEELAN, KEILAN, KEILLAN, KELDEN, KELLAN, KELLE]

Kelly: *(KEL-ee)* (Irish) "Lively; aggressive." [KELLER, KELLEY]

Kelvin: *(KEL-vin)* (English) "River man." [KELVAN, KELVEN]

Ken: *(ken)* (English) Short form of names beginning with *Ken-*. Ken (Japanese) "strong, physically healthy." Kenn is an English surname. [KENN, KENNAN]

Kenan: *(KEE-nan)* (Hebrew) "Acquire." Biblical: the great-grandson of Adam; an ancestor of Mary, mother of Jesus. See also Kain and Keenan.

Kendall: *(KEN-dal)* (English) "Royal valley." Surname referring to Kent, England. [KENDAL, KENDALE, KENDEL, KENDELL]

Kendrew: *(KEN-droo)* (Scottish) "Manly; brave." Variant of Andrew.

Kendrick: *(KEN-drik)* (English, Welsh, Scottish) "Royal chieftain." Surname. [KENDRIC, KENDRIK, KENDRIX, KENRICK, KENRIK]

Kenji: *(KEN-jee)* (Japanese) "Intelligent second son; strong and vigorous." Kenjiro: *(ken-jee-ROH)* "Second son who sees with insight." [KENJIRO]

Kennard: *(KEN-erd)* (English) "Brave chieftain." [KENDON, KENNER]

Kennedy: *(KEN-a-dee)* (Irish) "Head of the clan." [KENNADY]

Kenneth: *(KEN-eth)* (English, Scottish) "Good-looking, fair." See also Kenny.

Kenny: *(KEN-ee)* (Scottish) Surname and short form of Kenneth. [KENNEY, KINNEY]

Kent: *(kent)* (English) "Royal chieftain." [KENTON, KENTRELL]

Kentaro: *(ken-tah-ROH)* (Japanese) "Sharp; big boy."

Keoki: *(kee-OH-kee)* (Hawaiian) Variant of George.

Keon: *(KEE-an)* (Irish) Variant of Ewan, from John. See also Ewen. Kian is a Gaelic name meaning "ancient." [KIAN]

Keoni: *(kee-OH-nee)* (Hawaiian) Variant of John. [KEON]

Kerrick: *(KARE-ik)* (English) "King's rule." English surname.

Kerry: *(KARE-ee)* (Irish) "Dusky, dark." Surname and name of the county in Ireland. Kerrigan is an Irish surname with the same meaning. [KERRIGAN]

Kerwin: *(KER-win)* (Irish) "Little dark one." [KERVIN, KERWYN]

Kevin: *(KEV-in)* (Irish) "Handsome child." St. Kevin (seventh century) founded a monastery that became famous as an educational center. There are many spelling variants, but Kevin is by far the most popular. [KEVAN, KEVEN, KEVEON, KEVINN, KEVION, KEVIS, KEVON, KEVRON, KEVYN]

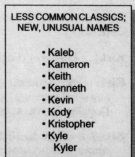

LESS COMMON CLASSICS; NEW, UNUSUAL NAMES

- Kaleb
- Kameron
- Keith
- Kenneth
- Kevin
- Kody
- Kristopher
- Kyle
  Kyler

Khalil: *(ka-LEEL)* (Arabic) "Friend." See also Kahlil. [KHA-LEEL]

Khanh: *(kahn)* (Turkish, Arabic) "Prince." Title used by central Asian tribal chieftains or ruling princes.

Kiefer: *(KEE-fer)* (German) "Barrelmaker." Variant form of Cooper. Noted name bearer: actor Kiefer Sutherland. [KEE-FER, KEIFER]

Kieron: *(KEER-en)* (Irish) "Dusky, dark-haired." St. Kieran (sixth century) was admired for his generosity. Notable in the 1990s: actor Kieran Culkin. See also Kiran. [KIERAN]

Killian: *(KIL-ee-an)* (Irish) "Small, fierce." [KILIAN]

Kim: *(kim)* (English) Short form of Kimball or Kimberly. Kim is also a Vietnamese name meaning "precious metal; gold." Literary: name of the boy hero of Rudyard Kipling's novel *Kim*.

Kimball: *(KIM-bul)* (English) "King's brave one." Variant of a medieval given name.

Kimo: *(KEE-moh)* (Hawaiian) Variant of James and Jim.

Kingsley: *(KINGS-lee)* (English) "King's field." King is one of several titles occasionally used as given names. Other male title names are Caesar, Count, Czar, Duke, Earl, Khanh, Prince, and Marquis. [KING, KINGSTON]

Kiran: *(keer-an)* (Hindu) "Beam of light." See also Kieron. [KYRAN]

Kirby: *(KER-bee)* (English) "Church farm." [KERBY]

Kirk: *(kerk)* (Scottish) "Church." In Scotland, *kirk* is still used as a word meaning "church." Noted name bearer: actor Kirk Douglas. [KERK, KIRKLAND, KIRKLIN, KIRKLYN, KYRK]

Kit: *(kit)* (English) Nickname for Christopher. Notable name bearer: frontiersman Kit Carson.

Knute: *(k'NOOT, noot)* (Scandinavian) "Knot." Variant form of Canute, the name of an 11th-century king of Denmark and England. Famous name bearer: Notre Dame football coach Knute Rockne.

Kody: *(KOH-dee)* "Helpful." See also Cody. [KODEY, KODIE]

Kolby: *(KOL-bee)* "Dark, dark-haired." Koby is a German/Polish short form of Jakob. See also Colby. [KELBY, KOBY]

Kolton: *(KOHL-ten)* "Coal town." See also Colton. [KOLT, KOLTEN, KOLTIN]

Konnor: *(KAHN-er)* "Desiring." See also Connor. [KONNER, KONOR]

Konrad: *(KAHN-rad)* (Polish, German) "Bold advisor." See also Conrad.

Korbin: *(KOR-bin)* "Raven-haired." See also Corbin. [KOR-BYN]

Kordell: *(kor-DELL)* "Cordmaker." See also Cordell. [KORD, KORDALE, KORDEL]

Kort: *(kort)* (Dutch) "Counselor." Variant of Cort and Kurt.

Kory: See also Cory. [KOREY, KORRY, KORREY]

Kraig: *(krayg)* "Rock, rocky." See also Craig.

Kris: *(kris)* (Scandinavian) Short form of names beginning with *Kris-*. Noted name bearer: singer/actor Kris Kristofferson.

Kristian: *(KRIS-t'-yun)* (Scandinavian) Variant of Christian. [KRISTAN, KRISTIEN]

Kristopher: *(KRIS-ta-fer)* (Scandinavian) Variant of Christopher. [KHRISTOPHER, KRISTOF, KRISTOFER, KRISTOFF, KRISTOFFER, KRYSTOF, KRYSTOPHER]

Kruz: *(krooz)* "Cross." See also Cruz.

Kurt: *(kert)* (German) "Brave, wise." Noted name bearer: actor Kurt Russell. See also Kort.

Kurtis: *(KER-tiss)* (French) "Courtier." An alternate form of Curtis. [KURTISS]

Kyle: *(kyl)* (Irish) Possibly a place name referring to "the narrows," "a wood," or "a church." [KYLER, KILE, KILEY, KYE, KYLAN, KYLAR, KYLEN, KYRELL]

L

La-: (American) Blends of *La-* plus various endings, with pronunciation emphasis on the second syllable. Second syllable may or may not begin with a capital. See also Lamar, Lamont, and *Le-*. [LADALE, LADELL, LAJON, LAMARCUS, LAMARIO, LARAY, LARELL, LARENZO, LARICO, LARON, LAROY, LAROYCE, LASEAN, LASHAWN, LATRELL, LAVAL, LAVANTE, LAVAR, LAVAUGHN, LAVELL, LAVON, LAVONTE]

Lachlan: *(LAHK-lin)* (Scottish "From the land of lakes."

Lafayette: *(lah-fay-ETT)* (French) Surname. Historical: the Marquis de Lafayette, a French nobleman, was only 20 when he came to serve four years in the American Revolutionary cause.

Laird: (Scottish) "Lord." Scottish landholder's title.

Lamar: *(la-MAR)* (French) "Of the sea." Surname. [LAMARR]

Lamont: *(la-MAHNT)* (Irish, Scottish) "Man of law." Lamond is a Scottish clan name. [LAMOND, LAMONTE]

Lance: *(lance)* (French) "Lance, lancer." Mythology: in the tales of King Arthur, Sir Lancelot was the most renowned Knight of the Round Table. Lantz is a Yiddish name meaning "lancet." See also Lanzo. [LANCELOT, LANTZ, LAUNCELOT]

Landon: *(LAN-don)* (English) "Landowner." Lando is familiar due to the character Lando Calrissian in the *Star Wars* film *Return of the Jedi* [LANDEN, LANDO, LANDYN]

Lane: *(layn)* (English) "Path, roadway." [LAYNE]

Langdon: *(LANG-don)* (English) "From the long hill slope." Related English surnames: Langley, "long meadow"; Langston, "long stone." [LANG, LANGLEY, LANGSTON]

Lanny: *(LAN-ee)* (English) Short form of names like Roland and Lanzo. [LANNIE]

Lanzo: *(LAHN-zo)* (Italian) Variant of Lance. See also Lonzo. [LANZA]

Laramie: *(LARE-a-mee)* (French) Surname with Western associations because of Laramie, Wyoming, a town on the Overland Trail, route of the Pony Express.

Larnell: *(lar-NELL)* (English) Blend of Larry and Darnell.

Larry: *(LARE-ee)* (English) Short form of Lawrence and Laurence, often used as an independent name.

Lars: *(larz)* (Scandinavian) Variant of Lawrence. [LARSEN, LARSON]

Lasalle: *(la-SAL)* (French) "The hall."

Lathan: *(LAY-then)* (English) Rhyming variant of Nathan. [LATHEN]

> **QUICK REFERENCE NAMES IN THE TOP 300**
>
> - Lance
> - Landon
> - Lane
> - Larry
> - Lawrence
> - Lee
> - Levi
> - Liam

Laurean: *(LAR-ee-an, LOR-ee-an)* (English) Variant of Lauren, from Laurence. [LAUREANO, LAURIAN, LAURIANO]

Lawrence: *(LAR-ens, LOR-ens)* (English) "From the place of the laurel trees." Lawrence, a later English form of Laurence, is the preferred form of the name in America. Laurens is a Dutch form; Laurent is French; Laurenz is German. See also Lars, Laurean, Loren, Lorenzo, Lorne, and Renzo. [LAURENCE, LAURENS, LAURENT, LAURENZ, LORANCE, LORENCE]

Le-: (American) Blend of *Le-* plus various endings, with pronunciation emphasis on the second syllable. See also *La-*. [LEMAR, LEONDRE, LERON, LERONE, LESEAN, LESHAWN, LEVELL, LEVELLE, LEVON, LEWAYNE]

Leandro: *(lee-AN-droh)* (Latin) "Lionlike man." Variant of Leander (Greek). St. Leander (seventh century) was a Spanish saint. [LEANDER, LEANDRE, LEANDREW]

Lee: *(lee)* (English) Surname frequently used in the American South as a given name in honor of Confederate general Robert E. Lee. [LEIGH]

Leif: *(life, layf, leef)* (Scandinavian) "Son, descendant." According to Norse legend, the Viking Leif Eriksson landed his longboat on American shores some 500 years before Columbus arrived.

Leighton: *(LAY-ton)* (English) "Meadow town." [LAYTON]

Leland: *(LEE-land)* (English) "Pasture ground." [LEELAND, LEYLAND]

Lemuel: *(LEM-yoo-el)* (Hebrew) "Belonging to God." Biblical: a king mentioned in Proverbs 31 who was given a detailed description of the value and capabilities of a good wife. Literary: Lemuel Gulliver of Jonathan Swift's *Gulliver's Travels*.

Lennox: *(LEN-iks)* (Scottish) Surname and clan name. Lennox, a Scottish nobleman, appears in Shakespeare's *Macbeth*.

Lenny: *(LEN-ee)* (English) Short form of Leonard. [LEN, LENN, LENNELL, LENNIE]

Leo: *(LEE-oh)* (Latin) "Lion." Leo was the name of numerous popes, including Leo the Great (fifth century), who successfully dealt with Attila the Hun when the Vandals conquered Rome.

Leon: *(LEE-ahn)* (Greek) "Lion." The lion is a central figure in the art and religious symbolism of many different cultures, usually meaning kingliness, grandeur, and courage. See also Lionel. [LION, LYON]

Leonard: *(LEN-ard)* (German) "Lion-bold." Notable name bearer of Leonardo (Italian, Spanish) is Leonardo da Vinci, considered to be one of the most brilliant and creative men who ever lived. See also Lenny. [**LEONARDO**, LENARD, LENNARD]

Leopold: *(LEE-oh-pold)* (German) "A bold man." A saint's name. [LEOPOLDO]

Leron: *(le-RON)* (French) "The circle." Also an Israeli name meaning "my song."

Leroux: *(la-ROO)* (French) "The red-haired one." [LARUE]

Leroy: *(LEE-roy, le-ROY)* (French) "The king." [LEEROY, LEROI]

Leslie: *(LEZ-lee)* (Scottish) The name of a prominent Scottish clan. Noted name bearer: actor Leslie Nielsen. [LES]

Lester: *(LES-ter)* (English) "Fortified place."

QUICK REFERENCE
NAMES IN THE TOP 300

- Logan
- Lorenzo
- Louis
- Lucas
- Luis
- Luke

Levi: *(LEE-vye)* (Hebrew) "Joined." Biblical: Levi, third of Jacob's 12 sons, became father of the tribe that was later assigned priestly duties.

Lewis: *(LOO-iss)* (English) "Renowned fighter." Variant of Louis. See also Louis and Luis. [LEW]

Lex: *(leks)* (English) Short form of Alexander. [LEXIS]

Liam: *(LEE-am)* (Irish) Variant of William. (Israeli) "My people." Noted name bearer: actor Liam Neeson. [LYAM]

Lincoln: *(LINK-en)* (English) "Lakeside colony." The name of an early Roman settlement in England. The surname, made famous by U.S. President Abraham Lincoln, is occasionally used as a given name. [LINC]

Lindell: *(LIN-del, lin-DEL)* (English) "From the linden tree dell." [LENDALL, LENDELL, LIN, LINDEL, LINWOOD]

Linus: *(LYE-nus)* (Greek) "Net." Biblical: a Christian companion to Paul in Rome. In modern times, Linus has been made familiar by the child character in Charles Schulz's cartoon *Peanuts*.

Lionel: *(LYE-a-nel)* (French) "Young lion." Leonel is a Spanish form. [LEONEL, LIONELL, LONELL, LONNELL]

Llewellyn: *(loo-ELL-en)* (Welsh) "Lionlike." [LEW, LEWELLYN]

Lloyd: *(loyd)* (Welsh) "Gray." Notable name bearer: actor Lloyd Bridges. See also Floyd. [LOYD]

Locke: *(lahk)* (English) Surname referring to a lock or a locksmith.

Logan: *(LOH-gan)* (Scottish) "Low meadow." [LOGEN]

Lonnie: *(LAH-nee)* (English) An independent name and short form of Lionel and Alonzo. [LON, LONELL, LONNE, LON-NELL, LONNY]

Lonzo: *(LAHN-zoh)* (Spanish) "Ready, eager." Short form of Alonzo. See also Lanzo. [LONZA, LONZELL]

Lorcan: *(LOR-ken)* (Irish) "Little fierce one."

Loren: *(LOR-en)* (English) Variant of Lorenzo and Lawrence. [LORAN, LORIN, LORREN, LORYN]

Lorenzo: *(lor-REN-zoh)* (Spanish, Italian) Variant of Lawrence. Notable name bearer: Lorenzo de'Medici, a Renaissance patron of Michaelangelo and da Vinci. In modern times: actor Lorenzo Lamas. Lorenz *(LOR-enz)* is a German form. See also Lawrence and Renzo. [LARENZO, LORENZ]

Lorne: *(lorn)* (Scottish) Surname; also a variant form of Lawrence. Familiar since the 1960s due to actor Lorne Greene. [LORNELL]

Louis: *(LOO-iss)* (English) *(loo-WEE)* (French) "Renowned fighter." A name used by 18 French kings and numerous saints. Noted name bearers of the 20th century: musician Louis Armstrong and writer Louis L'Amour. See also Lewis and Luis. [LOUIE, LOU, LUIGI]

Lovell: *(lo-VELL)* (English) "Young wolf." Lowell *(LOW-el)* is a later form of Lovell. [LOWELL]

Loyal: *(LOY-al)* (English) "Faithful, unswerving." See also Lyle. [LOYALL]

Lucas: *(LOO-kas)* (Latin) "Light, illumination." Variant of Lucius (Latin), a saint's name. Luc and Lucan are French forms; Lucio is Italian. See also Lucian and Luke. [LUC, LUCAN, LUCIO, LU-CIUS]

LESS COMMON CLASSICS; NEW, UNUSUAL NAMES
• Leo
• Leon
• Leonard
Leonardo
• Leroy
• Lewis
• Lincoln
• Lionel
• Lukas

Lucian: *(LOO-shun)* (French) Variant of Lucius. Luciano is an Italian and Spanish form. St. Lucian of Antioch (fourth century) was a noted scholar. [LUCIANO, LUCIEN]

Lucky: *(LUK-ee)* (English) "Fortunate." Lucky is also used as a nickname for Lucas and its variants.

Luis: *(loo-EECE)* (Spanish) Variant of Louis. See also Lewis and Louis. [LUIZ]

Luke: (Latin) "Light-giving." English form of Lucius. Biblical: a first-century Christian, called "the beloved physician," who wrote one of the four Gospel accounts of the life of Christ. Lukas is a Dutch form. See also Lucas and Lucian. [LUKAS]

Luther: *(LOO-ther)* (German) "Renowned warrior." Notable in the 1990s: singer Luther Vandross. [LOTHAR]

Lydell: *(lye-DEL)* (Scottish) Surname used as a given name. [LEDELL]

Lyle: *(LYE-el)* (French) "Islander." Lyell and Lyall are Scottish surnames meaning "loyal." See also Loyal. [LYALL, LYELL]

Lyndon: *(LIN-dan)* (English) "Place of linden trees." Noted name bearer: U.S. President Lyndon B. Johnson. See also Lindell. [LYNDALE, LYNDALL, LYNDELL]

Lysander: *(lye-SAN-der)* (Greek) "Liberator." Lysander is one of the main characters in Shakespeare's *A Midsummer Night's Dream.* Lisandro is a Spanish form. [LISANDRO]

M

Mac: *(mak)* (Gaelic) "Son of." Scottish and Irish surname prefix used as a given name or nickname. Mack is an ancient Scottish given name. See also Mackenzie, Maxwell, and *Mc-*. [MACK, MACKEY, MACKLIN]

Mace: *(mayce)* (English) Short form of names like Macy and Mason; also an English surname that may be a form of Matthew. Literally, a mace was a medieval weapon used by knights. Macerio may be a variant form of Macarius (Latin), a saint's name. [MACERIO, MACEY, MACY]

Mackenzie: *(ma-KEN-zee)* (Scottish) "Son of Kenzie; fair, favored one."

Madison: *(MAD-ih-sun)* (English) Surname derived from Matthew, "gift of Jehovah," or Matilda, "strong fighter."

Magnus: *(MAG-ness)* (Latin) "Great, greatness." A name favored by Scandinavian royalty; also a saint's name.

Major: *(MAY-jer)* (Latin) "Greater." Surname that is also a military rank.

Makani: *(mah-KAH-nee)* (Hawaiian) "Wind."

Makoto: *(mah-koh-toh)* (Japanese) "Good."

Malachi: *(MAL-a-kye)* (Hebrew) "Messenger of God." Biblical: a prophet and writer of the final book of the Old Testament. Malachy (12th century) was an Irish saint. [MALACHY, MALAKIA]

Malcolm: *(MAL-cum)* (Scottish) "St. Columb's disciple." Noted name bearer: publisher Malcolm Forbes. [MALCOM]

Malik: *(MAL-ik, ma-LEEK)* (Arabic) "Master." [MALEEK, MALEK, MALIQUE]

Manfred: *(MAN-fred)* (German) "Man of peace." [MANFREDO]

Mano: *(MAH-no)* (Hawaiian) "Shark." Figuratively, a passionate lover. Mano (Spanish) is a short form of Manuel.

Manuel: *(mahn-WEL)* (Spanish) "With us is God." Short form of Emmanuel. Noted name bearer: Manolito was one of Spain's greatest matadors. [MANNIE, MANNY, MANOLITO, MANOLO, MANUELO]

Manzo: *(mahn-zoh)* (Japanese) "10,000-fold-strong third son."

Mar-: (American) Blends based on Mark plus other names. See also Marshawn and Marquis. [MARKAINE, MARKEITH, MARQUEL, MARTRELL, MARZELL]

Marc: *(mark)* (French) See Mark.

Marcel: *(mar-SELL)* (French) Variant of the Latin Marcellus, from Marcus. Marcelo (mar-SAY-loh) is a Spanish form, Marceau *(mar-SOH)* is French. Marcelino and Marciano are Italian forms. Noted name bearer: the French mime, Marcel Marceau, combined two of the names in this entry. See also Marcus and Marcellus. [**MARCELO**, MARCEAU, MARCELINO, MARCELL, MARCIANO]

QUICK REFERENCE
NAMES IN THE TOP 300

- Malcolm
- Malik
- Manuel
- Marcus
- Mario
- Mark
  Marc
- Marshall
- Martin
- Mason

Marcellus: *(mar-SEL-us)* (Latin) A diminutive form of Marcus. Marcellus is the name of numerous saints. [MARCELLO]

Marco: *(MAR-koh)* (Spanish) Variant form of Marcus. Marcos is a Spanish and Portuguese form. [**MARCOS**, MARKO]

Marcus: *(MAR-kus)* (Latin) "Of Mars." Mythology: Mars, the Roman god of fertility, for whom the spring calendar month March was named, became identified with the Greek Ares, god of war. Markos and Markus are Dutch, German, and Hungarian forms. Marcas is Irish and Scottish. See also Marcel, Marco, Marcellus, Mark, and Marquis. [MARCAS, MARKOS, MARKUS]

Marden: *(MAR-den)* (English) Surname used as a given name. [MARDEL, MARDON, MARDYN]

Marek: *(MAR-ik)* (Czech, Polish) Variant form of Mark. [MARIK]

Mareo: *(mah-ray-oh)* (Japanese) "Rare, uncommon."

Mariano: *(mahr-ee-AHN-oh)* (Spanish) Masculine variant of Marie. Marion, the English form (Marian for girls) is very rarely used for American boys today.

Marino: *(ma-REE-no)* (Latin) "Of the sea." St. Marinus (third century) was a Roman centurion.

Mario: *(MAR-ee-oh)* (Latin) Masculine form of Mary. A number of male names have been created as variants of names attributed to the Virgin Mary. See also Mariano. [MARIUS]

Mark: *(mark)* (Latin) "Of Mars, the god of war." Variant of Marcus. Biblical: the Roman surname of John Mark, missionary companion to Peter and Paul and writer of one of the four Gospel accounts of the life of Jesus. Marc is a French form; Marco and Marques are Spanish. Marko and Markos are Slavic forms. See also Marcel, Marcellus, Marcus, Marek, Markell, Marquis, and Martin. [**MARC**, **MARCO**, MARKEY, MARKO, MARKOV, MARKUS, MARQ, MARQUE, MARQUES, MARQUEZ]

Markell: *(mar-KEL)* (German) Variant form of Mark. [MARKEL, MARX]

Marlon: *(MAR-lon)* (English) Possibly a variant form of Merle. Noted name bearer: actor Marlon Brando. [MARLAN, MARLAND, MARLEN, MARLIN]

Marlow: *(MAR-loh)* (English) "Marshy meadow." Marlowe and Marley are occasionally used for girls. [MARLEY, MARLOWE]

Maro: *(MAH-roh)* (Japanese) "Myself."

Marquis: *(mar-KEECE, MAR-kuss, mar-KEE)* (French) "Nobleman." Phonetic variants indicate that parents favor *mar-KEECE*, probably using Marquis as a title name, ranking below a duke and above an earl. Marquis *(MAR-kuss)* is a variant of a Scottish surname. [MARKEECE, MARKEESE, MARKESE, MARQUES, MARQUEZ, MARQUI, MARQUISE]

Marshall: *(MAR-shal)* (French) "Caretaker of horses." In America *marshal* is a law enforcement title similar to·*sheriff*. In France, the title refers to a high military rank. [MARSH, MARSHAL]

Marshawn: *(mar-SHAWN)* (American) A blend of *Mar-* and Shawn. [MARSEAN, MARSHON]

QUICK REFERENCE
NAMES IN THE TOP 300

- Matthew
  Mathew
- Max
- Maxwell
- Micah
- Michael
  Micheal
  Miguel
- Miles
- Mitchell
- Morgan

Marston: *(MARS-tun)* (English) "Town near the marsh." [MARSTEN]

Martel: *(mar-TEL)* (German) Variant form of Martin. [MARTELL]

Martin: *(MART-en)* (Latin) "Warrior of Mars." St. Martin de Porter (16th and 17th century), a man of mixed Spanish and Indian blood, is patron of work for interracial justice and harmony. Spanish pronunciation is *mar-TEEN*. Marten is a Scandinavian form; Martino and Martinus are Italian. Marti is a Swiss short form. [MARTEN, MARTI, MARTINO, MARTINUS, MARTON, MARTY, MARTYN]

Marvin: *(MAR-ven)* (English) Variant of Mervin. [MARVEN, MARVYN, MARWIN]

Mason: *(MAY-sun)* (English) "Worker in stone, stone mason." An occupational surname. See also Mace.

Matthew: *(MATH-yoo)* (Hebrew) "Gift of Jehovah." Biblical: the name of one of the twelve apostles, who wrote the first Gospel account of the life of Jesus. The alternate spelling Mathew is an English surname variant spelling. Mateo is a Spanish form; Matteo is Italian; Mateus is Portuguese. Mathieu and Matthieu are French forms. [MATHEW, MATEO, MATEUS, MATHIEU, MATT, MATTEO, MATTHIEU]

Matthias: *(ma-THYE-us)* (Hebrew) Variant form of Matthew. Biblical: the disciple selected by lot to replace Judas as an apostle. Mathias is a Scandinavian and Welsh form; Matias is Spanish. [MATHIAS, MATIAS]

Maurice: *(maw-REESE)* (French) "Dark-skinned; Moor." St. Maurus (sixth century) was a French saint. Mauricio is a Spanish form; Mauro is Italian and Portuguese. See also Merrick and Morris. [MAURICIO, MAURELL, MAUREO, MAURIN, MAURIO, MAURO, MAURUS, MORINO]

Maverick: *(MAV-rick)* (American) A 19th-century American named Maverick refused to brand his calves as other ranchers did; his name entered the common language signifying an independent man who avoids conformity. [MAVRICK]

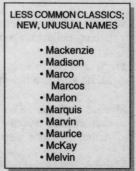

LESS COMMON CLASSICS; NEW, UNUSUAL NAMES

- Mackenzie
- Madison
- Marco
  Marcos
- Marlon
- Marquis
- Marvin
- Maurice
- McKay
- Melvin

Max: *(maks)* (Latin) "The greatest." Short form of Maxmillian or Maximo, the name of three Roman emperors and various saints. Maxime *(max-EEM)* is a French form. [MAXIM, MAXIME, MAXIMILIAN, MAXIMILIANO, MAXIMILLIAN, MAXIMINO, MAXIMO, MAXX]

Maxfield: *(MAKS-feeld)* (English) "Field belonging to Mack." Noted name bearer: artist Maxfield Parrish.

Maxwell: *(MAKS-wel)* (English, Scottish) "Mack's well." See also Mac.

Mayer: *(MYE-er)* (German) "Headman, mayor." Also an alternate form of Meir (Hebrew), "shining." [MEIR, MEYER]

Maynard: *(MAY-nerd)* (French) "Powerful." [MAYNE, MAYNOR]

Mc-: (Scottish, Irish) Surnames occasionally used as given names. See also Mac. [MCARTHUR, MCCAIN, MCCARTHY, MCCAULAY, MCCLAIN, MCCORMICK, MCKADE, MCKAY, MCKINLEY]

Meade: *(meed)* (English, Irish) "Honey wine; meadow."

Melvin: *(MEL-vin)* (English) Meaning uncertain; possibly "friend of Michael." [MEL, MALVIN, MELVON, MELVYN]

Mercer: *(MER-ser)* (French) "Merchant." Rare. Noted name bearer: children's books author/illustrator Mercer Mayer.

Merle: *(merl)* (French) "Blackbird." Country-western singer Merle Haggard has made this name familiar.

Merlin: *(MER-lin)* (Welsh) "Sea fortress." Mythology: Arthurian tales describe Merlin as the wizard who was King Arthur's mentor. See also Mervin. [MERLYN]

Merrick: *(MARE-ik)* (Welsh) Variant of Maurice. [MYRICK]

Merrill: *(MARE-ul)* (English) "Shining sea." [MERRIL]

Merritt: *(MARE-it)* (English) "Worthy." [MERITT]

Mervin: *(MER-ven)* (Welsh) Variant of Merlin. See also Marvin. [MERVYN, MERWYN]

Micah: *(MYE-cah)* (Hebrew) "Who is like God?" A variant of Michael. Biblical: a prophet and writer of the Book of Micah.

Michael: *(MYE-kal)* (Hebrew) "Who is like God?" Michael the archangel (chief or principal angel) and Gabriel are the only two angels given personal names in the canonical Bible. Many saints, emperors, and kings have borne the name, and there are many variants, male and female. In this century, Michael has been among the top 50 names for at least seven decades. Micheal, the Gaelic spelling, is frequently used. This may be intentional, or it may be an accidental transposition of the *ae* vowels. Michael and Angelo are frequently blended in Latin-based language–speaking countries, as in Michelangelo Buonarroti, the Italian sculptor-artist. Miguel *(mee-GEL)* is a Spanish and Portuguese form. Of the many national variants, several are indicated here. See also Mike, Mischa, and Mitchell. [MIGUEL, MICHEAL, MICHEL (FRENCH, DUTCH); MIKAEL, MIKELL, MIKKEL (SCANDINAVIAN); MICHAIL, MIKHAIL (RUSSIAN); MICHAL (POLISH); MIKO (SLAVIC); MIKEL, MIQUEL (BASQUE, FRENCH); MICHAELANGELO, MYCHAEL, MYCHAL, MYKEL]

Michio: *(mee-chee-oh)* (Japanese) "Man with strength of three thousand."

Mike: *(myk)* (English) Short form of Michael and Micah, often used as an independent name. The nicknames Mick and Mickey are considered to be particularly Irish. See also Mischa. [MICKEY, MICK]

Miki: *(MEE-kee)* (Japanese) "Tree." Mikio *(mee-kee-OH)* "Three trees together. [MIKIO]

Miles: *(myls)* (English) "Merciful." Noted name bearers: historically, the Pilgrim leader, Miles Standish. In the 1990s, the character Miles O'Brien in the TV series *Star Trek: Deep Space Nine*. See also Myles. [MILO, MYLO]

Miller: *(MIL-er)* (English) "One who grinds grain." Occupational surname. [MILLARD, MILLEN]

Milton: *(MIL-ton)* (English) "Mill town." Noted name bearer: comedian Milton Berle.

Minoru: *(mee-noh-roo)* (Japanese) "Bear fruit."

Mischa: *(MEE-sha)* (Russian) Nickname for Michael. See also Mike.

Mitchell: *(MITCH-el)* (English) Variant of Michael. [MITCH, MITCHEL]

Modesto: *(mo-DESS-toh)* (Latin) "Modesty, moderate." A Spanish saint's name.

Mohammad: *(moh-HAH-med)* (Arabic) "Praiseworthy, glorified." Name of the founder of the Islamic religion. Listed here are only a few of the dozens of names and name variants attributed to Mohammad. See also Ahmed and Hamid. [MAHMOUD, MOHAMAD, MOHAMED, MOHAMET, MOHAMMED, MUHAMMAD, MUHAMMED]

Monroe: *(mun-ROH)* (Scottish) "From the river's mouth."

Montaine: *(mon-TAYNE)* (French) "Mountain." [MONTANE, MONTAYNE]

Montana: *(mon-TAN-nah)* (Latin) "Mountain." The name of the western state as a given name. May also be used in reference to Montanus, a saint's name (third century). [MONTANNA, MONTANUS]

Montaro: *(mon-tah-roh)* (Japanese) "Big boy."

Monte: *(MON-tee, mon-TAY)* (Latin) "Mountain." Short forms of Montague and Montgomery. Noted name bearer: Montel Williams, TV talk show host. [MONTAE, MONTAY, MONTEL, MONTES, MONTEZ, MONTIE, MONTREL, MONTRELL, MONTY]

Montgomery: (English) "Mountain of the one who rules." A surname of English and Scottish earls.

Morell: *(moh-REL)* (French) "Dark one; the Moor." [MAU-RELL]

Morgan: (Welsh) "Of the sea." Surname. [MORGEN]

Morio: *(mor-ee-oh)* (Japanese) "Forest boy."

Morland: (English) "Marsh, wet land." [MORLEY]

Morris: *(MOR-iss)* (English) "Dark." Variant of Maurice. [MORREY, MORRIE, MORRISON, MORSE]

Moses: *(MOH-ziz)* (Hebrew) "Saved from the water." Biblical: name of the Hebrew child pulled out of the River Nile and adopted by the Egyptian Pharaoh's daughter. Moses lived one of the most eventful lives recorded in Scripture (see the Book of Exodus). Moss is an English medieval form of Moses. Moises *(moh-EE-says)* is a Spanish form; Moshe is Hebrew. Mosiah probably is a blend of Moses and Josiah. [MOISES, MOSHE, MOSIAH, MOSS]

Murray: *(MUR-ee)* (Scottish) "From the sea." Surname of an ancient Scottish clan, occasionally used as a given name.

Myles: (English) Variant of Miles.

Myron: (Greek) "Myrrh, sweet oil."

N

Naman: *(NAY-man)* (Hindu) "Salutations." Naaman (Hebrew) means "be pleasant." [NAAMAN]

Namir: *(nah-MEER)* (Israeli) "Leopard."

Napoleon: *(na-POH-lee-an)* (Italian) "Man from Naples." Famous name bearer: the Corsican soldier who became emperor of France (19th century).

Nardo: *(NAR-doh)* (Latin) "Strong, hardy." Short form of names like Bernardo and Leonardo.

Nathan: *(NAY-than)* (Hebrew) "Given." Biblical: Nathan was God's prophet during the reigns of David and Solomon. Famous name bearer: American Revolutionary hero Nathan Hale. [NAT, NATE]

Nathaniel: *(na-THAN-yel)* (Hebrew) "God has given." Biblical: one of the 12 apostles. [NATHANAEL, NATHANIAL]

Navarro: *(na-VAR-oh)* (Spanish) "Plains." The name of a medieval kingdom in Spain. Navarre is a French form. [NAVARRE]

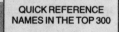
Neal: *(neel)* (English) Variant form of Neil. [NEALE]

Ned: (English) Nickname for Edward.

Nehemiah: *(nee-ah-MYE-ah)* (Hebrew) "Jah comforts." Biblical:

the prophet assigned to lead the Jews on their return to Jerusalem from exile in Babylon.

Neil: *(neel)* (Gaelic) "Champion." Scottish variant form of Niall. See also Neal, Nelson, Niall, Niles, and Nyles. [NEILAN, NEILL]

Nelson: *(NEL-sun)* (English) "Son of Neil." Historical: Admiral Lord Nelson, the English naval hero of Trafalgar. [NELS]

Nestor: *(NES-tor)* (Greek) "Remembers." In legend, the learned Greek general who gave counsel during the Trojan War.

Nevada: *(ne-VAH-dah)* (Spanish) "Snow-clad." The name of the western state used as a given name.

Nevan: *(NEV-en)* (Irish) "Little saint." [NEVIN]

Neville: *(NEV-il)* (French) "New village." [NEVIL, NEVILL]

Niall: *(NYE-al)* (English) *(NEE-al)* (Irish) "Champion." Historical: Niall of the Nine Hostages founded a dynasty of Irish kings. See also Neil, Nigel, Niles, and Nyles.

Nicholas: *(NIK-oh-lus)* (Greek) "Victorious; conquerer of the people." Biblical: one of seven "qualified men" in the first-century Christian congregation. St. Nicholas (fourth century) is known as the patron saint of Greece and Russia, children, scholars, sailors, and pawnbrokers. Because Nicholas was such a popular name over the centuries, many variant and short forms were created for men and women. Five popes and two emperors of Russia have borne the name. See also Cole, Colin, and Nick. [**NICKOLAS, NICOLAS, NIKOLAS**, NICHOLAI, NICOLAI, NIKLOS (SLAVIC); NICKOLAUS, NIKOLAUS (GERMAN); NIKOLAI (POLISH, RUSSIAN); NICCOLO, NICOLI, NICOLO, (ITALIAN); NIKOLOS (GREEK); NICHOLAUS, NICOLAUS, NIKLAS]

Nick: *(nik)* (English) Short form of Nicholas. Mythology: the name Nicholas refers to Nike *(NYK-kee)*, the Greek goddess of victory. Nikki and Nikko are also Japanese surnames with the potential meanings "two trees" and "daylight." [NICCO, NICO, NICKSON, NICKY, NIKKI, NIKKO, NIKO, NIKOS, NIXON, NYKKO]

Nicol: *(nih-KOL, NIK-ul)* (Scottish, English) Variant of Nicholas.

Nigel: *(NYE-jel)* (English) Variant of Niall. The name traveled well. Niall in Ireland and Scotland became Njal in Scandinavia, was latinized to Nigellus in Normandy, then became Nigel in England. Niguel *(ni-GEL)* is a Spanish variant. [NIGUEL, NIJEL, NYGEL]

Nikhil: *(nih-KEEL)* (Hindu) "Whole, all." [NIKHEL]

Niles: *(nyles)* (English) Variant of Niall. May also be used in reference to Nilus (Greek), a saint's name. Perhaps more familiar in the 1990s due to the character of Dr. Niles Crane in the TV sitcom *Frasier*. See also Nyles. [NILO]

Noah: *(NOH-ah)* (Hebrew) "Rest, consolation." Biblical: the patriarch survivor of the Great Flood. According to the biblical account, all the world's nations are descended from Noah's three sons. Noe is a Spanish form. [NOE]

Noel: *(NOH-el)* (French) "Birthday." Commonly used in reference to Christ's birth, Noel is also an alternate name for Christmas.

Nolan: (Irish) "Renowned; noble." [NOLAND, NOLEN, NOLYN]

LESS COMMON CLASSICS; NEW, UNUSUAL NAMES

- Nathanael
- Neil
- Nelson
- Nikolas
- Noel

Norbert: *(NOR-bert)* (German) "Shining from the north." St. Norbert (12th century) was a German saint. [NORBERTO]

Norman: (English) "Man of the north." Famous name bearers: author Norman Mailer, artist Norman Rockwell, and U.S. General Norman Schwarzkopf. Normando is a Spanish form. [NORMAND, NORMANDO]

Norris: *(NOR-iss)* (Scottish, English) "From the north."

Nuri: *(NOOR-ee)* (Israeli) "My fire."

Nuru: *(ner-ROO)* (Swahili) "Born at night."

Nyles: *(nyls)* (English) Variant of Niles, from Niall.

O'- : (Irish) "Descendant of." Surnames occasionally used as given names. [ODELL, O'KEEFE, O'SHAY, O'SHEA]

Octavio: *(ahk-TAH-vee-oh)* (Latin) "Eighth." From Octavius, a Roman family clan name. [OCTAVIUS, OCTAVIAN]

Olaf: *(OH-loff)* (Scandinavian) "Ancestor." [OLAV]

Oliver: *(AH-lih-ver)* (English) "The olive tree." Biblical: the olive tree is a symbol of fruitfulness, beauty, and dignity. Today "extending an olive branch" traditionally signifies an offer of peace. Literary: the title character in Dickens' *Oliver Twist*. Notable in the 1980s–1990s: film director Oliver Stone.

Omar: *(OH-mar)* (Arabic) "Long-lived." (Hebrew) "Speaker." Biblical: a sheik of Edom and son of Esau. Omar Khayyam (12th century) was a Persian poet, astronomer, and mathematician. Caliph Omar II made Islam an imperial power. Notable in modern times: General Omar Bradley and actor Omar Sharif. [OMARR]

Omari: *(oh-MAR-ee)* (Swahili) "God the highest."

Orel: *(OR-el)* (Russian, Slavic) "Eagle." Variants may be American creations. Noted name bearers: evangelist Oral Roberts and baseball player Orel Hershiser. [ORAL, OREL, ORIEL, ORREL, ORRY]

Oren: *(OR-en)* (Hebrew) "Pine tree." See also Orrin. [ORIN, ORAN]

Orion: *(oh-RYE-on)* (Greek) "Rising in the sky; dawning." Greek mythology: Orion was a mighty hunter, the son of Poseidon. The Orion constellation contains three of the most conspicuous stars in the nighttime sky.

Orlando: *(or-LAHN-doh)* (Spanish) "Renowned in the land." Variant form of Roland. [ORLAN, ORLAND, ORLIN, ORLONDO]

Orrin: *(OR-en)* (English) The name of a river in England. Familiar today due to Utah Senator Orrin Hatch. See also Oren. [ORRAN, ORREN]

Orson: *(OR-sun)* (Latin) "Little bear." Notable name bearer: actor/director Orson Welles. [ORSINO]

Orville: *(OR-vil)* (French) "Gold town." Famous name bearer: inventor/aviator Orville Wright. [ORVELLE, ORVIL]

QUICK REFERENCE NAMES IN THE TOP 300

• Owen

LESS COMMON CLASSICS; NEW, UNUSUAL NAMES

• Oliver
• Omar
• Orlando
• Oscar

Oscar: *(OS-ker)* (English) "God's spear." [OSKAR]

Osman: *(OZ-man)* (Scandinavian) "Godly protection." [OSMIN, OSMOND, OSMUND]

Oswald: *(OZ-wald)* (English) "God's power." Oswin means "God's friend." [OSWALDO, OSWIN, OZZIE, OZZY]

Otto: *(AW-toh)* (German) "Wealthy." [OTIS]

Owen: *(OH-en)* (Welsh) "Well-born." Variant of Ewan. [OW-YNN]

P

Palmer: *(PAHL-mer)* (English) "Bearing a palm branch."

Pancho: *(PAHN-cho)* (Spanish) Nickname for Francisco or Frank.

Paris: *(PARE-iss)* (French) The name of the French capital used as a given name. Greek mythology: Paris was the prince of Troy whose love affair with Helen led to the Trojan War. [PARRIS, PARRISH]

Parker: *(PAR-ker)* (English) "Keeper of the forest, forest ranger." A surname made familiar as a given name by actor Parker Stevenson.

Parnel: *(par-NEL)* (English) Surname derived from a medieval given name. Use of Parnell may be in honor of Charles Parnell, 19th-century Irish nationalist. See also Pernell. [PARNELL]

Pascual: *(pahs-KWALL)* (Spanish) "Passover." Pasquale is an Italian form; Pascal is French. [PASCAL, PASCOE, PASQUAL, PASQUALE]

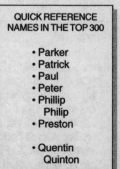

QUICK REFERENCE
NAMES IN THE TOP 300

- Parker
- Patrick
- Paul
- Peter
- Phillip
  Philip
- Preston

- Quentin
  Quinton

Patrick: *(PAT-rik)* (Latin) "Patrician, noble." The Romans once were divided socially and politically into plebeians (commoners) and patricians (aristocrats). Patrick, patron saint of Ireland (fourth and fifth century), has given the name its Irish associations. Padric and Padraic are Irish variants; Patric is French; Patricio is Spanish and Portuguese. See also Peyton. [PADRAIC, PADRIC, PAT, PATRIC, PATRICIO]

Paul: (pahl) (Latin) "Little." Biblical: the apostle evangelist. Paul's letters to early Christians form the majority of the books of the New Testament. Some of the many language variants are shown here. [**PABLO** (SPANISH); PAOLO (ITALIAN); PAULINO, PAULO (PORTUGUESE); PAL, POUL (SCANDINAVIAN); PAUEL (DUTCH); PAULUS (LATIN); PAVEL (SLAVIC); PAVLIK, PAVLO (RUSSIAN); PAULSON (ENGLISH); PAULSEN (DUTCH, SCANDINAVIAN)]

Pedro: *(PAY-droh)* (Spanish, Portuguese) Variant form of Peter. Pietro is an Italian form. See also Peter. [PIETRO]

Percy: *(PER-see)* (French) "Pierces." [PERCEVAL, PERCIVAL]

Pernell: *(per-NEL)* (English) Surname. Variant form of Peter. Made familiar in the 1960s by actor Pernell Roberts. See also Parnell.

Perry: *(PARE-ee)* (Latin) "Wanderer." Surname and a short form of Peregrine *(PARE-a-green)*. The peregrine falcon is the bird most favored in the ancient sport of falconry. [PEREGRINE]

Peter: *(PEE-ter)* (English) "A rock." Variant of Petros (Greek). Biblical: one of the 12 apostles, Peter the fisherman is remembered for his impulsive nature as well as for his rocklike faith. In Catholic tradition, the first pope. There are dozens of variants of the name in many languages. Pieter is a Dutch form; Petrov and Pyotr are Russian. See also Pedro, Pernell, Pierce, and Pierre. [PETE, PETERSON, PETROS, PETROV, PIETER, PYOTR]

Peyton: *(PAY-ten)* (Irish) Variant of Patrick. Paden is a Scottish variant. [PADEN, PAYTON]

Phillip: *(FIL-ip)* (Greek) "Fond of horses." Biblical: one of the 12 apostles. Philippe *(fil-LEEP)* is a French form. See also Felipe. [**PHILIP**, PHIL, PHILIPPE]

Philo: *(FYE-loh)* (Greek) "Loves, loved." Noted name bearer: Philo T. Farnsworth, inventor of television.

Pierce: (English, Irish) Variant of Piers, from Peter. [PEARCE, PEARSON, PIERSON]

Pierre: *(pee-AIR)* (French) Variant form of Peter. Per and Peer are German and Scandinavian forms. [PEER, PER, PIERS]

Prentice: *(PREN-tiss)* (English) "Apprentice, learner." [PRENTISS]

Prescott: *(PRESS-kut)* (English) "Priest's cottage."

Preston: *(PRES-ten)* (English) "Priest's town."

Prince: *(prince)* (English) "Principal one; first." The rock musician Prince made the royal title familiar as a given name, but has changed his name to an unpronounceable symbol. [PRINCETON]

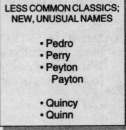

LESS COMMON CLASSICS; NEW, UNUSUAL NAMES

- Pedro
- Perry
- Peyton
  Payton

- Quincy
- Quinn

Q

Quade: *(kwayde)* (Gaelic) From McQuade, a Scottish clan name.

Quentin: *(KWEN-tin)* (English) "Fifth." Quent and Quint are short forms. [QUENT, QUENTON, QUINT, QUINTEN, QUINTIN, QUINTON]

Quincy: *(KWIN-see)* (French) "Fifth," from a Roman clan name. Noted name bearer: music producer Quincy Jones. [QUINCEY]

Quinn: *(kwin)* (Gaelic) "Counsel." A Scottish and Irish surname used as a given name from very ancient times. Quin *(keen)* is a Spanish short form of Joaquin. [QUIN, QUINLAN, QUINNELL]

Quintrell: *(kwin-TREL)* (English) "Dashing; elegant." Surname. Quantrell is a surname made famous during the Civil War by the soldier-brigands known as Quantrell's Raiders. [QUANTRELL, QUENTRELL]

R

Radames: *(RAH-da-mays)* The name given the Egyptian hero of Verdi's opera *Aïda*.

Radford: *(RAD-ford)* (English) "From the reedy ford." Old English surname. [REDFORD]

Rafael: *(rah-fah-EL)* (Spanish) "God has healed." Variant form of Raphael.

Rafe: *(rayf)* (Scandinavian) A short form of Rafer or Raphael. [RAFER]

Rai: *(RYE-ee)* (Japanese) "Trust; lightning, thunder." Also a Spanish short form of Raimundo.

Rainer: *(RAY-ner)* (German) "Strong counselor." Variant form of Raynor. Related surnames are occasionally used as given names. Use of Rainier *(ray-NEER)* may be influenced by Prince Rainier of Monaco. See also Raynor. [RAINIER, RANIER, RAINOR, REINER]

Rajan: *(rah-JAHN)* (Sanskrit) "King." Raja *(RAH-jah)* is an Indian or Malay princely title; Raj *(rahzh)* means "rule." [RAJ, RAJA, RAJAH]

Raleigh: *(RAH-lee)* (English) "Deer's meadow."

Ralph: *(ralf)* (English) "Wolf counsel." Rolf is a German form. Ralston, "Ralph's town," is an English surname. See also Raul. [RALSTON, ROLF]

Ram: *(ram)* (Sanskrit) "Pleasing." (Hebrew) "High." Mythology: as the seventh incarnation of Vishnu, Rama's story is told in the Hindu *Ramayana*. Biblical: an ancestor of King David and Jesus. [RAMA, RAMOS]

Rami: *(RAH-mee)* (Arabic) "Loving." [RAMEY, RAMY]

Ramiro: *(ra-MEER-oh)* (Spanish) "Wise, renowned."

Ramón: *(ra-MOHN)* (Spanish) Variant of Raymond. [RAMONE, RAYMAN, RAYMON]

> **QUICK REFERENCE NAMES IN THE TOP 300**
>
> - Randall
> - Randy
> - Raymond
> - Richard
>   Ricardo
> - Ricky
> - Riley

Ramses: *(RAM-zees)* (Egyptian) "Begotten by Ra, the sun god." Ramses or Rameses was the name of at least eleven kings of Egypt. Ramzan is a Russian form. [RAMESES, RAMZAN]

Ramsey: *(RAM-zee)* (English) "Ram's island." [RAMSAY, RAMZEY, RAMZI]

Randall: *(RAN-dal)* (English) Randall and the other English surnames listed here are variants of Randolph. [RAND, RANDAL, RANDALE, RANDEL, RANDELL, RANDON, RENDALL, RENDELL]

Randolph: *(RAN-dolf)* (Teutonic) "Wolf's shield." See also Randall. [RANDOLF, RANOLF, RANULFO]

Randy: *(RAN-dee)* (English) Short form of Randall and Randolph. More frequently used than the longer forms.

Raphael: *(rah-fah-EL)* (Hebrew) "God has healed." The name of an archangel in the Apocryphal book of Tobit. Noted name bearer: renowned Italian Renaissance artist Raphael was a contemporary of da Vinci and Michelangelo. See also Rafael.

Rashad: *(rah-SHAD)* (Arabic) "Thinker, counselor." [RASHAAD, RASHEED, RASHID, RASHIDI]

Rashaun: *(ray-SHAWN)* (American) Blend of Ray and Shawn, or a variant form of Roshan (Sanskrit), "Shining light." See also Roshan. [RASHAE, RASHANE, RASHAWN, RAYSHAUN, RAYSHAWN]

Raul: *(rah-OOL)* (Spanish) Variant of Ralph. Raoul is a French form. Noted name bearer: actor Raul Julia. See also Ralph. [RAOUL]

Ravi: *(RAH-vee)* (Sanskrit) "Sun." A name made familiar by Ravi Shankar, renowned sitar player and composer. Mythology: the Hindu god of the sun.

Ray: (English) "Counselor." A short form of Raymond often used in contemporary blends. See also Raynor. [RAYCE, RAYDER, RAYDON, RAYFORD, RAYLEN, RAYNELL]

Raymond: *(RAY-mund)* (French) "Guards wisely." St. Raymond (13th century) was a Spanish saint. See also Rainer, Ramón, Ray, and Redmond. [RAIMOND, RAIMUNDO, RAMOND, RAYMUND, RAYMUNDO, REYMOND, REYMUNDO]

Raynor: *(RAY-ner)* (Scandinavian) "Strong counselor." Variant of Ragnar, an ancient personal name. See also Rainer. [RAYNER, RAGNAR, RANE, RANELL, RAYNE, RAYNELL, RAYNORD]

Redmond: *(RED-mund)* (Irish, English) Surname; a variant of Raymond.

Reece: *(reece)* (Welsh) "Ardent; fiery." See also Rhys. [REESE]

Reeve: *(reev)* (English) Surname. The medieval reeve of a castle or landholding had oversight of all matters of feudal obligations. *Rêve* is the French word "dream." [REEFORD, REEVES, REVE]

Reginald: *(REJ-a-nald)* (English) "Counselor-ruler." Variant of Reynold. [REGGIE, REGINALDO, REGINO]

Regis: *(REE-jis)* (Latin) "Rules." The name is familiar today due to TV morning show host Regis Philbin of *Live with Regis and Kathie Lee.*

Rei: *(RAY-ee)* (Japanese) "Law, rule; strive." Reizo *(ray-ee-ZOH)* can mean "cool, calm; well-groomed." [REIZO]

Reid: *(reed)* (English) "Red-headed." English and Scottish surname. [READE, REED, REDD]

QUICK REFERENCE
NAMES IN THE TOP 300

- Robert
- Rodney
- Roger
- Ronald
- Ross
- Roy
- Russell
- Ryan

Remington: *(REM-ing-tun)* (English) The character on the TV show *Remington Steele* may have influenced increased use of this English surname as a given name. St. Remi (fifth century) was a French saint. [REMI, REMO, REMY]

René: *(re-NAY)* (French) "To rise again." Renato is a Spanish form. Rene without the accent may be pronounced *(REN-ee)*. [RENATO, RENNE, RENNIE, RENNY]

Renjiro: *(ren-jee-roh)* (Japanese) "Clean, upright, honest."

Reno: *(REE-noh)* (Spanish) Short form for names like Moreno. May sometimes be used in reference to the city in Nevada.

Renzo: *(REN-zoh)* (Italian) Short form of Lorenzo. The Japanese name Renzo can mean "third link" or "third son."

Reuben: *(ROO-ben)* (Hebrew) "See, a son." Biblical: Reuben was the firstborn of Jacob's 12 sons. Ruben is a Spanish and Scandinavian form. [RUBEN]

Rex: *(reks)* (Latin) "Chieftain, ruler." Notable name bearers: actor Rex Harrison and film critic Rex Reed. [REXFORD, REXTON]

Reyes: *(rays)* (Spanish) "Kings." [REY]

Reynard: *(ray-NARD)* (French) "Strong counselor." [RAYNARD, RENARD, RENARDO, REYNARDO]

Reynold: *(REN-ald)* (English) "Counselor-ruler." See also Reginald and Ronald. [RAYNALDO, REINALDO, RENALDO, REYNALD, REYNALDO]

Rhett: *(ret)* (Welsh) Variant of Rhys. Rhett is most familiar as the hero of Margaret Mitchell's *Gone With the Wind*.

LESS COMMON CLASSICS;
NEW, UNUSUAL NAMES

- Rafael
- Ralph
- Raul
- Ray
- Reid
- Rhett
- Roberto

Rhys: *(rees)* (Welsh) "Ardent; fiery." See also Reece.

Richard: *(RICH-erd)* (English, French) "Powerful, strong ruler." A Teutonic name that developed in several European countries during the Middle Ages, with many variants. England's King Richard Coeur de Lion gave the name lasting impressions of kingliness and the exploits of a crusading knight. Ricardo is a Spanish and Portuguese form; Riccardo is Italian; Rikard is a German form. See also Dick, Ricky, and Ryker. [RICARDO, RICARD, RICCARDO, RICHARDO, RICKARD, RIKARD]

Ricky: *(RIK-ee)* (English) Short form of Richard. Rikk and Rikki are Norwegian forms. See also Richard. [RICK, RIC, RICCO, RICHIE, RICKEY, RICKIE, RICO, RIKK, RIKKE, RIKKI, RIQUE, RITCHIE]

Rigel: *(RYE-jel)* (Arabic) "Foot." In the Orion constellation, Rigel is the blue star of the first magnitude that marks the hunter's left foot.

Riley: *(RYE-lee)* (English, Irish) "Rye." Variant of Ryley. [REILLEY, REILLY]

Rinji: *(rin-jee)* (Japanese) "Peaceful forest."

Rio: *(REE-oh)* (Spanish) "River." An independent name and short form of names ending with -rio. Rito is a male short form of Margaret. [REILLY, RITO]

River: *(RIV-er)* (English) A name from nature. Literally, a flowing body of water. Made familiar in the 1980s by actor River Phoenix.

Roald: *(ROH-al)* (Scandinavian) "Renowned; powerful." Famous name bearers: Norwegian explorer Roald Amundsen and author Roald Dahl.

Robert: *(RAH-bert)* (English, French) "Famed; bright, shining." One of the all-time favorite names for boys since the Middle Ages. Especially favored by the Scots due to 14th-century king Robert the Bruce (see Bruce) and to poet Robert Burns. Roberto is a Latin form of the name. See also Bobby, Robin, and Rupert. [**ROBERTO**, ROB, ROBB, ROBBIE, ROBERTSON, ROBBY]

Robin: *(RAH-bin)* (English) Variant of Robert, in popular use as a boy's name since the medieval days of Robin Hood. Notable in the 1990s due to actor/comedian Robin Williams. [ROBBIN, ROBINSON]

Rocky: *(RAH-kee)* (English) Nickname for Rocco (Italian), the name of a 14th-century saint. Also used for the literal meaning ''rock.'' St. Roque (16th century) was a Spanish saint. The nickname is familiar today primarily due to champion boxer Rocky Marciano and his fictional counterpart, Rocky Balboa, of the *Rocky* series of movies. [ROCCO, ROCK, ROCKFORD, ROCKLAND, ROCKLIN, ROCKWELL, ROQUE]

Rodel: *(roh-DEL)* (French) Variant form of Roderick. [RODELL]

Roderick: *(RAH-der-ik)* (German) ''Famous ruler.'' Roderic and Rodric are Scottish forms. See also Rodel and Rodrigo. [ROD, RODD, RODDRIC, RODDRICK, RODDY, RODERIC, RODERIK, RODRIC, RODRICK]

Rodman: *(RAHD-man)* (English) ''Guard wisely.''

Rodney: *(RAHD-nee)* (English) ''Island of reeds.''

LESS COMMON CLASSICS;
NEW, UNUSUAL NAMES

- Roderick
- Rodrigo
- Roland
- Roman
- Ronnie
- Ruben

Rodrigo: *(roh-DREE-goh)* (Spanish, Portuguese) Variant form of Roderick.

Roger: *(RAH-jer)* (German) ''Renowned spearman.'' Rogelio is a Spanish form. Rutger is a Dutch form, made familiar in the 1990s by actor Rutger Hauer. [ROGELIO, ROJAY, RUTGER]

Rohan: *(ro-HAHN)* (Irish) "Red-haired; red." Also a Sanskrit name meaning "ascending." [ROANE, ROYAN]

Roland: *(ROH-land)* (French) "Renowned in the land." Roland is celebrated in French and Italian poetic sagas as a hero in the service of Charlemagne. See also Orlando. [ROLANDO, ROLLAN, ROLLAND, ROLLIE, ROLLIN, ROLLO, ROWLAND]

Roman: *(roh-MAHN, ROH-mun)* (Latin) "Man of Rome." Variant form of Romanus, a saint's name. Romain is a French form. Shakespeare used Romeo for his tragic young hero in *Romeo and Juliet*. [ROMAIN, ROME, ROMEO]

Ronald: *(RAH-nald)* (English, Gaelic, Scandinavian) "Rules with counsel." Variant of Reynold. Ranald is a Scottish form, Ronaldo is Spanish. Noted name bearer: U.S. President Ronald Reagan. [RONNIE, RANALD, RON, RONAL, RONALDO, RONDALE, RONN, RONNY]

Ronel: *(roh-NEL)* (Israeli) "Song of God." [RONELL, RONNELL]

Rory: *(ROR-ee)* (Irish) "Red." Literary: tales of Rory O'More, 16th-century rebel chief, are celebrated in Irish poetry. Rorik is a Scandinavian and Slavic form. [ROREY, RORIK, RORRIC, RORRY]

Rosario: *(roe-ZAR-ee-oh)* (Latin) "Rosary." The name refers to devotional prayers honoring Mary.

Roscoe: *(ROS-koh)* (Scandinavian) "Heathland of the roe deer." [ROSCO]

Roshan: *(roh-SHAHN)* (Sanskrit) "Shining light." See also Rashaun.

Ross: (Scottish) "Red." [ROSSITER, ROSSTON, ROTH]

Rourke: *(RORK)* (Irish) An ancient given name of uncertain origin, adopted as an Irish clan name. [ROARKE, RORKE]

Rowdy: *(ROW-dee)* (English) "Boisterous." Western nickname. Rowdon (English) means "rough hill." [ROWDON]

Roy: *(roy)* (Gaelic) "Red." As a short form of names like Leroy, Roy means "king." [ROYDEN, ROYER]

Royal: *(ROY-al)* (English) "Of royal family, royalty." Roi (French) means "king." [ROI]

Royce: *(royce)* (English) "Famous."

Rudolph: *(ROO-dolf)* (German) "Fame of the wolf." Rodolfo is a Spanish form. See also Rudy. [RODOLFO, RUDOLFO, RUDOLPHO]

Rudy: *(ROO-dee)* (German) Short form of Rudolph. [RUDELLE, RUDI]

Rufus: *(ROO-fuss)* (Latin) "Red-haired." Biblical: the name of two first-century Christians. See also Russell. [RUFINO]

Rupert: *(ROO-pert)* (German) Variant of Robert. St. Rupert of Salzburg (eighth century) was instrumental in the founding of Salzburg on the ruins of an old Roman town.

Russell: *(RUSS-el)* (French) "Red-haired." Variant of Rufus. In the news in the 1990s: Rush Limbaugh, radio personality and commentator. [RUSH, RUSS, RUSSEL]

Rusty: *(RUS-tee)* (English) Nickname for a red-haired person; also a short form or nickname for names like Russell and Ruston. [RUSTAN, RUSTEN, RUSTIN, RUSTON, RUSTYN]

Ryan: *(RYE-an)* (Irish) "Kingly." Noted name bearer: actor Ryan O'Neal. [RIAN, RION, RYEN, RYON]

Ryder: *(RYE-der)* (English) "Horseman, rider." Rydell is a contemporary variant. [RYDELL, RYDEN]

Ryker: *(RYE-ker)* (Dutch) Surname form of Richard occasionally used as a given name, perhaps due to the character Commander Riker on the TV show *Star Trek: The Next Generation*.

Ryley: *(RYE-lee)* (Irish) "Island's meadow." Also used for girls, though usually in variant forms like Rylee and Rylie. See also Riley. [RYE, RYLAN, RYLAND, RYLEIGH]

S

Sabino: *(sa-BEE-noh)* (Latin) "Of the Sabines." A saint's name in use since at least the second century. [SAVINO]

Sachio: *(sah-chee-oh)* (Japanese) "Fortunately born."

Sage: (English) "Wise one." Sagan is a Slavic surname. [SAGAN, SAIGE]

Salem: *(SAY-lem)* (Hebrew) "Peace." Biblical: name of the ancient city that later was identified with Jerusalem. [SHALOM]

Salim: *(sa-LEEM)* (Arabic) "Peaceful." [SALEEM]

Salvador: *(SAL-va-dor)* (Latin) "Savior." Famous name bearer: Spanish artist Salvador Dali. Salvatore is an Italian form. [SAL, SALVATORE, SALVINO]

Sami: *(SAH-mee)* (Arabic) "Honored."

Samson: *(SAM-sun)* (Hebrew) "The sun." Biblical: a judge of ancient

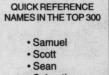

QUICK REFERENCE
NAMES IN THE TOP 300

- Samuel
- Scott
- Sean
- Sebastian
- Seth
- Shane
- Shawn
- Skyler
- Spencer
- Stephen
- Steven

Israel, endowed by God with superhuman strength. [SAMP-SON]

Samuel: *(SAM-yoo-el)* (Hebrew) "Name of God." Biblical: the prophet and judge who anointed Saul and David as kings of Israel. [SAM, SAMMIE, SAMMY, SAMUELE]

Sandy: *(SAN-dee)* (English, Scottish) Short form of Alexander. Sandro is an Italian form; Sandor is Hungarian. [SANDINO, SANDOR, SANDRO]

Sanjiro: *(sahn-jee-roh)* (Japanese) "Praise; admirable."

Santana: *(san-TAN-ah)* (Spanish) A blend of Saint and Anna, after the fashion of Sinclair. Rock guitarist Carlos Santana has made the name familiar. [SANTANNA]

Santiago: *(sahn-tee-AH-go)* (Spanish) A blended form of Saint Diego; Diego is a Spanish form of James. James the Greater (of the two apostles by that name) is the patron saint of Spain.

Santos: *(SAHN-tos)* (Latin) "Saints." Santino means "little saint." [SANTEE, SANTINO]

Saul: *(sahl)* (Hebrew) "Asked; inquired of God." Biblical: the first king of Israel; also the Hebrew name of the apostle Paul.

Saxon: *(SAKS-un)* (German) "Knife." English surname. Saxons were among the Germanic tribes that invaded and settled England in the fifth century. [SAXTON]

Schaeffer: *(SHAY-fer)* (German) "Steward." [SCHAFFER]

Schuyler: *(SKY-ler)* (Dutch) "Scholar." See also Skyler. [SCHYLAR, SCHYLER]

Scott: *(skaht)* (English) "From Scotland, a Gael." Noted name bearer: basketball player Scottie Pippen. [SCOT, SCOTTIE, SCOTTY]

Seamus: *(SHAY-mus)* (Irish) Variant of James. In America, *seamus* is sometimes used as a name for a private detective.

Sean: *(shon)* (Irish) Variant of John, from the French Jean. Occasionally used in hyphenated names. Noted name bearers: Sean Connery and Sean Penn. See also Shane and Shawn. [SEAN-CARLO, SEAN-MARK, SEAN-PATRICK]

Sebastian: *(se-BASS-tian)* (Greek) "Revered." Shakespeare gave the name to the twin brother of Viola in *Twelfth Night*. St. Sebastian was a third-century martyred centurion who became a patron saint of soldiers. [SABASTIAN, SEBASTIEN]

Seiji: *(SAY-jee)* (Japanese) "Lawful; manages affairs of state." Noted name bearer: symphony conductor Seiji Ozawa.

Sergio: *(SER-jee-oh)* (Latin) "Protector; shepherd." Sergei *(sare-GAY)* is a Russian form. St. Sergius (14th century) was a much-loved Russian saint. Noted name bearer: the late figure-skating champion, Sergei Grinkov. [SERGE, SERGEI, SERGEO, SERGIUS, SERJIO]

Seth: *(seth)* (Hebrew) "Appointed." Biblical: the third named son of Adam and Eve. Eve said Seth had been appointed to take the place of Abel, killed by Cain.

Severin: *(SEV-er-in)* (French) "Strict, restrained." Variant of Severus, a saint's name. See also Soren. [SEVERN, SEVERNE, SEVERO, SEVRIN]

Seymour: *(SEE-mor)* (English) "St. Maurus, the Moor."

Shaan: *(sha-AN)* (Hebrew) "Peaceful." (Hindu) "Pride."

Shad: *(shad)* (English) Short form of the biblical Shadrach, the Bab-

---

LESS COMMON CLASSICS;
NEW, UNUSUAL NAMES

- Sam
- Saul
- Sergio
- Shannon
- Shaquille
- Shaun
- Shelby
- Sheldon

ylonian name of one of the three young Hebrew men who were cast into a fiery furnace and miraculously survived. Notable in the 1990s: radio/TV personality Shadoe Stevens. [SHADD, SHADOE, SHADRACH, SHADRICK]

Shadi: *(sha-DEE)* (Arabic) "Singer." [SHADAY, SHADE]

Shaka: *(SHAH-kah)* (African) The name of a Zulu tribal leader (sometimes compared to Attila the Hun) who shaped an amalgamation of tribes into the great Zulu nation in the early 19th century.

Shane: *(shayn)* (Irish) Variant of Shaun, from John. Shan is also a Gaelic name meaning "old, wise." See also Sean and Shawn. [SHAINE, SHAN, SHANDON, SHANDY, SHANN, SHAYNE]

Shannon: *(SHAN-en)* (Irish) "Old, wise."

Shaquille: *(sha-KEEL)* (American) Variant of Shakil (Arabic), "handsome." Made familiar in the 1990s by basketball player Shaquille O'Neal, also well known by the short form of his name, Shaq. [SHAKEEL, SHAKHIL, SHAKIL, SHAQ, SHAQUE, SHAQUILE]

Sharif: *(sha-REEF)* (Arabic) "Illustrious." A name of descendants of Mohammed. [SHAREEF, SHEREEF, SHERIF]

Shaw: *(shaw)* (English) "Woods."

Shawn: *(shawn)* (Irish) Variant of John, from Sean. Like others of the John, Jean, Sean group, Shawn is used in hyphenated names like Shawn-Lee, Shawn-Luke, Shawn-Michael. Shaundre is a contemporary blend of Shaun and Andre. See also Sean and Shane. [SHAUN, SHAUGHN, SHAUNDRE, SHAWNN, SHONN]

Shea: *(shay)* (Irish) "Courteous." Surname occasionally used as a given name or middle name. [SHAE, SHAI, SHAY, SHAYE, SHAYLON]

Shelby: *(SHEL-bee)* (English) "Willow farm." English surname used more for girls than for boys.

Sheldon: *(SHEL-den)* (English) "Deep valley." [SHELDEN, SHELTON]

Shem: *(shem)* (Hebrew) "Name; renown." Biblical: first named of the three sons of Noah.

Sheridan: *(SHARE-a-den)* (Irish) "Bright."

Sherman: *(SHER-man)* (English) "Shireman." (German) "Shear-man." In medieval times, a shireman served as governor-judge of an English shire or county; a shearman worked as a sheep shearer or finisher of cloth. [SHERMANN, SHERMON]

Sherwin: *(SHER-win)* (English) "Swift." [SHERWEN]

Sherwood: *(SHER-wood)* (English) "Shire-wood." Surname and place name, referring to the forest that harbored the legendary Robin Hood and his men.

Shiloh: *(SHYE-loh)* (Hebrew) "The one to whom it belongs." Biblical: a prophetic name for the Messiah. Shiloh is also significant as the site of a crucial battle in the American Civil War.

Shoda: *(SHOH-dah)* (Japanese) "Flat, level field."

Sidney: *(SID-nee)* (French) "From St. Denis." Sidney is favored for boys; Sydney is almost entirely used for girls. See also Cydney. [SID, SYD, SYDNEY]

Sigmund: *(SIG-mund)* (German) "Victory, protection." A name made famous by the Austrian psychoanalyst Sigmund Freud.

LESS COMMON CLASSICS; NEW, UNUSUAL NAMES

- Sidney
- Simon
- Skylar
- Stanley
- Stephan
- Sterling
- Steve

Silas: *(SYE-las)* (Latin) Variant of Sylvanus, from a Greek name meaning "forest, woods." Biblical: Silas was a missionary companion to Paul and Timothy.

Silvano: *(sil-VAHN-oh)* (Latin) Variant of Sylvanus, referring to the mythological Greek god of trees. A number of saints bore the name, and variants were formed in several language groups. See also Silas and Sylvester. [SILVERIO, SILVINO, SILVIO, SYLVANUS]

Simon: *(SYE-mun)* (English) Variant of a Hebrew name meaning "hear, listen." Biblical: Simon was the name of two of the apostles, including Simon Peter. Simeon *(SIM-ee-on)* was the second-born of Jacob's 12 sons. [SIMEON, SYMON]

Sinclair: *(sin-KLARE)* (English) "From St. Clair." Through long usage, some saints' names have been blurred into a single name. Sinjin *(SIN-jin)* is a blurred form of St. John favored in England. Noted name bearer: author Sinclair Lewis. See also Santana and Seymour. [SINCLAIRE, SINJIN]

Skye: *(sky)* (English) Name used in reference to the Isle of Skye in Scotland, as a nickname for the Skyler variants, or as a nature name referring to the sky. See also Schuyler and Skyler. [SKY]

Skyler: *(SKY-ler)* (English) Phonetic spelling of Schuyler. See also Schuyler and Skye. [SKYELAR, SKYLAR, SKYLOR]

Slade: *(slayd)* (English) "Valley." [SLAYDEN]

Sloan: *(slohn)* (Scottish) "Fighter, warrior." Surname in rare use as a given name; Sloane is used as a feminine form.

Solomon: *(SAH-lah-mun)* (Hebrew) "Peace." Variant of Shalom. Biblical: Solomon, son of David and Bathsheba, succeeded his father as king of Israel. He wrote the Book of Proverbs, Ecclesiastes, and the Song of Solomon. The wisdom of Solomon is proverbial because when asked what gift he would have from God, he asked only for the wisdom he would need to rule. [SALOMON, SOL]

Sonny: *(SUN-ee)* (English) "Son." A nickname in steady use as a given name for boys. Also a short form of Santino. [SONNIE]

Soren: *(SOR-en)* (Scandinavian) "Strict." Variant of Severin, a saint's name. Noted name bearer: philosopher Sören Kierkegaard.

Spencer: *(SPEN-ser)* (English) "Dispenser, provider." Familiar since the 1930s primarily due to actor Spencer Tracy. [SPENCE, SPENSER]

Stacy: *(STAY-see)* (English) "Productive." Short form of Eustace. Noted name bearer: actor Stacy Keach. [STACEY]

Stanley: *(STAN-lee)* (English) "Stony meadow." Related surnames mean "stony ford" and "stone town." [STAN, STANFORD, STANTON]

Steele: *(steel)* (English) "Hard, durable."

Stephen: *(STEE-ven)* (English) "Crown, wreath." Variant of Stephanos (Greek). Biblical: Stephen was the first Christian martyr. Stefan *(stef-FAHN)* is a German, Scandinavian, and Slavic form. Steffan and Steffon *(STEH-fen)* are Welsh forms. American parents have created spelling variants to ensure similar pronunciations. See also Esteban, Etienne, Steve, and Steven. [STEPHAN, STEFAN, STEFANO, STEFFAN, STEFFEN, STEFFON, STEFON, STEPHANO, STEPHANOS, STEPHENSON, STEPHON]

Sterling: *(STER-ling)* (English) Variant of a name meaning "easterner" given to pre-medieval refiners of silver. Today *sterling* means "of high quality, pure." This name became familiar as a given name in the 1950s–1960s due to actor Sterling Hayden. [STERLYN, STIRLING]

Steve: *(steev)* (English) Short form of Steven and Stephen used as an independent name. See also Stephen and Steven. [STEVIE]

Steven: *(STEE-ven)* (English) Variant form of Stephen. See also Stephen. [STEVAN, STEVENSON, STEVON, STEVYN]

Stewart: *(STOO-ert)* (English, Scottish) "Steward." A medieval steward was charged with the care of castle and estate affairs. See also Stuart.

Stoney: *(STOH-nee)* (English) Nickname based on the word *stone*. [STONE, STONER]

Storm: *(storm)* (English) Surname with the literal meaning of a storm. The German form, Sturm, is a saint's name (12th century). [STURM]

Stuart: *(STOO-ert)* (English, Scottish) Stuart and Stewart are clan names of the royal house of Scotland; Stuart was the family name of English kings during the 18th century. See also Stewart.

Sullivan: *(SUL-ih-vun)* (Irish) "Dark eyes."

Sydney: *(SID-nee)* (English) See Sidney.

Sylvester: *(sil-VEST-ter)* (Latin) "Trees; sylvan." Silvestre is a French form. Noted name bearers: actor Sylvester Stallone and rock singer Sylvester "Sly" Stone. See also Silvano. [SILVESTER, SILVESTRE]

T

Tabor: *(TAY-bor)* (Hebrew) Biblical: Mt. Tabor, a landmark mountain near Nazareth. Taber is an Irish name meaning "well." The nickname Tab became familiar in the 1950s due to actor Tab Hunter. [TAB, TABER]

Tad: *(tad)* (English) Short form of Thaddeus. Tadeo *(ta-DAY-oh)* is a Spanish form. [TADD, TADEO]

Tadao: *(tah-dah-OH)* (Japanese) "Complacent; satisfied."

Taj: *(tahzh)* (Sanskrit) "Crown." Taji *(TAH-jee)* (Japanese) "Silver and yellow color." [TAHJ, TAJI]

Takeo: *(tah-kay-OH)* (Japanese) "Strong like bamboo."

Tal: *(tal)* (English) "Tall; fierce." With related surnames. Tal is also an Israeli name meaning "dew." [TALBERT, TAL-FORD, TALLON]

Tanjiro: *(tahn-jee-roh)* (Japanese) "High-valued second son."

Tanner: *(TAN-er)* (English) "Worker in leather."

Tariq: *(TAHR-ik)* (Arabic) "Morning star." Historical: the Islamic military leader (eighth century) who conquered Spain for the Moors. [TAREK, TAREQ, TARICK, TARIK, TARIQUE]

Taro: *(tah-roh)* (Japanese) "Big boy."

Tarun: *(TAH-run)* (Hindu) "Youth." Notable in the 1990s: actor Taran Noah Smith. See also Terran. [TARAN, TAREN]

Tate: *(tayt)* (Scandinavian) "Cheerful." (Irish) "Measure of land." [TAIT]

Tau: *(TAH-oh)* (African) "Lion."

Taurean: *(TAH-ree-an)* (Latin) "Bull-like." From Taurinus, a saint's name. Taurus is a constellation picturing the forequarters of a bull and is the second sign of the astrological zodiac. *Toro* is the Spanish word for "bull." [TAURINO, TAURO, TAURUS, TORO]

Tavis: *(TAV-iss)* (Scottish) Variant of Thomas. Tavio is a Spanish short form of Octavio. Tavin is a nickname for Gustav. Tavis and its variants may also have a connection with *teeve,* an Irish word meaning "hillside." In the news in the 1990s: singer and rock bandleader Tav Falco. [TAVEON, TAVIN, TAVIO, TAVION, TAVON, TEVIS]

Taylan: *(TAY-lan)* (American) A blend of Taylor and Dylan. [TAYLON]

Taylor: *(TAY-ler)* (English) "Tailor." Surname used as a given name. Also used for girls. [TAYLER]

Tayson: *(TAY-sun)* (English) A variant form of Tyson or a rhyming variant based on Jason.

Teague: *(teeg)* (Irish) "Handsome." [TAG, TIGHE]

Ted: *(ted)* (English) Short form of Theodore. Tedrick is a variant of the old German name Theodoric, "ruler of the people." Tedman refers to St. Edmund. [TED, TEDDIE, TEDDY, TEDMAN, TEDMUND, TEDRIC, TEDRICK]

Teiji: *(tay-ee-jee)* (Japanese) "Righteous; well-governed." Teijo: *(TAY-joh)* "established." [TEIJO]

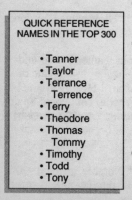

QUICK REFERENCE
NAMES IN THE TOP 300

- Tanner
- Taylor
- Terrance
  Terrence
- Terry
- Theodore
- Thomas
  Tommy
- Timothy
- Todd
- Tony

Templeton: *(TEM-pel-tun)* (English) "Temple-town." The surname refers to the medieval priories and settlements of the Knights Templar, a military religious order. Temple is in rare use today. [TEMPLE]

Teo: *(TAY-oh)* "God." (Spanish) Short forms of names like Mateo and Teodor. [TEYO]

Terran: *(TARE-en)* (English) "Earthman." Variants are contemporary rhyming blends of *Ter-* plus Darin. See also Tarun. [TARRIN, TERRIN, TERRON]

Terrance: *(TARE-ence)* (English) Variant form of a Roman clan name. Terence is the older English and Irish form. [TERRENCE, TARRENCE, TERENCE]

Terrell: *(TARE-el)* (English) "Powerful." See also Tyrell. [TERELL, TERRALL, TERREL, TERRELLE, TERRILL]

Terry: *(TARE-ee)* (English) Short form of Terrance and Terrell. Terry is also an Anglicized phonetic form of the French given name Thierry, from an older Germanic name meaning "powerful; ruler of the people."

Tevin: *(TEV-in)* (American) Contemporary rhyming variant of Kevin. [TEVYN]

Thaddeus: *(THAD-ee-us)* (Greek) Biblical: one of the 12 apostles. See also Tad. [THAD, THADDIUS, THADEUS]

Thane: *(thayn)* (English, Scottish) Title of Anglo-Saxon and Scottish feudal lords. Shakespeare's Macbeth was Thane of Cawdor.

Theodore: *(THEE-a-dor)* (Greek) "God-given." See also Ted. Teodor *(TAY-oh-dor)* is Spanish; Teodoro is Italian and Portuguese. [TEODOR, TEODORO, THEO, THEODON, THEODOR, THEODRIC]

Theron: *(THER-on)* (Greek) "Untamed." [THEON, THERRON]

Thomas: *(TAH-mas)* (Aramaic) "Twin." Biblical: one of the 12 apostles. Tomás *(toh-MAHS)* is a Spanish form. See also Tavis. [TOMMY, TOMAS, THOM, THOMPSON, TOM]

Thor: *(thor)* (Scandinavian) "Thunder." Mythology: Thor was the Norse god of thunder, one of the sons of Odin. Thursday was named for Thor. Noted name bearer: explorer Thor Heyerdahl [THORIAN, THORIN, THORSSON, THURMAN]

Thornton: *(THORN-ten)* (English) "Town of thorns." Noted name bearer: author Thornton Wilder. Thorn variants are English surnames occasionally used as given names. [THORN, THORNE]

Thurl: *(therl)* (Irish) "Strong fort." [THURLE]

Thurston: *(THER-sten)* (English) "Thor's stone." [THURSTAN]

Timon: *(tee-MOHN)* (Greek) "Honorable." Biblical: a man noted for his wisdom in the first Christian congregation. Shakespeare used the name in his play *Timon of Athens*.

Timothy: *(TIM-oh-thee)* (Greek) "One who honors God." Biblical: Timothy was an energetic, well-trained young Christian to whom Paul wrote, "Let no man look down on your youth." Timoteo and Timo are Spanish forms. [TIM, TIMMY, TIMO, TIMOTEO]

QUICK REFERENCE
NAMES IN THE TOP 300

- Travis
- Trent
  Trenton
- Trevor
- Trey
- Tristan
  Tristen
- Troy
- Tucker
- Ty
- Tyler

Titus: *(TYE-tus)* (Latin) Meaning uncertain. Biblical: a Greek Christian missionary to whom Paul wrote the canonical letter Titus. [TITO]

Toby: *(TOH-bee)* (English) Short form of Tobiah, a Hebrew name meaning "Jah is good." Tobias is a Greek form. [TOBEY, TOBIAH, TOBIAS, TOBIE, TOBIN, TOBYN]

Todd: *(tahd)* (English) "Fox." Tod is a Scottish nickname meaning a clever or wily person. [TOD]

Tomeo: *(toh-MAY-oh)* (Japanese) "Cautious man."

Tony: *(TOH-nee)* (English) Short form of Anthony and its variants, frequently used since medieval times as an independent name. Tonio is a Latin short form. [TONIO]

Torin: *(TOR-en)* (American) Contemporary. Torin and its variants probably are based on Torrance and Dorian. [TORAN, TOREAN, TOREN, TORION, TORRAN, TORRIAN]

Torio: *(toh-ree-oh)* (Japanese) "Bird's tail." Torrio is a Spanish short form of Victor. [TORRIO]

Torrence: *(TOR-ence)* (Irish, Scottish) "From the craggy hills." Tor is a name for a craggy hilltop and also may refer to a watchtower. The Scandinavian Tor refers to Thor, god of thunder. [TOR, TORENCE, TORRANCE]

Toru: *(toh-roo)* (Japanese) "Sea."

Tory: *(TOR-ee)* (English) Surname based on Tor, Torrence, or Tower. Tory variants may also be short forms of Victor. Torre (Italian) means "tower." [TOREY, TORRE, TORREY, TORRIE, TORRY]

Toshiro: *(toh-shee-roh)* (Japanese) "Talented, intelligent."

Tracy: *(TRAY-see)* (French) "From Thracia." Surname dating from before the Norman conquest. Notable name bearer: Tracey Walter. [TRACE]

Travis: *(TRAV-iss)* (English) "Crossing, crossroads." Noted name bearer in the 1990s: country-western singer Travis Tritt.

LESS COMMON CLASSICS; NEW, UNUSUAL NAMES

- Tate
- Terrell
- Tevin
- Toby
- Triston
- Tylor
- Tyree
- Tyrone
- Tyson

Travon: *(tra-VAHN)* (American) Contemporary blend of Travis with various name endings. See also Trevin. [TRA-VAUGHN, TRAVEON, TRAVION, TRAYVON, TREVONN]

Tremayne: *(tre-MAYNE)* (English) "Town built with stone." [TRAMAINE, TREMAIN, TREMAINE]

Trent: (English) Refers to the River Trent in England. [TRENTON, TRENTEN, TRENTIN

Trevin: *(TREV-in)* (English) "Fair town." Short form of Trevelyan. Variants are probably influenced by Devon and Davion. See also Travon. [TREVAN, TREVEN, TREVIAN, TREVION, TREVON, TREVYN]

Trevis: *(TREV-iss)* (English, Welsh) Variant of Treves, French surname and place name. Contemporary American usage may be as a blend of Travis and Trevor.

Trevor: *(TREV-er)* (Welsh) "Goodly town."

Trey: *(tray)* (English) "Three." May also be a variant of *traigh* (Irish), "strand."

Tristan: *(TRISS-tan)* (English) "Tumult, outcry." From a Celtic name. In Arthurian legend, Tristan was a Knight of the Round Table and the tragic hero of the medieval tale *Tristram and Isolde*. Tristram *(TRISS-tram)*, an English form, is difficult to pronounce and rarely used in modern times. [TRISTEN, TRISTIAN, TRISTIN, TRISTON, TRISTYN, TRYSTAN]

Troy: *(troy)* (English) As a given name, Troy may derive from the ancient Greek city or from an Irish surname meaning "soldier." [TROI, TROYE]

Tucker: *(TUH-ker)* (English) "Clothmaker."

Ty: *(ty)* (English) Short form for names beginning with *Ty-*. [TYE]

Tyler: *(TY-ler)* (English) "Tile layer" or a variant of Taylor. An English surname frequently used as a given name. [TYLOR]

Tyrell: *(tye-REL, TER-el)* (Scandinavian) Derivative of Tyr, the name of the Scandinavian god of battle. Tuesday was named for Tyr. See also Terrell. [TYREL, TYRELLE, TYRRELL]

Tyrone: *(TY-rohn, ter-ROHN)* (Irish) "From Owen's territory." County Tyrone in Ireland has been made familiar as a boy's given name primarily due to actor Tyrone Power. [TYRONNE]

Tyrus: *(TY-rus)* (American) Blend of Tyrone and Cyrus, or a reference to the ancient Phoenician city of Tyre.

Tyson: *(TY-sun)* (English) "Fiery." [TYCE, TYESON]

U

Udell: *(yoo-DEL)* (English) "Yew-tree valley." [UDALE]

Ugo: *(YOO-goh)* (Italian) "A thinker." Variant form of Hugo.

Ulric: *(UL-rik)* (English) Variant of Wulric (German), "wolf-people." A saint's name. [ULRICH, ULRICK]

Ulysses: *(you-LISS-ees)* (Latin) Variant of the Greek name Odysseus. Mythology: Ulysses was the clever and resourceful hero of Homer's *Odyssey*. Ulises is a Spanish form. [ULISES]

Uriah: *(yer-RY-ah)* (Hebrew) "My light is Jehovah." Biblical:

one of King David's warriors, the Hittite husband of Bath-sheba. Urijah was the name of a prophet. [URIJAH]

Uriel: *(OOR-ee-el)* (Hebrew) "Angel of light." In the Apocrypha, Uriel is one of seven archangels. In Muslim tradition, he is the angel of music who will sound the trumpet on Judgment Day.

Ursus: *(ER-sus)* (Latin) "Bear."

V

Valente: *(va-LEN-tay)* (Italian, Portuguese) "Valiant." Variant form of Valentine.

Valentine: *(VAL-en-tyne)* (Latin) "Strong." Variant of Valentinus, the name of more than 50 saints and three Roman emperors. Valen *(VAL-en)* is a short form. [VAL, VALEN, VALENTIN, VALLEN]

Van: *(van)* (Dutch) "Of." Equivalent of *de* in French names. Van was sometimes converted from a surname prefix to a given name by early immigrants to America. The name became familiar in the 1950s due to actors Van Johnson and Van Heflin.

Vance: *(vance)* (English) "Marshland."

Vaughn: *(von)* (Welsh) "Little." Von is the German equivalent of Van. [VAUGHAN, VON, VONDELL, VONN, VONTELL]

Verdell: *(ver-DELL)* (French) "Green, flourishing." [VERNELL]

Vernon: *(VER-non)* (French) "Alder tree grove." Aristocratic surname brought to England at the time of the Norman conquest. Vern and Verne are related English/French surnames frequently used as short forms of Vernon or Lavern. [VERN, VERNARD, VERNE]

Victor: *(VIK-tor)* (Latin) "Conqueror." A very popular saint's name. At one time, more than 200 were listed in the Catholic Dictionary of Saints. Vittorio is an Italian form; Viktor is Czech. [VIC, VICTORIANO, VICTORINO, VICTORIO, VIKTOR, VITTORIO]

Vidal: *(vee-DAL)* (Latin) "Life." Several language groups (French, English, Spanish, and Portuguese) use Vidal as a surname or given name. Notable name bearer: hairstylist Vidal Sassoon. See also Vito. [VIDEL]

Vijay: *(VEE-jay)* (Hindu) "Victor." [VEEJAY]

Vincent: *(VIN-sent)* (Latin) "Conquering." Vincenzo and Vincente are Italian forms; Vicente is Spanish. Noted name bearer: film director Vincente Minnelli. [VICENTE, VINCE, VINCENTE, VINCENZO, VINNIE, VINSON]

Virgil: *(VER-jil)* (Latin) "Flourishing." The writings of Virgil, the Roman poet-philosopher, have provided classic texts for the study of Roman history and the Latin language for the past 2,000 years.

Vito: *(VEE-toh)* (Latin) "Life." See also Vidal. [VITALE]

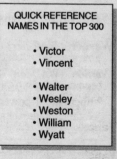

QUICK REFERENCE
NAMES IN THE TOP 300

• Victor
• Vincent

• Walter
• Wesley
• Weston
• William
• Wyatt

W

Wade: *(wayde)* (Scandinavian) Medieval given name taken from Scandinavian mythology. Also an English surname referring to a water crossing. [WAYDE, WAYDELL]

Waldo: *(WAL-doh)* (German) "Powerful." Short form of Oswald. [WALDEN, WALDRON]

Walker: *(WAHL-ker)* (English) "Worker in cloth."

Wallace: *(WAL-iss)* (English, Scottish) "Welshman." [WALLIS]

Walter: *(WAL-ter)* (German) "Rules, conquers." [WALLY, WALT, WALTON]

Ward: *(ward)* (English) "Protector." [WARDE, WARDELL]

Warner: *(WAR-ner)* (English) "Warrior."

Waylon: *(WAY-lon)* (Scandinavian) Variant of Wayland. Mythology: the Scandinavian Wayland was a blacksmith with supernatural powers, corresponding to the Roman Vulcan. Notable name bearer: singer Waylon Jennings. See also Wylan. [WAYLAN, WAYLAND, WAYLIN]

LESS COMMON CLASSICS;
NEW, UNUSUAL NAMES

- Wade
- Walker
- Warren
- Wayne
- Willie

Wayne: *(wayne)* (English) "Wagon driver."

Webster: *(WEB-ster)* (English) "Weaver." (Note: the *-ster* ending on English occupational surnames like Webster and Brewster is an indication that the work was originally a female occupation. When the occupations were taken over by males, the names were adopted as well.)

Wendell: *(WIN-del)* (German) "Traveler, wanderer." [WEN-DALE, WENDALL]

Wesley: *(WEZ-lee, WES-lee)* (English) "West meadow." Variant of the English surname Westley. Noted name bearer: actor Wesley Snipes. [WES, WESTLEY]

Weston: *(WES-ten)* (English) "West town." [WEST, WESTEN, WESTIN]

Wilbert: *(WIL-bert)* (German) "Willful; bright." [WILBER, WILBUR, WILBURN, WILBURT]

Wiley: *(WYE-lee)* (English) "Well-watered meadow." [WY-LIE]

Wilfred: *(WIL-fred)* (German) "Desire peace." St. Wilfred (seventh century) was an English saint. [WILFREDO, WIL-FRID, WILFORD]

Willard: *(WIL-erd)* (German) "Bold, resolute."

William: *(WIL-yum)* (English) "Resolute protector." For a long time after the Norman conquest in A.D. 1066, three out of four English boys were given some form of the conqueror's name, William. Short forms and variants came into being with a common basic meaning of "will," "determined," or "resolute." The firstborn son of the current Prince of Wales is named William. Wilhelm is a German form; Willem Dafoe has made the Dutch form familiar since the 1980s. See also Guillermo, Liam, Willard, Willie, Wilmer, and Wilson. [WILHELM, WILLEM, WILLIAMS, WIL-LIS]

Willie: *(WIL-ee)* (English) Short form of names beginning with *Wil-*. Noted name bearer: country-western singer Willie Nelson. Actor Wil Wheaton has made his unusual form of the name familiar to fans of *Star Trek: The Next Generation.* [WIL, WILL, WILLY]

Wilmer: *(WIL-mer)* (German) "Resolute; famous." [WILMORE]

Wilson: *(WIL-son)* (English) "Son of Will."

Winston: *(WIN-stun)* (English) "Stone marker of friendship." Famous name bearer: former British prime minister, Sir Winston Churchill. [WIN, WINN, WINFIELD, WINSLOW]

Woodrow: *(WUD-roh)* (English) "From the cottages in the wood." Noted name bearer: United States President Woodrow Wilson. The nickname "Woody" is familiar today due to actor Woody Harrelson and actor/director Woody Allen. [WOODY]

Wyatt: *(WY-ut)* (English) "Lively." Variant of Guy. [WIATT]

Wylan: *(WYE-lan)* (English) Variant of Waylan. [WYLAND]

Wyler: *(WYE-ler)* (English) "Wheelmaker." An occupational surname. [WYLIE]

Wynn: *(win)* (English) "Friend." Variants are English surnames in rare use as given names. [WYNDELL, WYNTON]

X

Xander: *(ZAN-der)* (Greek) Short form of Alexander. [XAN-DRO]

Xavier: *(ecks-ZAY-vee-er, ZAY-vee-er)* (Spanish, Arabic) "Bright; splendid." See also Javier.

Xiomar: *(zhoh-MAR)* (Spanish) "Famous in battle." Variant of Geomar.

Y

Yale: *(yayl)* (Welsh) "Heights, upland." Yael: (Israeli) "God's strength."

York: *(york)* (English) Place name and surname.

Yuri: *(YER-ee)* (Russian) Variant of George.

Yves: *(eve)* (French) Variant of the Germanic name Ivo, meaning "archer's bow." St. Yves (14th century) was a French lawyer and priest described in history as "an attorney who was an honest man." Familiar since the 1940s due to couturier Yves St. Laurent and singer/actor Yves Montand. See also Ivar.

Z

Zacchaeus: *(za-KAY-us)* (Hebrew) "Clean, pure." Biblical: a tax collector who became one of the disciples of Jesus.

Zachariah: *(zak-a-RYE-ah)* (Hebrew) "Jehovah has remembered." Variant of Zechariah. Biblical: the name of 31 men, including the prophet who wrote the Book of Zechariah. Zacarias is a Spanish and Portuguese form. See also Zachary. [ZACARIAS, ZACHARIA, ZACHARIAS, ZACKARIAH, ZECHARIAH]

Zachary: *(ZAK-a-ree)* (English) Variant of Zachariah; Zachary is one of several names from the Bible that have enjoyed a revival of favor in modern times. See Jacob, Jared, and Joshua. [ZACHERY, ZACKARY, ZACH, ZACK, ZACKERY, ZAK, ZAKARI, ZAKARY]

Zadok: *(ZAY-dok)* (Hebrew) "Just." Biblical: the most prominent Zadok was a priest who showed great courage during the reigns of the first three kings of Israel.

Zander: *(ZAN-der)* (Slavic) Short form of Alexander. Also a German Yiddish name. See also Sandy.

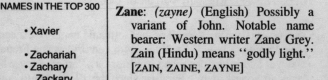

QUICK REFERENCE
NAMES IN THE TOP 300

- Xavier

- Zachariah
- Zachary
  Zackary
  Zackery
- Zane

Zane: *(zayne)* (English) Possibly a variant of John. Notable name bearer: Western writer Zane Grey. Zain (Hindu) means "godly light." [ZAIN, ZAINE, ZAYNE]

Zarek: *(ZAR-ek)* (Slavic) "God protects."

Zeke: *(zeek)* (English) Short form of Ezekiel.

Zeno: *(ZE-noh)* (Greek) ''Of Zeus.'' Zenon was the name of two Greek philosophers. Zeno of Verona (fourth century) was an Italian saint. [ZENON]